Christmas Greetings From a Remarkable Life

Harleigh Thayer Knott

Edited by Kevin & Kimberly Meyer

Contents

Foreword

We first met Harleigh when we moved to a house across the street from her in Morro Bay in late 2000. Her cat, Whiskers, was lost, and being cat people ourselves, we helped locate him. We soon learned that Harleigh was a fixture of our small fishing village, and was often seen walking along the street, tall and slender and always dressed in proper English fashion.

Over the next nineteen years we got to know Harleigh quite well – or so we always thought. We helped her change lightbulbs, set up printers, and provide rides to the train station. In return she'd tell us stories of her travels around the world. Her interests were wide and varied, which we often realized in a sudden, unexpected manner. At dinner one evening she was telling us how she was planning one of her frequent trips to Santa Barbara for shopping and to watch a polo match but needed to be back home by Sunday afternoon. We asked why. She said she couldn't miss her Indy car race on TV. Wait… what? Sure enough, she also had a passion for car racing.

Harleigh's father, Arthur Harold Knott (going by Harold), was born in Canada but moved to Vermont soon after. He studied art at the Pratt Institute in New York, then settled in Carmel, California, and would become rather famous for his watercolor landscapes. Harleigh's mother, Rachel Louise Thayer, was a descendant of 17th century English settlers, and the daughter of the mayor or Norwich, Connecticut. After high school she left to travel and live in South America and Europe, where she married a Canadian doctor. Her husband was killed during WWI. She returned to the U.S. and enrolled at Stanford, double majoring in English and Classics. After some time in Santa Fe, New Mexico, she found her way to Carmel, where she met Harold who would become her second husband.

Harold and Rachel soon moved down the coast to Morro Bay, where they bought a home and eventually added an artist studio. Morro Bay at the time had a lively British colony, which especially appealed to Rachel. Harleigh and then Nona were born and raised in the home. During WWII they moved to a neighbor's house for a few years so that military officers could rent their home. Harleigh followed in her mother's footsteps, going to Stanford to receive a degree in history, and then exploring the world. Her mother died in 1957, then her sister in 1962, and her father in 1976. Harleigh eventually returned to spend the rest of her days in her childhood home.

Harleigh had a thirst for knowledge and subscribed to innumerable newspapers and magazines. The librarian side of her took that one step further with a massive filing system with clippings related to her interests. Opera, travel, politics, even Indy cars and frogs. Her friends knew that if they brought up a topic over dinner there would often be a small plastic bag on our doorstep the next morning with clippings related to that topic – some from decades ago.

A highlight for many of us was her annual Christmas letter, which she labored over for months – sometimes to the point that she never finished it until the following year. They were exceptionally detailed, especially when describing her world travels, and humorous even when describing the aches and pains of aging.

Harleigh never married and was a very private person, especially about her personal and family life. When she passed unexpectedly earlier this year, we discovered she had a wealth of friends from the many phases of her life, as well as some distant relatives. At her memorial we shared stories of the thoughtful, eclectic, and humorous Harleigh we loved.

To preserve the memory and legacy of this remarkable lady we have tried to compile as many of her famous Christmas letters as we could locate, keeping the few grammar and spelling errors. We also included some of her other public writing and speeches, as well as some photographs and other materials. Mindful of respecting her privacy, we have not included private letters or information.

Rest in peace, Harleigh.

Kevin and Kimberly Meyer
Morro Bay, California - April 2019

Christmas Letters

1957

Greetings!

Please excuse this method of "mass communication" but my correspondence has gotten way out of hand and this is about the only way I can cope. Some (few!) people will have heard parts of this year's news already and will, I trust, bear with the repetition.

The year got off to a very sad start, for my mother died on January 18th. I spent 2 difficult months at home attending all the legal and other responsibilities and looking after my family. They now have a housekeeper, and I was able to return to my job in London in March. I was completely worn out and very depressed for a long time, and gradually began to pick up the pieces of my life here.

I have had many interesting trips and experiences, although this summer was not as fruitful in this respect as the previous ones, since I was poisoned by a severe sunburn (over-exposure on an overcast day at the beach) in July, and was laid up for some time. In fact, it was about 6 weeks before I really recovered. Of all of the ridiculous things to happen in England! Even in my misery I had to admit it was funny. Then I went up to Scotland for my vacation, and after a rather hectic time seeing plays, etc. at the Edinburgh Festival, caught what I assume must have been the famous Asiatic flu, and spent a week being ill in a place called Ullapool, on the northwest coast of the Highlands. There I was quite spoiled by the zealous Highland hospitality of the landlady, who fed me 6 times a day and thereby established a habit pattern which has resulted in my gaining about 20 lbs. since I returned in mid-September. I'm delighted, of course, but it means a lot of frantic letting out of skirts to accommodate the expanding girth.

In May I spent a weekend in the city of Norwich, which proved to be one of the most interesting places in England, with many historic features, yet not "touristy." I have also made trips to Rottingdean, Guildford, Exeter, Torquay, Oxford, Lynmouth & the Doono Volley, Jordans Meeting House (old Quaker place where Wm. Ponn is buried), Ystradgynlais (there's a neat Wolsh mouthful for you!--near Swanson--where I visited friends, who drove me down the Gower Peninsula and also to Brocon). But the most hilarious long weekend I think I've ever had was the trip to Laugharne, the Welsh village where Dylan Thomas lived and which was his chief inspiration for the play "Under Milk Wood." My friend and I decided the original was even crazier than the play, and agreed we'd never laughed so hard so continuously for 3 days in our lives. The Welsh are quite mad, and delightfully witty.

I have continued to see lots of plays, London being such a treasure-house of theatres; I especially enjoy seeing all the Shakespeare productions at the Old Vic, and have also been to some parties there were one can talk with the actors. I have also been to a number of productions (free!) by the students at the Royal Academy of Dramatic Art, which is England's no. 1 training ground for actors.

I watched the Duke of Edinburgh play polo one day at Cowdray Park, and went to the famous Ascot races* (England's big fashion show-- like the Easter Parade in New York) and saw the Queen and other members of the royal family there. I also attended the opening of the Royal Academy of Arts summer show, and the types attending this were just as interesting as the exhibit--everything from the nobility to seedy Bohemian-type art students, etc.

*People go to look at each other, not at the horses!

Probably my most outstanding experiences this year were the occasions when I dined at the House of Commons and at Lambeth Palace. The first mentioned was as a guest of an English lady whose local Conservative Party Association and their M.P. (Member of Parliament) hold the dinner, which was preceded by a guided tour around both the House of Lords and the House of Commons. We had a fine meal of pheasant, etc., followed by toasts and political-type speeches. It is interesting and amusing to see how politicians are basically the same in all parts of the world "Hurrah for our

4

party, and the country will go to the dogs if the other party gets in!"

The dinner at Lambeth Palace (which is the London residence and "headquarters" of the Archbishop of Canterbury) was an even more exclusive event, and a rare privilege indeed, since not even English people get to go there, let alone lay foreigners. I was the guest of an archdeacon, which is an office I don't think we have in our Episcopal Church in the U.S., but is a sort of administrative position next in line to a bishop. The occasion was the annual ecclesiastical dignitaries from foreign churches, but the only one they had this time was the hand of the Armenian Church in England. We first had sherry in the Great Hall (which contains the library) and I was introduced to the Archbishop and his wife--both very jolly and good-natured types, as, in fact, everyone there seemed to be. Then we went upstairs to the dining hall. I must say it was quite an experience to be at a dinner where the Archbishop says the grace! He gave a short informal talk after the meal and the toasts. I was seated between my host and the Bishop of Lincoln, and opposite a Canon Somebody-or-other MacLeod-Campboll of Charterhouse, and Sir Henry Dashwood, "a noted ecclesiastical lawyer."

It was a very colorful gathering (about 100 people) because of the various types of ecclesiastical and academic dress the men wore. Most of the women were in evening dress. There were red cassocks, purple cassocks, and black cassocks, academic robes with different colored hoods, ordinary priest's clothing, and ordinary evening dress. But what I thought were the most picturesque "outfits" were the ones like my host's, which consisted of a sort of black frock coat, short knee-length cassock-like affair, knee brooches, long black silk stockings & black patent leather shoes with big silver buckles. Some of the bishops, including the ones sitting next to me, wore this same outfit in purple--very striking indeed.

After the meal we returned to the library and heard a concert of 15th and 16th century music played by a recorder ensemble, while we strolled about looking at the special exhibit of early Americana manuscripts etc., showing aspects of Church life and history in our colonial days.

Needless to say, it was an unforgettable occasion, and I could hardly believe I was really there. I hope I didn't look too wide-eyed and open-mouthed, but that was the way I felt!

I wish I had time to write everyone more often and more fully, but as you can see, life here is terribly busy, on top of the fact that I work from 9 to 6! So trusting you understand, I wind up with best wishes for a happy Christmas and New Year.... And please don't let my failure as a correspondent deter you from writing! All letters eagerly devoured and much appreciated!

1958

Christmas Greetings!

Here goes for the second annual mass-produced Christmas letter. Let's face it--I can't write nearly 200-odd individual letters, so it's either this or nothing.

****

Before I launch into this, let me say that I will be finishing this job in London at the end of March, and after a few last-minute travels in this part of the world, will be returning to the U.S.

****

Last winter instead of going into hibernation as in previous years, I made a number of sightseeing expeditions with an American friend who was to leave England in the spring and wanted to see as much as possible before going. This was sheer madness, but fun in a way, because of course there were no other tourists about and we could see the places as they really were, and also the beauty of Olde England covered with snow (even if the physical suffering entailed did tend to obscure one's appreciation of some). We went to York on the coldest, snowiest weekend of the year--and there was NO HEAT in our hotel room. Agony. In a way we were better off outdoors. At any rate, at one stage of the game, as we ploughed doggedly along through slush and mud, bundled in numerous layers of woollen underwear, sweaters, scarves, wool socks, fleece-lined boots, mittens and heavy coats, purple and raw and chattering with cold, we were recognized as foreigners in spite of this disguise by a hearty man coming along the street, who beamed cheerfully at us. "This is England at its best!" His timing couldn't have been better. I think our laughter helped keep our circulation going the rest of the day.

We also made a trip to Chester in the snow, although it was somewhat less cold there, and we made a specific point of booking a room with an electric stove in it. Both York and Chester are extremely interesting and picturesque "Olde England" cities with medieval walls and lots of old Tudor buildings, and look more like what-the-foreigner-thinks-England-should-be-and-mostly-isn't. We also took cold one-day trips to Lincoln (made no impression on me, cathedral withstanding) and St. Alban's (noted for its Roman ruins and dreadful hodge-podge-of-architectural-styles cathedral). I was dragged round Ipswich, which has a number of interesting old buildings, by an English friend--in pouring rain.

In the spring and summer I made a few trips including Ayot St. Lawrence to see Shaw's Corner, the home of G.B.S. Pewtheaud in Wales to visit friends, and Bath, the attractive Georgian spa town (where I had been several times before).

There was of course the usual round of theatres, concerts, etc., and the Old Vic Shakespeare Birthday Party in April and sherry party in the fall. At these functions one gets a good look at various actors and actresses. One evening during the winter I was sitting next to Charles Laughton at the theatre (at "Epitaph for George Dillon" to be exact); this gentleman is so corpulent he bulged over the edge of his seat into mine. I enjoyed eavesdropping on his comments on the play, and was highly amused when during the course of some jazzy music on the stage he started jumping and jiving around in his seat.

The chief event of the year was a 16-day "Hellenic Cruise" to Greece and Turkey. We went from London to Venice by train, and there embarked on the T.S.S. "Mediterranean," a Greek ship of the Typaldos Line, rather ancient, but fun. There were about 300 passengers. We had a number of leading authorities on board to lecture us, so it was something of a floating education. For classical topics, Sir Maurice Bowra of Oxford, Prof. W.B. Stanford of Trinity College, Dublin, and F. Kinchin Smith, University of London, did the honors. Mr. Michael Maclagan of Oxford expounded on Byzantine matters, and Lord William Taylour gave us the word on Mycenaean archaeology, having done considerable "digging" in this field. The Rev. G. Pentreath, Headmaster of Cheltenham College, filled in with miscellaneous bits, showing colored slides each evening of sites we were to see the next day. It was a very strenuous trip, what with getting up at the crack of dawn, eating, piling overboard (usually into small boats which took us ashore to the different sites), clambering all over ruins and up and down acropolises all day, returning quite bushed to try and clean up, dress for dinner, listen to more lectures, eat dinner, and collapse into one's bunk.

First we attacked the Peloponnese with a bang: Old Corinth, which has not much left in the way of classical period ruins except the temple of Apollo, but its Roman area offers the rostrum from which St. Paul is supposed to have addressed the Corinthians. Then we roared across the countryside by bus to Mycenae--the Palace of Agamemnon, in an impressive setting, with its famous Lion Gate, "beehive tombs" and secret underground cistern. Tiryns, another fortress-city of that period, was nearby, but not so impressive. Thence to Epidauros with its marvelous theatre--perfect acoustic--from the very top at any angle you could hear someone speaking in a low voice from the "stage" area. Epidauros was the first "Asclepeion" or health resort where people went to be healed by the god Asclepios, perhaps with the assistance of snakes (whose licking was considered beneficial) and in the course of the rest-cure, enjoy the theatre, music, dancing, and athletics, all in a very lovely and peaceful setting.

Our next day was less hectic. We visited the lovely "sacred island" of Delos, where the god Apollo and the goddess Artemis were born, and where masses of fascinating ruins, both ancient Greek and Roman, are beautifully surrounded by a carpeting of wild flowers, and there is no modern settlement whatever apart from a museum. Nearby Mykonos, next, offered no ruins or anything to distract one from the enjoyment of the beach. It is a most charming island with neat, spotless, whitewashed, flat-topped houses. Even the stone-paved alleyways were whitewashed.

The island of Rhodes next: The city of Rhodes is primarily a medieval city, having been the stronghold of the crusader Knights of St. John, and has a more European flavor so did not appeal to me as much as the purely Greek places, although it was chiefly Greek in population. There is also a considerable Turkish element here however, as evidenced by the sprinkling of mosques. But the village of Lindos about 35 miles away was utterly charming, nestled round a lovely beach, with a gorgeous acropolis on a steep hill just above it, on the edge or a sheer cliff dropping to the sea below. One speculated on how many ancient laborers must have been lost over the edge in the course of building. In addition to the temple of Athena and other typical acropolis ruins, there was an intriguing relief of an ancient galley ship carved right into the rock wall at the entrance, no doubt done at the behest of an earlier Onassis-type.

We now left Greece for the time being to venture into another civilization altogether. Greece and its heritage belongs to us all and we feel at home there. But Turkey was a different cup of tea (or should I say coffee..) altogether--really foreign.

The outside, Western world seemed never to have touched Kusadasi, a tiny, obscure seaside village where we first landed in turkey. Women wafted along with veiled heads and baggy trousers (perhaps following the lordly husband at a respectful distance) or peered furtively out of doors and windows at the strange outsiders who had suddenly descended on their soil. There was a great silence one hesitated to break by speaking above a whisper. Not hostility exactly, but definitely "otherness" you might say. Occasionally strange, snaky music would be heard coming from some crackling wireless set. (My great regret is not having tried to buy some Turkish records! The music was fascinating.) Eventually, we "shoved off" in vintage buses, grinding over twisted mountain roads enveloped in clouds of chalky dust. Suddenly ahead of us out of the cloud loomed a fierce galloping figure with robes flying, whom we could not overtake, chills ran up and down my spine and I expected to see a whole horde of warriors charge down the slope at us brandishing scimitars. We subsequently reached more placid surroundings, where storks nestled cosily on the housetops and one splendid bird stalked majestically in the wake of a ploughing farmer, picking up overturned bugs.

We reached the site of Priene, ruins of an early Greek colony, the first example of "town planning" with its orderly terraced, criss-cross geometrical layout. Here we noted that schoolboys have not changed much over the centuries: Masses of Greek lads' names were carefully carved into the stone walls round their gymnasium washbasins.

You really haven't meandered, may I say, until you do so along the Meander River! In the course of its meandering, it so silted up as to leave both Priene and the nearby and even greater Greek city of Miletus high and dry. The latter was once one of the richest and most important of the Greek Cities in Asia Minor, but now there is nothing but a tiny Turkish village and herds of sheep with pleasantly-tinkling bells and a few heavily-laden camels lounging about the ruins of a great theatre and several other remnants of marble and stone. I was rather unnerved when some Turkish men came out and decided to shoot crows willy-nilly in our midst.

The next Turkish port we hit was a fairly large village called Dikili, and we gathered quite a crowd of native gawkers on our arrival and departure, particularly children in their national black school uniform with white collars. Following a hectic bus ride, punctuated by frequent breakdowns which the driver could not overcome despite repairs with assorted spare parts carried along, we were rescued by another bus and tackled Bergama, for a look at the ruins of the ancient Greek city of Pergamon. Drank from the sacred spring at the Asclepeion, which had a nice little theatre, and the world's first public toilets, built by the Roman Emperor Vespasian as a means of raising revenue. Learned that a member of his court told him that was an undignified and unworthy operation for an Emperor, whereupon he retorted "Mind your own business!"

Zeus apparently began to look on us with disfavor by the time we got to the top of the acropolis at Pergamon, unleashing thunderbolts and torrents of rain. (Turkey is altogether colder, rainier, and also more fertile than Greece, anyway.) Soaked and chilled to the bone I could not work up much enthusiasm for this site, spectacular though its theatre was, reaching up an almost perpendicular cliff wall, and important though the place may have been ("the capital of an Hellenistic Kingdom, inferior in importance only to Macedonia and Egypt....famous for its school of sculpture and its library second only to that of Alexandria!!) We consoled ourselves with the museum in the modern town of Bergama, and wandered about buying sticky sweet Turkish confections, one of which drooled honey all over me and my friend the entire journey back to the ship, and continued to drool from the shelf on which I set it over my bunk. When I decided to put a stop to this nonsense the following day by eating it, I thought surely it must have drained itself dry by that time, and was somewhat miffed to say the least when it continued dripping all over the bunk and on me when I attempted to eat it.

The magic of the name Istanbul, or Constantinople, is somewhat shattered for me in that as a city, despite an attractive situation, it is what one would call "a real dump" - terribly dingy, dirty and dilapidated, and its overrated Bazaar is full of second-rate, rather shoddy and not very exotic gods. However, the "architectural gems" such as St. Sophia Byzantine cathedral (which was later converted to a mosque by the Turks and is now just a museum), the Sultan Ahmet (or "Blue") Mosque and the Suleymaniye Mosque were the most impressive, and the museum of priceless china and all kinds of jewel-encrusted treasures in what used to be the Sultan's Palace were absolutely fabulous, like something out of the

11

Arabian Nights, to be sure! I was particularly struck by one emerald on a turban belonging to one of the Sultans, which looked about 3"x4" in size. One section of the museum held a terrifying collection of frightful looking weapons which gave one a pretty good idea of how the Turks managed to sweep across so much of the Mediterranean area as they did one time--particularly in view of the extremely fierce eyes these men still have today. Another item, in the Archaeological Museum, which was impressive was a beautifully carved sarcophagus intended for Alexander the Great (which he never used, however).

I think the thing that fascinated me the most in Istanbul was going to a service in a mosque--which I did with a small party led by a Turkish lady guide in the evening. We left our shoes at the door, shuffled, awe-struck, over the carpets inside, and sat quietly listening to the priest chanting from the front, the muezzin chanting from his perch near the back, and watching the huge congregation go through the assorted motions peculiar to their worship as one man. The sight of all those bodies "bottoms up" simultaneously was quite something. The congregation consisted almost entirely of men, and the few women were segregated in a small space at the back.

During the day an interesting sight is the men busily washing their face, hands and feet in special fountains outside the mosques prior to going inside for prayers.

Heading back for Greece again, we landed at Mytilene on the island of Lesbos, which was the home of the poetess Sappho and the scene of the romance of "Daphnis and Chloe." It was a lovely spot, mountains covered with silvery olive groves and colorful wild flowers. We went to a mountain village called Ayasso to look at a celebrated ikon (supposed to have been painted by St. Luke) in the local church. The natives of this village found us particularly fascinating and lined the streets as we went past. I felt as if I were in a parade of freaks or something. Which I suppose, in fact, we were! They put on an exhibit of folk dancing for us in return, however, outside the local taverna!! When this assemblage broke up and I was wandering around trying to find the right bus, I became separated from our crowd and found myself suddenly surrounded by excited Greek youths and accosted by a large handsome Greek woman dressed in red, who chattered excitedly, obviously exclaiming over my size. Apparently I was the first woman she'd ever seen as tall as she was, and she carried on at a great rate, measuring herself alongside me, etc., all this to the delight of the lads standing around us laughing and throwing in their two-cents-worth (or two-drachmas-worth). Not being able to speak Greek, of course, I couldn't readily communicate, but managed to look amiable (I hope) and shook hands vigorously. If I had had my wits about me (too flustered by all the attention) I should have got someone to photograph us together.

Our next island was Aegina, a sort of resort-escape for tired Athenians, with one ruined temple (not badly ruined at that, however), beaches, and numerous open-air tavernas for light refreshment.

By that time we reached Athens I think I was so saturated with ruined temples, acropolises, etc., that I was not as bowled over as I might otherwise have been on seeing that great city; nevertheless it was a thrill to see the things I'd read about, to reel off a few--the Temple of Athena Nike, the Parthenon, the Erechtheum, the Theseum, etc., and the Theatre of Dionysus, where we sat spellbound by one of our lecturers, Prof. Stanford, on the Greek Drama, in the very spot where Aeschylus, Sophocles, Euripides, and Aristophanes put on their plays (Approaching the Acropolis, I was quite charmed by a small plump man festooned with sponges for sale near the entrance. These sponge men seemed to appear conveniently wherever suitable crowds might be.) We also raced round the National Museum (with many lovely sculptures and other relics) and the Byzantine Museum, and were treated to a surprise performance of a ballet on a theme from ancient mythology, performed in the open air by the sea at nearby Vouliagmeni, with the sun just setting in the background....really lovely. An additional excursion was to Daphni to look at a noted Byzantine church, and Eleusis, at the ruined site which was the centre of the old Eleusinian Mystery religion. (Factory smokestacks now seem to be of more importance there.) I should add here that the modern city of Athens struck me as most attractive in architecture -

even its ultra-modern designs seemed extremely harmonious and pleasing to the eye - so the Greeks have not lost their early gifts at all.

Our last stop in Greece was at Olympia here the ancient Olympic Games were held every 4 years for over 1000 years. The site was silted over by a nearby river, and excavations are not yet completed, so if any would-be athlete now tries to take off from the runners' starting line, he will plunge headlong into a 12-foot bank of soft dirt. There are the usual lot of temple and other ruins here, and a museum with some wonderful sculpture, including the famous Hermes by Praxiteles.

When we arrived back at Venice and did a quick tour round there, I was so full of the wonders and beauties of Greece that Venice and things Roman and/or Italian just left me cold. They looked so "new" and "upstart-ish." I did the glass-factory interesting, however!

It was a considerable come-down to return to smog-covered, rain-soaked England after all the warmth and sunshine of Greece (which in its climate, geography and plants reminded me very much of home, i.e. California). I really loved it, and thought the people most charming, courteous, pleasant, and had an outstanding dignity. And of course it was the thrill of a lifetime to see so many of the famous places, ruins, and statues that I had always heard about, to see these beautiful examples of architecture and sculpture that the rest of the world has been copying ever since. I felt I had seen "the real thing" and that undoubtedly no trip would ever equal it, wherever I might travel.

This cruise was televised by the BBC, incidentally, and later in the summer I saw a special showing of the films at the BBC studios. Pangs of nostalgia! I even saw myself on the screen - rear and side view! (in the course of going through the Corinthian Canal, standing at the front of the ship)

****

The "summer" in England was like winter anywhere else - cold, cloudy and rainy. I made an escape to the sun the latter part of September to the Spanish island of Mallorca.

This is a sort of international Coney Island type place, terribly commercialised "tourist trap," filled with holidaymakers from all over Europe frantically trying to have a good time and all getting in each other's way. (There are more isolated spots one could stay, but too isolated, and local transportation is almost nil.) The only "sight" really noteworthy, to my mind anyway, was the Carthusian Monastery at Valldemossa, where Chopin spent a winter with his mistress George Sand; it was cold, rainy, and uncomfortable, and in this atmosphere he composed some of his famous "melancholy preludes." They should have gone there in the summer (but the who knows what kind of hot jazz he might have composed?!) It was scorching hot. The sunny climate, parched earth and familiar plants and trees reminded me of California, plus of course the Spanish-ness--I never realised how great the Spanish influence on California was, in fact, until I had this look at Spain.* I was particularly interested to learn that the "Founder of California," the Franciscan Father Junipero Serra, who built all our "mission" churches, was born in Mallorca. I went to a bullfight, exciting but gruesome, and was lucky in seeing two of Spain's leading toreros, a glum-faced lad named Chamaco (nicknamed rather), and a proud, elegant gentleman named Angel Peralta, who fought bulls from horseback, on beautiful and beautifully-trained horses, which is apparently more of a skill and rarer than the usual ground-fighting method. It was a wonderful show of horsemanship.

The brilliant colors of the stained glass in the cathedral in Palma were noteworthy, and I found the Chamber of Deputies, which is the seat of government for the 3 Balearic Isles (Mallorca, Menorca, and Ibiza) most interesting in its samples of local handicrafts - lovely wrought-iron light fixtures and hand-carved olive wood furnishings etc. Indeed, the handicrafts were the greatest draw in Palma, to my mind, and I had a wild shopping spree amongst the hand-embroidered linen blouses, table-linen, attractive wrought-iron decorative items, leather goods, tiles, etc. - all extremely reasonable.

*In fact, I really got no feeling of being in a foreign country at all--I might as well have been right at home!

Jumping from sunny Spain back to the now smog-choked England (we're getting off early from work frequently now as the fog gets so thick it takes some people hours to drive home)....the last big news item I can report to you is the dedication of the American Memorial Chapel at St. Paul's Cathedral here in London on Nov. 26th. This was built by contributions from British people in memory of American servicemen stationed in this country who were killed in World War II. The English are good at colorful and impressive ceremonial affairs and this "do" was no exception. It was a lovely service. I had an excellent seat and got a good look at the Queen, Prince Philip, the Queen Mother, Princess Margaret, the Princess Royal, the Duchess of Kent, Princess Alexandra, the Prime Minister Mr. MacMillan, Vice Pres. & Mrs. Nixon, the Lord Mayor of London (bearing a "pearl sword"!) and his entourage, the Archbishop of Canterbury, and assorted other ecclesiastical and political and military dignitaries. It was quite a treat to see so many famous people concentrated all in one spot--particularly as an invited guest! (Having over the years spent many weary hours standing in crowds out in the cold just to get a distant glimpse of some celebrity or other, I fully appreciate this privilege!)

****

WELL! If your eyeballs haven't either fallen out or capsized into your head by this time, let me wish you a happy Christmas and New Year, which is the whole point of this anyhow!

And do let me hear your news, whether potted like this or otherwise!

1959

Greetings!

Lolling about in a fairly easy job with a lot of free time has softened me up to the point where I can hardly bring myself to compose and produce this smooth annual effort, and the glorious California sunshine I'm basking in every day (in grateful contrast to this cold, damp, clouds and fog of England) is not conducive to a Christmassy frame of mind...so if this reaches you late, that's just too bad!

This has been a year of upheaval, since I completed my employment in London after four wonderful years there, and following a few last-minute travels in Europe, returned to the U.S. to feel completely foreign and out of place--in fact, I'm still not "re-adjusted" to this country. It was quite a wrench to uproot myself from a place I'd grown attached to, and to leave so many wonderful friends... the theatres... and the endless opportunities for travel.

I finished my job at the American Embassy in London just before the Easter holidays and went on another Hellenic Cruise as I had done last year. We went to many of the same places as before (Athens, Olympia, Dalos, Rhodes, Istanbul) and had quite a few of the same passengers (and distinguished lecturers) abroad too, so it was like "old home week." The new places we visited were Delphi, Sparta, Mistre, Crete and Sounion in Greece, Troy and Ephesus in Turkey, and Dubrovnik in Yugoslavia.

Delphi is a dramatic site on the slope of a mountain overlooking a huge valley & more mts. on the other side....you've no doubt heard about its famous Oracle....and maybe how Aesop was pitched over a cliff for his irreverence to the gods, and so on...there are some lovely bits of sculpture & firezes in the little museum, too....

Sparta has practically nothing left of its ancient self so there was nothing to see there in it is a quiet and ordinary town but a few unprepossessing fragment sin the museum. Nearby Mistra is more exciting, a Byzantine city (ruins of course) built right up to the side of a very steep hill, so steep in fact that I couldn't drag myself all the way up but had to be content with viewing the rosy-gold tile domed churches, etc. through the opera glasses.

If you read Mary Renault's "The King Must Die," you have a fair idea of some of the things we saw at Knossos (Crete)....King Minos' "labyrinth" palace has been partially restored, and really is a good place to get lost in. The remains at Phaestos, on the other side of the island, were the real thing though not restored therefore somehow more appealing. The drive from Heraklion to Phaestos over rough, winding roads through spectacular mountain scenery was exciting, especially when one of the rickety buses in our party lost a wheel, broke down and blocked the road so that nearby Cretan farmers had to come to the rescue by building a wide spot on the road, enabling the rest to get around. We also stopped at Gortyne, a place noted for having its early code of laws inscribed on a large wall.

The ruins of Troy's 9 layers are almost impossible to "reconstruct mentally," yet still is was thrilling just to be there, and to hear one of the Greek guides read, from the original Greek, a selection from Homer's "Iliad" on the walls of the city where it took place. The swarm of Turkish rural types (including many baggy-trousered, black-veiled women) found us all pretty entertaining, too.

Ephesus, which we reached via Izmir (Smyrne--the fig country!) was a fascinating site; since there is more of it left standing, it was a little easier to visualize what it had been like. Many of the ruins were marked with signs, conveniently written in Turkish, German, and English--e.g. "Ask Evi -- Freudenhaus -- Brothel"! Ephesus, one of the various places lived in (and written to) by St. Paul, was the great center of the worship of Diana (Artemis, a sort of lascivious, fertility-type goddess, (her temple, now vanished, was one of the Seven Wonders), and a brisk trade in images of her was beginning to be sabotaged by St. Paul and his new-fangled religion. One Demetrius and other fellow-silversmiths whose business was thus threatened caused "no small stir" to arise against Paul & Co. We sat in the very theatre where the riot took place and one of our lecturers read the account to us from the Bible (Acts XIX: 23-41), as exciting as if it had just taken place... the typical mob scene, "...And the whole city was filled with confusion...they rushed with one second into the theatre...some therefore cried one thing, and some another: for the assembly was confused, and the more part knew not wherefore they were come together....but when they know.............all with one voice about the space of two hours cried out, "Great is Diana of the Ephesiens!" "

Sounion, a short & scenic ride along the coast from Athens, boasta an attractive enough ruin (temple of Poseidon) but was too "touristy," and unfortunately many people followed the deplorable... I won't describe "last year's places" and save in mentioning that in Istanbul, where my English companion and I went to a record shop to buy a bit of Turkish folk music, we found the place full of Turkish teen-agers buying all the latest American jazz and rock & roll....laughing at us for listening to their corny local stuff.

We were scheduled to visit Cyrene in Libya, but the sea was too rough for us to lend at the port of Derus, so my knowledge of the North African coast is somewhat superficial still...the offshore view was not much help.

Dubrovnik (Yugoslavia) proved to be an attractive small medieval city (formerly known as Saguea, a fairly powerful independent city-state in its time, with its own fleet, etc.) and in fact looked more like "The Merchant of Venice" then Venice does... we fully expected to see Shakespearean characters pop out of doorways and side alleys any minute. There is a cathedral there built by Richard the Lion-Hearted, by the way. The Dubrovnik of today apparently exists mostly on the tourist trade (summer holidaymakers from colder climates) and the natives, although quite a good-looking people, seemed a bit glum in temperament.

As before, the cruise ended in Venice (gondola travel with a full load of passengers and suitcases in the rain is not the gay, romantic mode of transport generally ballyhooed in the films, in once you're interested---but has its amusing moments!), I left the party there, and proceeded up to Austria--Innsbruck & St. Johann in the Tyrolean Alps--brr! and those mountains are just too big for my taste--Salzburg (where a Prince-Bishop of some centuries past built a lovely palace for his mistress and 11 children, and another summer palace full of practical jokes, i.e. spraying water all over his unsuspecting guests at every turn in the garden, etc.)--and Vienna. The latter still retains some of its charm and spirit despite all it has been through, and has the added beauty of being relatively cheap; a good place to indulge in a bit of "luxury" at a low price. Schonbrunn Palace was really gorgeous... where old Frans Joseph slept amidst gilded decor in a small, plain iron bed. A ride through the "Vienne Woods" is lovely too... and the opera...the food...etc. etc. but the outstanding show was, I think, the performance of the Spanish Riding School, a lovely fragment of the aristocratic past, with the Lipizzan horses and their handsome riders in a sort of "equestrian ballet: as it were, to music, in a riding hall that looked more like a ballroom.

I returned to London for various Cruise reunions and then went up to Scotland for a short and less glamorous "cruise" by local mail & cargo ships to the Orkneys and Shetlands. Cold, bleak and treeless, pest bogs, Shetland ponies, and fishing boats from various Northern countries ind, clear invigorating air, white sands blue sea... Shetland was appealing in its way. (Orkney not so interesting, apart from the Scapa Flow where so many ships were sunk and a little Nissen hut converted into a Baroque-type chapel by Italian prisoners of war with considerable artistic flair.) But on the mainland of Shetland we had a bus trip to Sumburgh, where the various ruins (called "Jarlshof" - Sir Walter Scott's idea) of iron oge, Pictish, Viking, and some medieval Scottish dwellings are tidily preserved. (Shetland was settled by Vikings, and only came into Scottish hands because the King of Denmark pawned it to the King of Scotland as part of his daughter's dowry and never redeemed it). Proceeding farther north by smaller ship, the sea became rougher and rougher, and I only left my healthy bunk when we stopped to load or unload some of the local cargo (maybe a cow, a sheep, a sick man on a litter, a few carts of food or other vital supplies) but at one point before I had retreated back to the bunk, the Captain invited me up to the bridge, and I just COULDN'T be sick there, so queasily & politely listened to his tales of island life, and the Norwegian weather forecast, which he could understand and give a running translation of, even the various Norse dialects. We made our most northerly stop at Baltasound (island of Unst) where we had a little bus ride up to view the Muckle Flugga Lighthouse (yes, Muckle Flugga) which is the northernmost point in Great Britain, and I'd say it would be a toss-up as to which is the loneliest outpost at which to be stationed, that, or the nearby RAF station; but the natives, a happy, contented and very nice looking people, say it is a very busy and pleasant place to live.

Incidentally, Shetland has some of the most marvelous place names: Mouses, Grutness, Fitful, Haad, Pepa Stour, Scatote, Vidlin Voe, Lunna Nose, Yell!

That cruise ended at Aberdeen, and from there I proceeded down to the North of England to visit friends in Billingham, who took me to see Durham Cathedral - one of the most imposing in the country. I had long wanted to see Hadrian's Wall, and there were not ours running this early in the year, so I made my way from Newcastle by local trains and buses to one of the Roman camps ("Checters") and there found a party of school boys in chartered buses, whose headmaster kindly let me come along with them, to see other sites of interest along the wall, including the best preserved portion of Housestenda. I can't think of a better way to "do" this well than with this bright bunch of lads, who were most amusing playing "Picts" and "Romans" fighting on the wall.

My last sightseeing in the North was the so-called Holy Island (Lindisfarne), accessible only by dilapidated taxi at low tide, not frightfully thrilling when you got there, but an historic site from the standpoint of early British Christianity, the abbey founded by St. Aidan from the parent community at Ions in Scotland.

I returned to London for a last farewell, and sailed from Southampton May 27 on a ghastly military transport ship (my own fault, I could have flown). Arrived in New York June 3 in my heavy British woolens and nearly collapsed in the 96°-or-so heat, but crawled around dazed and awestruck at the variety and volume of beautiful clothes, feeling like a foreigner, with my profusion of pleases and thank-yous and sorrys and waiting for buses on the wrong side of the street and thinking every American I saw was a tourist till I remembered I was back on home ground...felt very strange indeed. I spent awhile on the east coast and then came home to California & spent the summer at home in Morro Bay, unpacking, sorting, washing, cleaning (the English soot will never come out), and then re-packing to come up north, i.e. to Palo Alto, to look for a job.

There are a lot of aircraft and electronics firms around here but I'd had such a bellyful of that kind of subject matter on my previous job, so I decided to investigate office jobs at Stanford University (the "alma mater"): however, on seeing my application (dazzled by this "American Embassy - London" background) they seemed to think I was just the thing for the directorship of one of the girls' dormitories (Union Res. to be exact). My reaction was "ugh!" - not my cup of tea at all - the prospect of having to cope with 80 adolescent American females was, to say the least, revolting. However, the university was desperate (the previous lady having suddenly quit on them at the last minute, school was about to start, and no staff), so they gave me a big line of bull about how the academic standards had risen to unprecedented heights, students now more serious minded, etc. (not much!) But what really enabled them to railroad me into this job was sheer greed on my part -- for the room & board, long vacations, daily maid service, & lots of free time during the day, so I capitulated, and plunged right in with all four feet and fur flying, an exhausting round of orientation meetings for new staff, then the tribulations of getting the place opened and everyone settled in, and so on. The first month was pretty hectic, but now things have calmed down and I'm beginning to have some idea of what I'm doing. It's like being a hotel manager, mother confessor and general crying towel for all the little darlings under one's care. This particular dorm had always been the hangout for the Bluestocking-Bohemian set, who have recently been inundated by a swarm of more conventional sweet young things and social butterflies, etc., arbitrarily assigned here under the university's new housing policy. This mixing may have a salubrious effect on both camps.

As jobs go, it's fairly easy, as I say with free time during the day, but being "on call" 24 hours a day, 7 days a week, and having to eat with - and listen to - nothing but adolescents all the time gets a bit annoying sometimes. However, for the present time, the many advantages make it worth my while, & it's nice being (for the most part) my own boss.

The only "trip" I've taken since I came here was a weekend down to Carmel and Monterey, most charming, and in fact almost like being back in Europe again!

****

Cheerio for now, and have a happy Christmas and New Year....

1964

Greetings and Merry Christmas!

I'm late getting my cards done -- but just discovered I could borrow a duplicating machine, so that will speed up the message somewhat as compared to the handscrew method.

I resigned from my London job in early April, and for a last-fling trip coming home, took a tour of the Holy Land and other areas of interest in the Middle East -- through four countries to be exact -- Lebanon, Syria, Jordan, and Israel. We flew from London to Beirut where we stopped a few days, taking excursions to various sites in Lebanon-- Sidon, bait-ed-Din, the Dog River, and the Cedars (a skiing resort!) into Syria, stopping to see Chevaliere (Crusader castle: Incidentally, we got an absolute bellyful of Crusader castles on this trip -- they're everywhere), (just a revolt there shortly after we left), the Syrian desert to the ruined city (gorgeous!), and then down to a city with wonderful bazaars, beautiful mosques, and of course the places associated with the life of St. Paul.

Then we proceeded into Jordan -- via the ruined city of Jeresu - to Jerusalem, our headquarters for seeing the places associated with the life of Christ and various other sites. We also had a swim in the Dead Sea, a look at the caves where the

"Dead Sea Scrolls" were found, climbed down onto the walls of buried Jericho, and viewed the Promised Land from Mt. Nebo, as did Osea and his followers. We thought Osea had made a mistake, because the area he had just come from looked more fertile, but were told that once the heat started the situation would be more or less reversed in favor of the "promised land."

Our tour ended in the Jordan side of Jerusalem, but about half our group continued on into Israel for further touring. Israel is more interested in showing its brand new features, but from our point of view we were more interested in seeing sites of biblical and historical interest. Our tour there covered Aere (Richard the Lion Hearted and more Crusaders!), Tiberias, Mt. of Bestidude, Sea of Galileo, Nazareth, etc. - various sites in the area associated with Jesus' life. I also took a tour down to camel market of the bedouins of the Negev and Ashkelon.

In summary, this was the most exciting and intriguing trip I've taken. The impact of actually being in the very places one knows from the Bible cannot be described. And the Arab world is absolutely fascinating. I used to think Lawrence and such types must be a bit goofy; now I see what it was all about - there is definitely something about the Feat that "gets you."

I stopped over briefly in Greece treking down St. Paul some more (Neapolia and Philip and a few more Greek Islands were also added to my collection (Kee Koni and Hydra) and on land...then back to London whence I reorganized and got myself back to the U.S. on the S.S. "France" - a very comfortable ship with delicious food and such gracious staff.

For real anti-climax, now, I've been bogged down at home ever since in household repairs, renovations, painting, etc. to the point where I feel there was a great deal to be said for the bedouin tents of the Arabian deserts. Though there is much left to be done I can't stick it much longer so hope to get away soon. Plans very vague and miscellaneous yet. But I switch from this growling note just in time to wish you a happy Christmas and New Year before I fall off the bottom of this page... and may your house never get into the crumbling state mine was!

1965

Greetings!

Christmas is at our throats once again--only this time the usual panic, rush, etc. is further complicated by the fact that at the time of writing this I'm not settled as to a job and a place to live, so I'll be doing very well if I can get greetings off at all, let alone on time.

In January, in spite of the preceding six horrible months of household painting, etc, I took off for New York to take up the study of interior design. I drove by the southernmost route to avoid snow. A long, wearisome journey... you realize how big this country really is when you start to drive across it. The Arizona and New Mexico desert were beautiful, and what bliss-- perfect peace, hardly another car or human being in sight.

School proved to be hectic, as it was a very high pressure course, involving vast amounts of leg work as well as work, so there was not much time for recreation. But the course was so fascinating it was worth it. I used to think of furniture as just some thing to sit on and a nuisance to dust and polish... but when you learn the whole history of architecture, art, decoration and furnishing, including all the "ingredients" that go into an interior (such as rugs, wallpaper, fabrics, ceramics, glass, etc.) from the time of the ancient Egyptians down to the present day, you see everything around you with new eyes. But imagine the struggle trying to remember it all for our final exam! We also studied room arrangement, trade information, color and antiques. All the instructors and special lecturers were practically architects, designers, decorators, etc. So we really got the expert "word." I stayed on for the summer course in design (drafting) and sketching which in New York's sweltering humid heat meant literally sweating over a hot drawing board. I loved all my courses and enjoyed the museums, stores, etc. that N.Y. has to offer, but think it is a vile place in which to live. In all my round-the-world travels, I've never seen such rude people anywhere-ugh! I marvel at the endurance of my friends who manage to stand it there.

In September with the little green bug loaded inside and outside (tons of books in a tarpaulin on the roof) I took off across country for home again, this time via the middle of the country, more or less, and managed to see several friends en route whom I had not seen for years--though couldn't manage to see everyone I would like to have seen. As it was the trip took 4 weeks and a day, 4,200 miles, driving, driving, driving, and I had really   begun to feel like the Flying Dutchman of the Highways, doomed to spend the rest of my life driving across flat miles of corn, bleak range lands, taking deserts, and crawling up and down endless mountain perks. Incidentally, the Rocky Mountains and English fords are not made for each other. I made the entire trip without any mechanical troubles or mishaps, but mountain climbing was slow, toilsome business, with frequent pauses to cool off the boiling radiator. Nevertheless I thought the mountain landscape interesting, especially in Wyoming. On this return trip I stopped to see Lincoln's home and grave in Springfield, Ill., and in the way of "natural wonders" found the badlands of South Dakota most fascinating, with all the millions of years of the earth's geological layers exposed in weird shapes by erosion; also liked the dinosaur and other prehistoric fossil remains exhibited in various places nearby. I think I was looking at about 60 million years worth of the earth's history. It makes you (and the world's current troubles) seem pretty small, after all. After that, the so-called "old west" history at Fort Laramie seemed pretty "new." I was further fascinated by the Bonneville Salt Flats of Utah--miles and miles of white desert composed of crystallized salt. Nice and crunchy to walk on; and plenty of disconcerting mirages out there, too.

The Middle West was pretty cold -- and down to around 20° sometimes in Nevada -- so trust good old California to give me a really warm welcome, 90° to 100° the whole first week I was back. October. Now, November, has evened the balance with two weeks of pouring rain, which has somewhat put the damper on my job-hunting activities, but I trust that in due course I can get settled up in the San Francisco Bay area.

A happy Christmas and New Year!

1971

Greetings!

At least I have something really newsworthy to report for the year. I FINALLY got back to Europe in the spring for another Hellenic Cruise, with a little time in London before and after. It was great to be back in London where I had spent so many interesting years, but frustrating not to have time to see everyone. And of course it was wonderful to be sailing the beautiful Mediterranean again.

The cruise visited several places we'd been on the 2 previous cruises I'd taken when I lived in London - such as Athens, Mykonos, Delos, Istanbul, Ephesus and Heraklion; plus some sites that were completely new to me-- Amphiareion, the Meteora, Thesos, Mt. Athos, Petmos, Megalopolis and Bassee in Greece; Ascos in Turkey; and Syracuse and Agrigento in Sicilyl plus Carthage and Tunis in Tunisia!

It was distressing to see how commercialized Greece had become in the intervening years, but I suppose it was inevitable; and it was even more of a shock to find the same thing creeping up on Turkey, which before had seemed so remote and untouched. Tourist shops and moneychangers all over the harbor village of Kusadasi, ticky-tacky cheap vacation resort springing up along the coast, and festival banners and litter in the theatre at Ephesus where centuries ago the silversmiths had stirred up the riot against St. Paul. But on the positive side it was interesting to see how much more of Ephesus had been dug up by archaeologists since we were there last; among ruined cities it's one of my favorites.

It was somehow sad to find that our creaking old Turkish ship the "Ankers" now had the conventional array of tiny individual plastic-encased English jellies messed on the breakfast tables instead of the big jars of gooey Turkish honey-based jams. And disciplined, organized service with even a slight grasp of the English language on the part of the stewards had no dulled all the fun of genuine and uncomprehending chaos that added so much amusement and adventure in the past when we met an endless barrage of "om-LET" every morning, regardless of what we had tried to order in the "good old days."

The Temple of Apollo way, way up the mountains at Bassae was handsome and spectacular as to scenic beauty of the location, remoteness and difficulty of access-involving a scary cliffhanging ride on unfurnished mountain roads which reduced one Greek guide literally to tears. Patmos was a charming and peaceful island where we had a very wobbly donkey ride up rocky paths to visit a monastery and the cave (now a chapel) where St. John wrote "Revelation."

Sicily was quite a surprise to me; I'd known of course that the Greeks had been there, but I hadn't expected so MANY temples and of such vast size. It seems that when they beat the Carthaginians in the Battle of Himera 480 B.C. they got so many slaves per capita and so much wealth that they went mad with ostentatious building projects.

Tunis and Carthage were exciting - some Punic remains (mostly graves of infants expended for human sacrifices); fantastic Roman baths (world's largest); the wonderful Berdo Museum full of magnificent Roman mosaics, plus some interesting Greek finds dredged up from an ancient shipwreck; and of course the colorful souks (bazaar) one expects in the Arab countries.

The cruise finished in Palme, Mellorce; having been there before I concentrated on shopping and enjoying a wonderful Spanish luncheon. And thence the flight back to London.. All in all the trip was a great morale builder, though strenuous, and I can't wait to get back to that part of the world!

All this is a far cry from the steady parade of heart patients where I'm still working in Cardiology at Stanford Medical Center. Coronary artery disease and impending myocardial infarctions (heart attacks) and the new approaches to some are the big thing now; and our heart transplant program continues with success. We had some top Russian health officials visiting this year; it seems Russia also has an extensive coronary artery disease problem so they came to see what we are doing about it.

1972

Greetings!

No exotic trips to report this year, but in Sept, a one -week "domestic" package tour in New Mexico proved to be most interesting. Based on Albuquerque (large, modern and highest crime rate in the U.S.(!), but a picturesque "old town" (early Spanish settlement quarter/now full of artsy-craftsy shops), and Santa Fé (oldest capital in the U.S., most attractive & charming - old-world Spanish feeling plus "Pueblo Indian" style architecture), we saw several Indian villages (Teos, Santo Domingo & San Ildefonso) where the Indians' way of life combines both primitive and modern features (e.g. mud buildings, outdoor ovens for baking bread in their traditional manner, and on the other hand, cars, washing machines, etc.); wild west ghost towns (most notably Cerrillos, former silver mining town owned by Tiffany's jewelers in New York, now being re-settled with restaurants, "antique" shops, and people fleeing modern civilisation); the atomic science and bomb museums at Los Alamos and at Sandie Air Base; 16th and 17th century Spanish haciendas & churches; Bandelier Natl. Park, a beautiful canyon filled with trees and wild flowers, the cliffs being "ruins" or former Indian cliff dwellings (caves, plus holes drilled for supporting poles to create lean-to type structures); and gorgeous scenery everywhere, a wide variety of geological formations, lovely wild flowers, and best of all, WIDE OPEN SPACES (the way California used to be!). Wish I'd had more time to spend in Santa Fé, and to explore further in this interesting state.

Enjoyed a number of performances of the San Francisco Opera this autumn, especially the complete Wagner Ring Cycle, which was magnificent.

Best wishes for a happy Christmas and New Year!

1973

Greetings!

This year I have a fairly off-bent trip to report, namely a camping trek around Tunisie on Algeria in May, with a small group in a Ford Minibug -- tents, sleeping bags and campfire cooking in the land of the Barbary Pirates, where Christians captured off European and American ships were sold as slaves for hundreds of years until the French took over in the early 19th century! Had to speak French everywhere, since the only alternative was Arabic, and I was gratified to find that even my mediocre French "worked." In fact I had to help intercept for some of the others in the group.

The natives of these countries are mainly of the Barber race, a Caucasian people of dark coloring somewhat resembling Malaysians. They have been occupied and ruled over several thousands of years by the Phoenicians, Romans, Vendals, Byzantines, Arabs, Spanish, Turks, and finally the French, and they have become independent and self-governing only in recent years. There are many contrasts of "the old and the new," modern features side by side with old-fashioned or primitive ones, and there are still even many bedouin tribes wandering about in their colorful costumes with their goats, camels, etc., and camping in their graceful tents of wool in broad earth-tone stripes. We saw a fantastic variety of scenery, architecture, costumes, plants, and (ugh) insects. Our itinerary took us through rolling hills and farmland, meadows carpeted with beautiful wild flowers, rugged mountains (some with a bit of snow on top), dramatic rock-hewn gorges, flat scrubby desert, sand-dune deserts, salt flats, palm-oases with voluminous irrigation streams, gorgeous beaches; Phenicien, Roman and even early Christian remains (the early Christians didn't last, what with Roman "discouragement" and then the later introduction of Islam by the Arabs), the full gamut of Arab/Turkish Moslem features such as welled Medines (old native quarters), souks (bezeers), mosques, ribats (fortified monasteries, to fight off Christian attackers); troglodytes' underground cave-houses, lovely French villes and other modern buildings, and attractive beach resort hotels where holidaymakers from the cold northern countries, mostly Germany, Scandinavia and Britain, come to soak up the sun, of which there is an abundance (we noted a temperature of 128° at one point).

The climate and plants are very much like California, as is much of the Mediterranean area, the familiar citrus, olives, eucalyptus, oleanders, hibiscus, bougainvillea, cacti, etc., plus perched earth and hot sun--the letter exceeding most of California's however except for our own deserts. We did most of our own cooking (frightful stews enlivened by the inevitable sand, and harsh, cheap local wines), but we did have occasions to try native cooking, some of which was very tasty and interesting, and some which was rather revolting (they make us of all entrails). They have particularly delicious and very fresh fish along the coastline. And of course the traditional French cooking could also be found in some places.

Our itinerary began at Tunis, where I'd been very briefly before. It's a large fairly modern (i.e. French) type city and has a wide main boulevard with a tree-lined central mall full of pretty flower stands, magazine stands, etc. The native Medine "teems" with life and colorful markets, and the Bardo museum on the outskirts of town has a fascinating collection (world's largest) of Roman mosaics I enjoyed seeing again. We travelled westward to Dougge (marvelous remains of a Roman city), crossing the border into Algeria with endless niggling formalities on both sides totalling nearly 3 hours, through the market town of Souk Ahras to Constantine, a city dramatically situated on a tremendous mountain gorge; it has been continuously inhabited since prehistoric times. Then we headed south, pausing for a look at the remains of the headquarters of the Third Augusta Legion of the Roman

Army at Lambesis, and the splendid Roman city of Timgad, which has one of the two known Roman library remains (the other being at Ephesus, Turkey, which I've seen on my Hellenic Cruises), and with roads rutted by the passage of many chariot-wheels in their day. The wind and heat here were nearly overpowering and I doused myself liberally at the same fountain used by the Romans. Then we went through the spectacular Aures mountains and gorges, an area where the hardy natives have always held out against foreign occupying powers, and apparently gave the Romans and the French a hard time; in fact, the final revolt against France began here.

We gradually came to flatter country, the heat intensifying with every passing day; in fact, it got so all we could think about every time we stopped was getting something to drink and water to slosh over ourselves, if it were available. The oasis town of Touggourt did little to cool us; it was entirely yellow-ochre, from the ground to the buildings to the air and the sky, from constant blowing sand, and I then fully appreciated the point of the native women's costumes, all-enveloping pale pastel-checked sheet-like wraps, draped in a way so that only one eye need peer out into the sand. (In the north of Algeria the costume was a somewhat nun-like black wrap and head-veil, with a small white face veil over nose and mouth. In Tunisian towns, and Tunis in particular, white sheet-like wraps were in vogue. However, in very rural areas where there had been less Arab influence, the women retained the Berbere traditional very bright multi-colored ensembles and did not cover the face. Very young women in cities wore modern European dress.... once there were, and how little scope they seemed to have (e.g. no women in restaurants or cafés).

We turned eastward across sand-dune deserts, nearly perishing with heat, and finding the highway partially covered with sand drifts and the telephone poles nearly buried with sand. The temperature was 113° inside our vehicle. These sand dunes are beautiful to the eye, but the roaring Sirocco is blowing so much of them into your eyes, teeth, hair, clothes, etc. that makes it almost impossible to walk, or care much about anything but getting out of there post-haste. Wind, sand, dirt, dust, heat, sweat, fatigue and thirst summarize the scene. (So much for all those romantic old Rudolf Valentino/Charles Boyer/Marlene Dietrich/Gary Cooper movies!!)

The next oasis town was El-Cued, "the city of a thousand cupolas," but architecture took second place to the search for a water-tap in the local market place where we drenched ourselves in very unseemly fashion, judging from the incredulity of the natives' expressions. The preoccupation with water and something to drink (survival instinct) is paramount at all times. Incidentally, no matter how remote or primitive a village appeared, they always seemed to have Coca Cola (the signs being equally recognizable in Arabic). Only one village did not, but it had Pepsi. I never touch these things at home but consumed quite a bit in North Africa, since synthetic "orange" drinks had even less appeal & I sometimes felt the need of more than just commercially bottled water. We carried some water with us from native springs or pumps along the way, to use for cooking, tooth-brushing etc., and I had my own plastic bottle to put some of this in (with chlorine tablets); however, as one goes south into the desert areas the water becomes more and more saline and quite unpalatable.

More desert, and another time-consuming border crossing back into Tunisie, &then we camped in a palm grove in the oasis town of Tozeur. We had white sand and lovely palms and huge irrigation streams, most welcome, to pollute somewhat by bathing, laundry and dishwashing on the part of some very tired and dirty travelers. We also met our first scorpion here (before he had a chance to sneak up on us). Much insect repellent daubed round entrance of our tent at all times, more so than ever here. This place had 200 springs flowing at 165 gallons per sec. into streams which water 2590 acres of date palms--statistics I found rather mind-blowing after miles and miles of parched deserts. The next leg of the journey took us across the Chott Djerid (salt flats), with plenty of disorienting mirages, and not a good place to get stranded. We made it through some old slave-trade post villages to the coastal city of Gabes, where a few of us (including me) sybaritically crawled into a hotel with real beds and real

French cooking and the rest of the group were nearly blown out to see camping on the beach in a windstorm.

Southward next through some World War II territory including the area of the Mareth Line, seeing a few German bunkers and German war cemetery, a stark, lonely place with one or two cacti among the rows of "iron cross" shaped crosses standing incongruously in the baked African earth and giving us some sobering thoughts of all that struggle in what now seems such an irrelevant place for the combatants and yet at the time had been important. At Metmets we visited some of the troglodytes' underground cave-homes, the rooms being dug out round a central core which formed the courtyard and which gave the landscape a pitted moon-scape appearance from a distance. Very sensible architectural style in which to keep cool in a beastly climate. Further south, we spent 3 nights on the lovely island of Djerba, timeless and peaceful, with miles of empty beaches (the Mediterranean gives good swimming, no huge waves to knock you down) and some very attractive hotels. Again a few of us opted for a couple of civilized nights with beds, showers, etc. at an hotel which also offered a campsite for the hardier souls. We camped for one night on a fairly isolated beach fringed with palms, which was great, although the next morning everything was drenched from the evening dew. Odysseus (Ulysses) is traditionally alleged to have landed on Djerba, which was thought to have been the "land of the lotos-eaters," but I've subsequently read a book which gives pretty good evidence that it was actually somewhere further east on the libyan coast. Djerba has a market town also, full of souvenir items for the tourists, and I watched some rug-weaving in a local etelier. Rugs in Tunisia were interesting but I couldn't cope with any bulky purchases on top of all my luggage so had to forego them.

We proceeded north along the coast area in to the large fairly industrial city of Sfax and camped in a wedi (dry river bed, the first "soft" ground I slept on the whole trip) and made a brief stop for a look at the huge Roman amphitheatre (colosseum) at El Djem, including the underground cells where gladiators, prisoners, lions, etc. were kept prior to the fights which furnished so much entertainment in roman days.

We headed for Keirounan, the holy city, where I think 7 visits to the Great Mosque equal one pilgrimage to Mecca, considered very beneficial from the Moslem point of view. Most Tunisien architecture is white with blue trim (to (a) keep cool and b) keep the flies away) but in Keirounen we saw some buildings with an apple-green trim as well as the usual white and blue ones, so it seemed a more "colorful"town, though ti had a more peaceful quality, owing presumably to its religious orientation.

Monestir is a resort town with a splendid big ribat on a cliff overlooking a nice beach, and President Bourguiba has his family mosque and mausoleum built here. By the way, the main street of every town is named after him. Sousee is another large and quite bustling modern city and Nabeul are smaller more residential and resort-type places; at Nabeul we camped in a "camping motel" among orange trees, bathed in real showers, used real toilets, and ate dinner a dining room, breakfast on a lovely terrace under fig trees. Such things as plumbing, soap and water now seemed to be utter luxuries. Camping in the Sahara gives one a whole new perspective on life.

Thence back to Tunis for a last look and dash round the souks, topping off the trip with two attractive nearby residential and resort areas of Carthage (Phoenician and Roman remains which I'd seen before) and Sidi Bou Said (gorgeous view across Gulf of Tunis towards Cap Bon), departing Tunis Airport, discarding one pair of worn out shoes there just before takeoff.

I had a bit of time in London before and after this North African tour, seeing a few old friends, but without enough time to see everyone, which was frustrating. I managed to take in a few plays, notably "Habeas Corpus" (Alec Guinness), "Dear Love" (Keith Michell & Geraldine McEwan as Robt. Browning and Eliz. Berrett), "A Doll's House (Claire Bloom)--all excellent. I also attended a delightful chamber music concert in a stately home, Hem House (once the seat of the Earls of Dysart), an experience which gives one an evening of feeling what it must have been like to live in such a place of grandeur during its 17th century heydey-- marvelous!

I found many changes in London, the main shock being a much higher cost of living, but it's still one of my favorite places!

1975

Greetings! It would take reams of paper to describe this year's off-beat travels, so I'll just try to hit the high spots, up to 1 oz. mailing weight! In August, I went, with considerable trepidation and apprehension, to East Germany on a specialized English group tour for art lovers, with a heavy sightseeing schedule of galleries, museums and palaces, etc.) and to Portugal (with even more trepidation and apprehension...on a general group tour, also English, covering a basic tourist route of historic, architectural and scenic interest). All this in the midst of Europe's biggest heat-wave in years.

Did not get swallowed up behind the Iron Curtain as I'd feared, and East Germany turned out to be more drab and bleek than anything else, with a great feeling of emptiness and joylessness & no bright lights, color, gaiety or night life to speak of. Since there were no policemen about (apart from a vehicle full lurking in the shrubbery near the huge Russian war memorial to prevent other Germans from desecrating it), one assumes there is an ample network of plain clothes police, Communist party, informers, etc. to keep the population in a subdued, guarded and circumspect state at all time.

The museum in East Berlin containing the magnificent Greek Altar of Pergamon and the Market Gate of Miletus (2 ancient sites I'd viste on my Hellenic cruises years ago, in what is now Turkey), and the Ishtar Gate and processional Way of Nebuchadnezzar II of Babylon, were of particular interest. At Potsdam we visited Sans Souci, Frederick the Great's palace complex, including his "Chinese Tea House," and I distinguished myself by being stung by a bee while eating lunch at the hotel where the Potsdam Agreement was signed. Schloss Moritzburg, hunting lodge of the Saxon King Augustus the Strong, set on an island in the middle of a lake in a pleasant little village, was a quick detour en route to Dresden, where we had a large dose of art at Augustus' Zwinger Palace. His collection of paintings, jewel and objets d'art, armor (elaborately decorated and inlaid weapons, uniforms, etc.) and porcelains, was quite staggering. The porcelains were from many places, but of course there was a great deal of Meissen, Augustus having been responsible for its existence. It seems he had imprisoned the alchemist Boettger with orders to make gold, but Boettger arrived at the secret of making porcelain instead (1709), hitherto a Chinese monopoly. We saw many examples of the work of the famous sculptor Kaendler of that early period--not only the well-known dainty rococo figures of coy damsels and gallant lovers, but also some large, strong, masculine figures of birds, animals, and busts of people, in solid white glaze, which were magnificent. Schloss Pillnitz, Augustus' residential summer palace across the river in a more rural area, was delightful on a steamy summer afternoon on the bank of the Elbe. A number of interesting objets d'art were on display here, including some very lacy Saxon glassware.

The little town of Meissen (untouched by the war) was quite charming and we enjoyed a visit to the porcelain factory, where the process of making and painting porcelain is demonstrated to visitors, and examples of their ware from the earliest times to the present may be seen in their museum. Leipzig turned out to be a city actually pulsating with a bit of life, a feeling we missed elsewhere on the trip. I speculated that the retention of some identity and morale here was perhaps the result of having been allowed to continue their 800-year-old right to have an international statue looking over it, just opposite the Maedler Passage where one enters Auerbach's Keller (utilized in "Faust"), was full of people who actually seemed to be enjoying themselves, a few even laughing and joking and clowning about. We visited Bach's St. Thomas Church, where he worked and is buried; his statue is just outside. Wagner's birthplace is gone, a modern store standing in its place. A friend and I went to have a drink in Auerbach's Keller one evening before dinner, and it was quite delightful--16th century or so, several rooms for drinking and dining, one with a pianist and violinist playing gaily away, all very lively and romantic and charming; the violinist apparently spotted us for "English" right away, as he immediately started playing songs from "My Fair Lady," with much bowing and smiling between numbers. Naumberg has a fine old cathedral with some particularly beautiful cathedral with some particularly beautiful stone carvings including the figure of the lovely Queen Uta. Weimar is a delightful town, where we visited the Goethe/Schiller mausoleum (not only permanent artificial wreaths here at this place of pilgrimage for the German people, but also little clusters of two or three fresh flowers that individual visitors had brought--very touching), the homes of Goethe (both his main house and his summer house), Schiller, and Liszt (where one sees many of his personal belongings including his treasured death-mask of Beethoven). We also raced past the Architecture School where the "Bauhaus" movement started, which has subsequently furnished the whole world with so much stark functional building, and one marvels that it should have started in such a pretty traditional-style town.

Wittenberg was of much historic interest, to see the church (actually, second re-building thereof) where Luther preached and pinned his famous Theses to the door, launching the Protestant Reformation. Visited the Augustinian monastery where he lived. Reflected again on the colossal courage of this man.

Miscellaneous observations: Dining rooms invariably had desserts sitting on table when one arrived. Food pretty good solid fare in most places, lots of meat, lots of beer. Evidently a child care system is in effect for working mothers; saw uniformed nursemaids wheeling giant prams containing 6 to 8 babies each. Every hotel room has one potted plant (and one radio). Washed off potted plant at each place in my shower; ("What am I doing here, showering potted plants all over Germany?!") Window sills of historic houses we visited also full of potted plants (usually flowering ones); this must be a German "thing." Recalled Erich Von Stroheim with his geranium in the fortress of the old movie "Grande Illusion." Shops rather dull--seemed to have ample "basics" but nothing much of interest. Visited small supermarket--practically no fresh vegetables, and a few of poor quality, possibly because of the drought and heat. Post and catalog counters at all palaces, art galleries, museums etc. mobbed with tourists. (all from other Iron Curtain countries) craving a bit of beauty to take home. Battled my way through a cluster of Polish Boy scouts to get myself some postcards of paintings etc. at Dresden. Russian Army troops, trucks, tanks, headquarters, etc. everywhere. Germans refer to the Russians as "Sasha" now (during WWII it was "Ivan.") Heard our driver refer to them as "Blancmangies." To anyone who has ever eaten a blancmange pudding, this puts Cold War in a whole new light. Must say Russians look sloppy; however, there are an awful <u>lot of</u> them. Tourists have to put on huge "slippers" made of something like thick carpet under-felting, over their shoes, while visiting palace rooms with elaborate parquet or marble-inlaid floors, ostensibly to protect the floors, but also a way of getting you to polish their floors, since you must slide around like an ice-skater to prevent the slippers falling off.

End of tour - time to cross through the <u>Berlin Wall</u> again. Our own driver not allowed to drive us through, since he was unmarried, and therefore regarded as more likely to try to escape, so we had to change into another bus with a married driver, the wife thus being hostage to ensure his return. (Wonder if they ever had any married drivers who wanted to escape not only the country but also their wives?)

After we had settled into the our second bus, our original driver and guide came in to say goodbye, and at this point, we all began to choke up, since it was not just a case of saying goodbye after a pleasant week's touring--it was the realization that we were free to go through that wall, and they were not. They too, of course, were feeling this same thing. An acutely poignant moment, which made it difficult to even speak, and left us with heavy hearts. Thus one realizes what freedom means.

As we entered the area for border-crossing formalities, our faces and passports were intently scrutinized to be sure we "matched," the bus and luggage compartments were carefully searched and a huge mirror rolled under the bus, looking for stowaways. In this hideous maze of electrified wire, nasty wall, tank traps, & gun towers for shooting escapers, would you believe more potted flowering plants in and around the guards and money-changing buildings!! Finally, having been cleared, we went through the wall and on to the famous "Checkpoint Charlie" where Allied military guards just wave jauntily as you pass through--no formalities at all on the West Berlin side.

Feeling rather tired, sloppy and seedy in our casual wear, we were then suddenly plunged into a smart and luxurious <u>West Berlin</u> hotel, to clean up, pull ourselves together, and enjoy fine service, facilities and food, a bit of "glamour," in staggering contrast to the drabness and dreariness of life on the East Side. After dinner we strolled outside on the famed Kurfurstendamm, to find West Berlin a really "swinging" city of bright lights, color, beautiful shops full of elegant things, cafes, restaurants, nightclubs, and people full of pep and zest for living, a terrific morale. Quite a unique little island of the West holding out against the Communist state surrounding it on all sides. Next day, a hectic city-tour, many very modern new (i.e. filling up bombed out areas) buildings, various old and new residential areas, historic sites from various periods including dismal memories of the Nazi regime (pointed out by guide, <u>not</u> marked as historic sites!), and the horribly pathetic graves of people who had been shot by East Berlin guards as they escaped over the wall to the West, to die in the attempt. It is hard to grasp that people can shoot their own citizens just because they want to live somewhere else. We visited the Berlin-Dahlem gallery, many marvelous paintings, including 26 Rembrandts, and the Egyptian museum, to see the bust of Queen Nefertiti, even lovelier than the photographs. Had a quick dash through part of Charlottenburg Palace, with a particularly lovely long elegant room in apple-green marble with fine gold rocaille. After lunch, departure from the Tempelhof Airport, famous from Berlin Airlift days. One would like more time for West Berlin, but at least it's a place one could get back to fairly easily.

The tour of <u>PORTUGAL</u> began with even more advance worry, in view of the revolution, anarchy and civil war type of activity going on there, played up so heavily in the press and TV everywhere. However, we experienced no untoward incidents, and for the most part the citizenry seemed to be going about their daily lives in the ordinary way. Since there were no other tourists, our little group of nine people (all of us having been too cheap to cancel the tour and lose all the money we had paid), had all the hotels, museums, etc. to ourselves, which made for easier, more relaxed ghostly feeling to be rattling around in big empty hotels etc. , and very sad, knowing the hotel trade would be completely ruined if this situation kept up indefinitely. Every building, wall, etc. all over the country was hideously defaced with political slogans, either painted on, or posters. This, combined with the apparently normal street garbage and litter and sewer smells, did not enhance the Portuguese scene. Only one pretty little "national historic monument" village (Obidos) had had the pride (and perhaps the <u>courage</u>) to clean the political slogans off its walls. Occasionally we would see groups gathering in public squares at night (carefully avoiding some) or hear the noise of their demonstrations at night after going to bed. We went through two towns where the Communist party headquarters had been burned out. (Santo Tirso and Braga), but saw one still quite intact in another village, with flag flying and party hack working late into the night. Portuguese soldiers were everywhere, with smouldering black eyes flashing about, missing nothing, lean and lithe like panthers in their camouflage suits, as if on perpetual jungle combat duty, giving one a slightly uneasy feeling, in view of the heavy political activity of all sorts in which the military are involved.

At any rate, after a few days I decided that since I looked like a harmless eccentric female in a floppy white hat and gloves, your basic bumbling Mr. Magoo-type-tourist, and was too big for anyone to attack (the Portuguese are rather short people), I was relatively safe no matter what happened; but as I mentioned, we did not encounter any dangers. The country is quite thick with pine forests in the north (tapped for pitch, for the manufacture of turpentine), olive groves, vineyards, rice paddles, and cork trees. The architecture is quite a strange mixture of styles, heavy Moorish influence, and in fact, the country itself has more of a Moorish feeling than European, with much poverty and squalor in evidence, and women carrying baskets of laundry or groceries on their heads, doing laundry in the rivers, and hanging laundry right out on public streets, even in cities. Our city started in <u>Porto</u> ("Oporto" to the British), quite a large and industrial city but with old seedy Mediterranean-looking central area, and is the headquarters of the port. We visited the cellars of the Calem company and tasted the various kinds of port; was enchanted with white port, a fry aperitif I'd never tried before. (I also tried the yards, table wine we'd have at lunch and dinner.) <u>Guimaraes</u> is the birthplace of the Portuguese nation, home of their first King, Alfonso Henriques, who fought off the Moors. <u>Bom Jesus</u> (good Jesus) is a lovely ape-cum-religious-pilgrimage place, attractive and peaceful, with the pilgrimage church and satellite chapels along an elaborate staircase all the way down the side of a mountain, and a gracious hotel serving fine food. <u>Luso</u> is a small spa town in the hills with springs producing the most delicious water I ever remember, and one can buy Luso water, bottled, all over the country for table use. <u>Bucaco,</u> noted for one of Wellington's defeats of Napoleon, has a park-forest of trees collected from all over the world, and there is also a tree labeled as "Wellington's tree" where he tethered his horse. <u>Coimbra</u> is the seat of Portugal's university (one of the oldest in Europe) and the library is absolutely magnificent, the richly ornate decor complementing the richness of the beautiful old volumes. Understand they have a system of using bats to remove any bugs from the library, then removing and cleaning up after the bats. How's that for harnessing the natural force of "ecology"? Was intrigued by the ruins of Santa Clara convent which has sunk 40 metres into the earth. "Children's Portugal," a sort of miniature village consisting of child-scale models of historic buildings all over the country, and also exhibition buildings for each of their overseas colonies, is meant for the entertainment and education of Portuguese children, but seems to delight adults very much as well. Large map exhibit showing routes of Portuguese explorers and their discoveries had me a little confused over a Fernão de Magalhães, until by studying the route shown I realized he was in fact our old friend, Magellan, in his own native spelling. Checked with guide and learned it's pronounced

"Mag's Lynech." Conimbriga appealed to my archaeology-fiend self, nice ruins of old Roman villas on the edge of a dramatic river-gorge. Fatima is a place of religious pilgrimage for Roman Catholics, because of some children's having had visions of the Virgin Mary there in 1913. Enormous arena and church provided for pilgrims. Masses of votive candles were melted in to hideous writhing tangle like waxen snakes in the boiling sun. Tomer - huge convent/castle of seafaring motifs such as shells, ropes, sea creatures, parts of ships, chains, etc.). Knights financed Prince Henry the Navigator's exploration projects, and then received much wealth back from the colonies and conquests. Evora was the most striking old Moorish walled city, of great architectural interest, and would have been for the most part all snowy white if it weren't for the political slogans defacing everything. Former Jesuit University, now a high school, had lovely pictorial tile facings throughout. (Pictorial tile found in many historic buildings, of Portugal, mostly from 17th-18th century, was lovely and most interesting.

*The fact that as a rule only men are seen out in public places such as cafes is also what one expects in Moslem countries or those formerly ruled by Moslems.

Portuguese cuisine very tasty, by the way, apart from the ubiquitous cabbage (kale) soup.

Portinho de Arrabida is an off-the-beaten-track seaside place somewhat reminiscent of Big Sur, pleasant for lunch in a restaurant built into an old fortress on a cliff over the sea.

Lisbon -- now it felt as if it were "back in Europe again," since the rest of the country felt a little more like North Africa or even the Middle East in many ways. Libson is quite a bustling and attractive city, mostly dating from the period since a major earthquake in the 18th century, but it was an old Moorish-type quarter still remaining with the most characteristic tiny houses, irregular, narrow, winding streets, etc. on a hill. The waterfront monument to Prince Henry the Navigator and the Portuguese Explorers is magnificent in conception and execution, with the figures (led by Prince Henry) arranged like the prow of a ship headed out to sea. I liked this so much I went back to look at it again on my own, as well as taking another look in the Naval Museum which has so many interesting exhibits pertaining to the Explorers and other items of naval history. The waterfronts of Lisbon are stacked up all over with crates of the belongings of Portuguese settlers returned from Angola, a pathetic sight, and these people are standing night and day filling the street in front of the Bank of Angola in fairly quiet demonstration, trying to get some financial assistance. Their return to Portugal at a time when it is itself in a state of upheaval is most difficult. Lisbon (and most other cities) has some fine broad sidewalk-pavings of white and black cobblestone designs, although they are not quite seen to best advantage, since street-cleaning in Portugal is apparently minimal. Probably they would look great right after a heavy rain. The Gulbenkian Museum was well worth a visit, particularly in its collection of French furniture, and also some interesting examples of Art Nouveau jewelry and accessories, among the wide variety of things Gulbenkian had collected.

Near Lisbon, we visited the Queluz 18th century royal palace; Sintra, considered a "romantic" vacation or honeymoon spot in the mountains; Pena summer palace of the royal family, on a mountain; and Cascais and Estoril, much-publicized seaside resorts, but which struck me as fairly uninteresting, and I couldn't see what all the fuss was about.

The high point of my stay in Lisbon was the bullfight. It was quite different from the Spanish type. Actually, two types were presented. The most gorgeous was done by gentlemen in 18th century noblemen's costumes, riding magnificent, fast, highly-trained horses which rush in near the bull while the rider puts the sticks into the bull's back, then rushes away, just avoiding its horns--the most spectacular riding imaginable. It was absolutely beautiful and exciting to watch. They don't kill the bull in Portugal--he is just escorted out of the arena by a group of steers wearing huge bells. (This style is very much like that of the "rejoneadores" of Spain except that the costume is different, and they do not dismount and kill the bull. The other kind of fight consists of some brave fellow who comes out jeering and taunting the bull to induce it to charge him right in the stomach. He is thus flipped over the bull's head and back, and all the men in his entourage rush up and try to hold the bull so he and others won't be gored or trampled on. However, somebody invariably gets trampled on anyway, and the brave bullfighter, very pained in the abdomen, limps around the rest of the evening looking miserable. The crowd goes mad with joy and admiration at the sight of such bravery. Quite crazy, but in its way exciting. I should add that these particular bulls have their horns tipped, to diminish the goring dangers somewhat. Incidentally, by going out to the bullfight stadium on the subway, I luckily avoided seeing some Army troops and tanks putting down anti-Communist demonstrators who were trying to get anti-Communists put back on their jobs at a newspaper office the Communists had taken over. One man in our group had gone out to the stadium on a bus, and saw this spectacle en route.

In summary, I'm glad to have seen Portugal, but it was saddening to see it in such a state of political and economic disaster. The political changes and turmoil are ruining their economy, and with the vast amounts of money and guns being poured in there by the Russians to boost the Communist minority, one wonders if, and how, the country will stay afloat. Thousands of business people and intellectuals have already departed, so this loss of talent and capability will not help matters.

No exciting news on the California front. I'm still working in the Cardiology Dept. at Stanford, and recently enjoyed the San Francisco opera season although it was not one of their better seasons. "Gianni Schicchi" was, I thought, the best production (the deft hand of Jean-Pierre Ponnelle), but I also enjoyed "Werther,." mostly because of so recently having "done" the Goethe sites in Germany.

Now, if you haven't gone totally blind from trying to read this crowded account, may I wish you a Merry Christmas and a Happy New Year!

P.S. I should add that between the German and Portuguese tours I spent some time in London, seeing friends and taking in a few plays, the best of which were Alan Bates in "Otherwise Engaged." Even England was having a terrific heat-wave, simply astounding--I couldn't believe it. Prices in

London struck me as out of sight, in many cases much worse than in the U.S. It was good to be back in London, although August is really not an ideal time, too crowded.

1976

Greetings!

Time once again for your Famous World Traveller's annual report. This time a Nile Cruise, in April. Does that phrase conjure up a vision of luxury, leisure, good food, relaxation, glamour, etc. in exotic settings reminiscent of the Pharaohs, Antony & Cleopatra, and the heyday of the British Empire? Right. Now add to that a combination of overpowering heat, dust, sandstorms, flies, sweat, gastroenteritis, beggars and sundry blackguardly types, and a gruelling sightseeing program that would serve the Army in good stead as commando training for desert warfare. We walked, climbed, and stumbled up hills and down into tombs, across desert sands, rocks, rubble, weeds, in and out of temples and other ruins, on foot, and were hurtled to and from some of the sites by rickety buses, rickety taxis, tractors, donkeys, and antique horse-carriages, sometimes having to disembark and board ship by means of makeshift planks, ropes and stones along the river edge when other boats got to the docking area ahead of us. In short, a trip something like a cross between "Lawrence of Arabia" and "The African Queen," with a touch of "The Desert Fox" thrown in. But once back on the boat after our commando-workouts, we reverted to vestiges of the good old British Empire way of wife, taking a sedate afternoon tea in the lounge-bar, dressing for dinner, sipping cool drinks while listening to erudite lectures by an Oxford Egyptologist, and dining on good meals served by Egyptian stewards dressed in bright red gold-trimmed galabiyehs and white turbans.

Our group consisted of 53 passengers, mostly English, with a sizeable number of Americans and Canadians thrown in. Our ship, the M.S. "Delta," was an old but quite gracious and comfortable number shaped something like a Mississippi steamboat, but of course without paddlewheel. Gliding along the silent river watching the daily life of the fellahin (peasants) along the shoes, especially in the very early morning when the rosy glow of the sunrise added to the beauty of the picturesque scene was a particularly enjoyable feature of the cruise. It gave one a marvelous and restful feeling of utter timelessness, watching a way of life that in many ways had literally not changed since the days of the pharaohs 6,000 years ago. Native-costumed women fill their clay amphorae with water from the river and men in loose galabiyehs lead a camel, donkey along the dusty pathways while a beatific-faced water-buffalo wallows happily in the water. Egypt is essentially this narrow strip of intensively cultivated land / (luxuriant crops) on either side of the Nile, the rest being desert which begins abruptly at the edge of this strip - perhaps rest being desert which begins abruptly at the edge of this strip - perhaps hilly, rolling or flat, but all desert, which flows with golden and rosy hues as the light changes in early morning or at sunset. Beautiful. Then occasionally a modern note may intrude, such as a jet plane roaring momentarily overhead, or the odd truck rumbling through a village. The ancient temples were built in the cultivated areas, but the dead were always buried (and still are) in the desert, so one must trek over into it to look into the famous tombs of the pharaohs, where of course the dry heat preserved the frescoes, mummies, and other objects buried with the dead, all these thousands of years.

Our trip started at Cairo, and we sailed some 600 miles up the Nile, stopping all along the way to look at the various points of interest, the voyage ending at Aswan, with an air excursion from there to Abu Simbel, and then a return to Cairo by air. Despite my having done quite a bit of preparatory "homework" reading, I still had a hard time grasping all the history and keeping the various sites straight in my mind, and I won't attempt to describe them all, but just hit the high spots. The ancient Egyptian religion with its assortment of bizarre gods, some with animal heads, the sacred animals, etc., and the pharaohs' role in all this, still strikes me as weird, and the stylized formality of the art work representing gods and pharaohs generally does not have a lot of appeal for me, except in regard to the artistic skill involved; but the art representing animals and daily activities of the people is full of life and charm as well as artistic beauty and skill, and I could really enjoy that sort of frescoes and carvings. And while the enormous pyramids are staggering in conception and execution, I was delighted by an appealing little "baby pyramid" the workmen who built the royal tombs at the Valley of the Kings at Thebes had built for themselves in the area of their own living quarters.

The "Step Pyramid" of Zoser at <u>SAKKARA</u>, the first pyramid ever built in Egypt, designed by their formidable architect/doctor/"deity." Imhotep, was the most impressive in a way - possibly because it took some considerable endurance see it at all, since at that point we were engulfed in a sandstorm (khamsin), which made struggling through the sand against such a stiff wind with sand blasting into your eyes, nose, mouth, hair, clothes etc. - despite hat, sunglasses and face mask (scarf tied round nose and mouth) - a real challenge. It was at this point, exhausted by heat, flies and the heavy sightseeing program, that I began to question that this could really be called a "vacation," muttering to myself that "Peter O'Toole got PAID for this sort of thing, and here we are paying to do it!" There are several interesting tombs around this area with marvelous carvings and frescoes. But don't travel as late as April if you want to avoid the sandstorm scene.

A visit to <u>TELL EL AMARNA</u>, where Pharaoh Akhenaton had set up his palace and tried to jettison all the gods except one, the sun-god, is notable in that his policy was so unpopular everything was razed to the ground after his demise, and our old friend Tut Ankh Amon subsequently reinstated the whole pantheon of gods, to everyone's relief. Lots of potsherds from Akhenaton's period are still lying around the area with a few remaining building foundations. On learning what an unprepossessing-looking pharaoh he was, I wondered what his beautiful wife Nefertiti thought about him. (Incidentally, a lovely natural stone carving of her head is in the Cairo Museum, and she's just as beautiful without paint as she is in the colored bust now in the Museum in West Berlin, which I saw last year.)

At <u>ABYDOS</u>, one is flabbergasted by "Om Seti," a genteel little elderly English lady who has lived in this ghastly hot, dusty, wretched village for years, acting as a guide to the temples, since she thinks she is the reincarnation of the mother of Pharaoh Seti I, and is "at home" here. Actually she is very intelligent and charming.

Also while moored at Luxor we turned out at 0600 hours to cross over to the West Bank to tackle THEBES, visiting all sorts of tombs and temples at the Valley of the Kings, Queens, etc., before the heat became totally intolerable. Must be one of the hottest places on earth. Tut Ank Amon's tomb is amazingly small for the quantity and size of his mummy-cases, statues, furniture and other art object crammed in there. One mummy-case is still there on display, and all the rest of the things are in the Cairo Museum (in fact, now just about to start touring the United States). Tut was only about 19 years old when he was apparently murdered by a heavy clout on the head (power politics in its more basic form). I liked Amenophis II's tomb with gorgeous dark blue ceiling with white drawings, and the tombs of the nobles Kaht and Menna, with charming paintings of scenes of daily life of the period. Carved reliefs in white limestone in the tomb of Vizier Ramo were beautiful too. The Ramesseum (Ramesses II) offers the fallen head and other bits and pieces of this famous pharaoh's gigantic statue, which was the "Ozymandias" of Shelley's poem ("My name is Ozymandias, King of Kings - Look on my work ye mighty, and despair!"). But Shelley never actually went there, so he failed to describe the scene accurately. The relief carving of Ramesses III hunting a wild bull on the temple wall at Medinet Habu is a beautiful piece of work, full of life and grace.

(I must insert a reminder here that because of the heavy dust in the air almost everywhere we went, many of our group were sathed in some sort of makeshift face-masks (scarves, handkerchiefs, towels, even a few genuine surgical masks). We were also constantly smearing ourselves with insect repellant and frantically swatting at thousands of flies with our Egyptian fly-whisks -- either the posh carved wooden ones with graceful horsehair whisks, or el cheapo ones made from split palm leaves -- the latter having greater clout, but less "class.")

Had great fun prowling round the Luxor souks (bazaars) -- little shops and street vendors with fascinating and beautiful displays of all kinds of exotic spices, baskets of dates in all shapes and colors, furniture makers, hardware, cloth merchants, galabiyeh-makers who can run up a garment with custom embroidery, and the whole place teeming with life and color, exotic sounds and scents. Bought some of the wonderful Egyptian cotton fabric to make dresses.

On Easter morning we each received a circular braided pastry with 2 colored eggs embedded therein, apparently the custom for the Coptic Easter, though I believe their Easter ws to be the following Sunday. A stop at ESNA to see the Temple of Khnum (Ptolemaic & Roman period) was dramatized by our having to be escorted by the ship's crew and local mounted tourist police to protect us against unfriendly natives (particularly those waving scorpions at us). Emperor Domitian is shown smiting his enemies on one wall and Trajan smiting his on another. We were told that up near the roof there are graffiti left by Napoleon's soldiers at a later date, but couldn't get up there to look. (Incidentally a few other villages had more casual (non-uniformed) versions of the tourist police to defend us against nuisance children/beggars etc. by literally beating them and driving them away, but they are something like the flies in their number and persistence.)

EDFU is noted for having the most complete temple remaining in Egypt (Ptolemaic period), but I remember this place chiefly for the wildest ride of my experience. Can you visualize a whole fleet of those 1905 carriages tearing through a dusty little village at a full gallop, literally racing each other to the temple, a scene something like the Den Hur chariot race or an old John Wayne movie. I was riding backwards on the footboard, hanging on for dear life, sharing the carriage with 3 other ladies who did not seem to find the whole thing as hilarious as I did.

KOM OMBO was pleasant - the air had cleared a bit, so with clear sky, bright blue Nile (instead of murky), and the

Ptolemaic temple attractively situated by the river with a few palms, it was a more appealing setting than most. This temple (like others located right on the river) has a Nilometer (well-like stair arrangement for measuring rise & fall of the river in the old days, which was useful in gauging success of future crops and thereby setting tax-rates.) There were some deep well-like pools to keep sacred crocodiles in and a small shallow "wading pool" for the baby crocodiles. A pile of old stinking crocodile mummies was stacked up in a small Roman temple at the side. Walls of the main temple had carvings illustrating the various surgical instruments in use at the time, which were all easily identified by a doctor in our group.

ASWAN was my favorite place - a pleasant town almost like our conception of a resort, with some trees, flowers, etc. (trees are very scarce in Egypt), and graceful felucca boats one can ride around in (fun) - we went over to Elephantine Island to see some ruins and the beautiful botanical gardens with herons, hoopoes & other interesting birds. The old Aga Khan is buried on the West Bank but we did not have time to go over there to his tomb. We inspected the Aswan High Dam (spectacular engineering feat, which left much of the surrounding countryside like a moonscape of red-rock rubble). Aswan's souks are fun, too, with fantastic spices, dates, bunches of garlic with leaves still on, etc. For a change of pace in transport, we roared off by Egypt Air's Boeing 737 to ABU SIMBEL to see the Great Temple of Ramesses II and smaller temple of wife Nefertari, which were so dramatically rescued from "drowning" in the rising waters of the Nile when the Aswan Dam was built a few years ago. These temples were cut up into blocks, moved piecemeal and reassembled in a new location, the back and top covered with a protective cement dome, in turn covered with natural-looking rock and earth. You can't even see where the "seams" are in the temple - a fantastic piece of work. The project was designed by a Swedish architectural/engineering firm and the work was carried out by a consortium of European companies, and concluded in 1969. The funds for this job were subscribed to by dozens of countries and the sands of individuals all over the world, an international effort that has made Abu Simbel a wonder of the modern world as well as of the ancient world, and Ramesses II would no doubt think no more than was his due, as Egypt's greatest pharaoh. (One can tell from the face of his statues, here was a man of strength.)

The cruise part of our trip ended at Aswan and we flew back to <u>CAIRO</u> to wind up our holiday at the Sheraton Hotel (!), where I was approximately roomed in no. 1,0001. Did a bit more sightseeing, including the Sphinx & pyramids at GIZEH which I had seen years ago. Cairo's urban sprawl has encroached out to the very edge of this desert now, with commercialised aspects such as amusement park, & a place for spectators to watch the Son et Lumiere show (far inferior to the one at Karnak), and so the poor old Sphinx and pyramids don't seem quite so remote, mysterious and dramatic as they were used to. We visited the Papyrus Institute in Cairo, to learn how papyrus paper was made, and one can buy pieces of same with painted copies of ancient designs, which are rather nice tourist purchase items. A half-visit to the Cairo Museum could only hit the high spots, including Tut Ankh Amon treasures (astounding). Cairo is more or less just another big noisy, smoggy city full of traffic jams like everywhere else, but it has perhaps a bit more local in its markets, mosques, etc., and the Nile winding through it. "People-watching" at the Sheraton was interesting, the guests being a fascinating mix of East-meets-West, where some Arabs in traditional costume mill about among others in fabulous, glamorous modern gowns or suits. Gambling casino a big draw here for affluent Arabs. There was a delightful Easter display in the lobby of live baby chicks, ducklings and rabbits in an enclosure decorated with a gorgeous big crepe paper "ball," swan and eggs. Children were delighted, and I also.

By tradition, Joseph and Mary and the infant Jesus are said to have taken refuge in a crypt in the Old Quarter of Cairo (at that time being the Jewish Quarter and known as "Babylon in Egypt"). This crypt was subsequently incorporated in St. Sargus' Church (4th or 5th AD). Christianity was brought to Egypt by St. Mark & St. Peter, A.D. 45. This Old Quarter remains the quarter of the Christians and Jews of Cairo to this day, and I visited this area on my own when we first arrived, going to St. Sargus' Church and one other, plus Ben Ezra Synagogue and the Coptic Museum. The Copts are the Egyptian Christians, and I marvelled at their tenacity in hanging on in Egypt all these years, despite severe persecution by the Roman Empire, the Islamic (Arab) Conquest, and the Orthodox Church, from whose doctrine they differed, in viewing the nature of Christ as purely divine (instead of as a combination of divine and human), and thus being condemned as heretics for this "Monophysite" view, at the Council of Chalcedon, A.D. 451. The little churches I visited resembled a non-affluent, somewhat primitive version of a Greek Orthodox church. I was also touched by the fact that in a country full of the most annoying, shameless beggars who pester you incessantly for baksheesh (handouts), the one person who really <u>deserved</u> a tip -- the chap who appeared out of nowhere and appointed himself my guide thru the confusing maze of little winding streets of Old Cairo -- refused to take my offering, and instead clasped my hand in his, as if to indicate that he was a fellow Christian and would not think of taking my money for his good deed.

It seems fitting to end this Christmas letter on a note of respect for these exotic and courageous Christians in a Moslem land. May I also say if any of you readers have an interest in visiting Egypt, contact me for a "nitty-gritty checklist" for some very basic pointers and items to take along, to make the trip a bit easier. It is a fascinating place to visit but one must be prepared, and be fairly hardy.

Meanwhile, Merry Christmas and Happy New Year!

1979

Greetings!

After three years with no vacation, I made up for lost time by taking two trips this year. I started the first trip (end of March) by spending a few days sightseeing and sampling the delicious cuisine in <u>New Orleans</u>. Found its French

Quarter a delightful and relaxing place, despite all the other tourists. It has a somewhat Mediterranean-cum-Caribbean ambiance and one has the feeling of being "abroad" rather than in the U.S. Went thru several period houses and enjoyed hearing real jazz at Preservation Hall, performed by elderly Negroes who had been in on jazz from its very beginnings. Never having paid any attention to jazz, I was amazed at how beautiful this was. A wonderful show for only $1.00!

Then I joined a Mississippi Steamboat Cruise on the "Delta Queen" paddlewheel steamboat, chartered entirely for a group of the Stanford University Alumni Association, and sailing from New Orleans, La., to St. Louis, Mo., stopping to visit lovely old Southern plantation houses and other historic sites along the way, and hearing our accompanying professors lecture on the history and literature of the South, as well as the geology and hydrology and history of the River itself (which proved to be fascinating as told by a dynamic live-wire retired Chief Geologist of the Army Corps of Engineers which has been responsible for coping with the River and its banks for the federal govt. since the overwhelmingly disastrous flood of 1928; prior to that the local citizenry had to take care of their individual segments of the banks).

The River was in a state of flood the whole time, which slowed down our course, causing us to miss several places originally scheduled on the itinerary. Trees along the banks and on islands were in many places "up to their knees" in water. One had the definite feel for the strength and "identity" of the River as a colossal and unpredictable force in nature, for which everyone in the area has a healthy respect. (The floods became serious after I got home, causing considerable damage in Mississippi.) The boat was fun it itself, and we enjoyed a visit to the Bridge watching the Pilot, a crusty old chap in the Mark Twain mold, steering his way among the swirls and eddies and barges and other shipping craft, speaking with them by radio and tooting the horn in the traditional manner. The engine room was an incredible mass of Rube-Goldberg-type machinery, noise, grease and steam, and the engineer obviously enjoyed his job as much as the Pilot and Captain did theirs. They all seemed to feel they were having fun and getting paid for it - I believe the Captain said "It beats working."

The boat's "Interlocutor" (master of ceremonies and leader of the lively orchestra) lectured on the various forms of music indigenous to the South, and a steam calliope played wildly every time we set sail following a shore excursion. We were stuffed with excellent food, including all kinds of local specialties, and everyone gained about 8 lbs in weight. We were also entertained lavishly at several of the mansions we visited, by hostesses in Scarlett O'Hara costumes (and with behaviour to match). It was really like stepping back into the past to experience a bit of that "Gone with the Wind" sort of life.

To run quickly through the itinerary, we visited "Oak Alley" plantation (sugar cane, and my first look at crawfish architecture in the form of little mud-chimneys in the irrigation ditches, quite an interesting surprise), then in the city of Baton Rouge, La., including a reception at the Old State Capitol (fantastic food and mint juleps), the Rural Life Museum (which includes examples of slave houses, school, shop, and the overseer's house with a broad-brimmed sun hat, pistol and whip for keeping slaves in line--how's that for Nostalgia?!). Then on to Natchez, Miss., celebrated for many beautiful old houses, of which we visited a few, "Stanton Hall," "Rosalie," "Longwood," and "Melrose," where we were treated to another fabulous reception of food and all sorts of drinks as well as the usual mint juleps, and a display of Civil War period dancing on the lawn by a group of young people in appropriate costume. Then on to Vicksburg, Miss., where the huge cemetery vividly reminds us of the terrible sacrifice involved in this decisive battle that, in conjunction with the battle of Gettysburg in the North, turned the tide of the Civil War ensuring a Northern victory. We were entertained at another reception (gasp…) at "Cedar Grove" house, which carefully preserves a cannon-ball lodged in the drawing room wall during the Civil War (that's over 100 years, mind you) as well as a gash made in the floor by another cannon-ball, and which is neatly framed with a glass cover, the carpeting being cut out and fitted round this display. (Compare this treatment with what one normally does to repair and cover up damage to one's house.) The U.S. Corps of Engineers Waterways Experimental Station, also at Vicksburg, offers interesting models which are research projects concerning rivers and harbors all over the country.

Memphis, Tenn., has Beale Street, birthplace of the "Blues" music, and a visit to a cotton warehouse and the Cotton Exchange were an interesting look at one of the staples of the Southern economy. We had a concert of Blues music at an old theatre, which I left early to have a some medical attention for a fingernail smashed in the Delta Queen window-shutter earlier that morning, so I experienced some more Southern hospitality, hospital-emergency-room variety. They were most helpful and solicitous. (Memphis has a long history of dealing with riverboat casualties, as you will find in reading Mark Twain's Life on the Mississippi.)   Cairo, Ill., is a depressed area following race riots and subsequent flight of industry and continuing conflicts, but we saw an interesting 19th century house in which Gen. Grant had slept. The River had risen so high by the time we got here that the local authorities had to open the flood gates and build some special wooden steps for us to climb up over into the town.

Cape Girardeau, Mo., has a number of interesting FRENCH colonial houses; the loveliest French house, however, was nearby Pierre Menard house (nr. Ellis Grove, Ill.) referred to as "The Mount Vernon of the West." The cruise ended at St. Louis, Mo., where I made a quick tour of the Westward Expansion Museum (underneath the "Gateway to the West" Arch right on the riverbank) and also visited the fine arts museum in the city.

Then off by train to Chicago on my own, never having "done" that city, and despite the bitter cold (our trip had progressed from about 80-85° in the South to 29-40° in the North) and biting wind off the Lake, not to mention intermittent rain, I managed to do a city sightseeing tour and a visit the Chicago Board of Trade (hub of the grain market, and just about as lively and exciting as the New York Stock Exchange).   I spent TWO DAYS in the Chicago Art Institute, feasting upon the marvelous collection of Impressionist and Post-Impressionist paintings (one of the world's largest and best), as well as many other wonderful things. It was a real treat....

****

<u>NOW FOR A CHANGE OF SCENE</u>! The next trip (June) was more or less a short-notice spur-of-the-moment dash off to another Hellenic Cruise (British group, Greek ship). I went off somewhat ill-prepared and helter-skelter but it had turned out to be one of the best trips I ever had. I had expected, too, to be jaded after having been to so many of the Mediterranean sites on 3 previous trips, but there were so many new places on this itinerary I'd never seen that it was like a "whole new bag."

We had a the usual busy (strenuous) program of sightseeing this company offers, with lectures on the history and archaeology of the area by various British professors. The company had decided to try out a sketch group for the first time, so I joined that as I thought it would be a good way to spend time when we got to places I'd already seen, as indeed it did. Though I hadn't done any sketching for years, it was great fun to brush up, and it also resulted in some diverting comments and conversations with local Greek and Turkish citizenry, with or without benefit of a common language. The ship, although about 22 years old and refurbished (like most Greek shipping), was more modern and spruce than the battered Turkish number we used to use. Another major difference between this trip and my earlier ones was the fact that Greece is now <u>overrun</u> with foreign tourists (most from Northern Europe), and the coastal ports and villages swarm with sunburnt, sun-oiled bikini/disco/swinger types. A multitude of shops has sprung up catering to visitors (even bushy fur coats bristling from every other doorway for the Scandinavian bargain hunters, in the 98°+ heat....) One could say Greece has been "ruined," but on the other hand, all this has brought some greater degree of prosperity to a country that used to be "unspoiled" but poor. Turkey is not yet quite as touristy but even there there are signs of development of the sites, and the bleak mess of ruined foundation of Troy now have a fancy new giant wooden horse on display! We had smooth seas and blazing heat all the way, balmy nights at sea with only a gentle breeze as you watch the moonlight ripple across the water. The food was good, especially the buffet luncheons featuring Greek specialties and lots of fresh fruit. Passengers were mostly British, with a larger sprinkling of Americans than before as well as people from various parts of the British Commonwealth.

Places we visited which I'd seen before were <u>Olympia</u>, <u>Delphia</u>, <u>Heraklion</u>/Knossos (Minoan gold jewelry always worth seeing again!), <u>Istanbul</u> (one of the world's most architecturally-fascinating cities and it was good to see Santa Sophia again, as well as pop in to revisit old friend Alexander the Great at the Archaeology Museum, and also the so-called "Alexander Sarcophagus" built for a King of Sidon, depicting scenes from life and battles of Alexander carved on the sides). Thassos, Delc, and Mykonos...Athens... the museum at the latter has several new things since I was up there last, including frescoes (lovelier than the Minoan ones at Knossos) and other objects dug up at Akroteri on the island of Santorini.

The places on our itinerary that I'd never seen before were <u>Corfu</u> (rather too "European", not very "Greek" in feeling, <u>Santorini</u> (astonishing whitewashed city built on rim of volcanic crater which the sea has filled so that it has become the entry harbor; a dreadful mule-ride up a steep winding cobblestone path, (alternative: WALKING up) is the only way to get to the town); <u>Perge</u> and <u>Aspendos</u> in Turkey offer an impressive Roman aqueduct near the former and the most nearly interesting Roman theatre at the latter (only one I'd seen with the back wall still on--and with the usual fantastic acoustic of that period); <u>Bodrum</u> (Turkey) is an attractive little harbor town with a castle-museum and the foundation remains of the Mausoleum of Halicarnassus (the statuary of which is in the British Museum in London). This had been one of the Seven Wonders of the Ancient World. <u>Tinos</u> (Greek) is a fairly low-key island noted for a church which attracts religious-healing pilgrimages--somewhat the Greek Orthodox of Lourdes, I gather.

One of the highlights of the trip was the remains of <u>Nestor's palace near Pylos</u>, where his decorated ceramic "built-in" bathtub is still in good condition. Nestor was one of my favorite characters in the <u>Iliad</u> so I was pleased to see his home. The island of <u>Samothrace</u> was lovely--a peaceful wooded mountain-island with the ruins of the various temples associated with the "mystery religion" cult, which was visited by Greeks from all over, including Philip of Macedon, who met and fell in love with his subsequent wife Olympias at this place, in due course producing Alexander the Great. There is no harbor, and even our landing boats could not make the trip so we had to go ashore in lifeboats (which added to the novelty), and there are NO SHOPS, NO TOURISTS, ETC.--hurrah! The "Winged Victory" statue stolen by the French Consul in the 19th century, now in the Louvre, Paris, came from this island, and the French govt. generously gave Samothrace a plaster model of its statue the little island museum!

The Island of <u>Kos</u> was pleasant, not quite as touristy as some, and of interest as the home of Hippocrates, father of modern scientific medicine, as opposed to religious/mystical ideas of healing which were concurrently practiced at the time as well; in fact, Kos was also a center of the religious healing cult featuring the god Aesclepios. There is a giant plane tree in the center of town, its branches all propped by bits and pieces of old marble columns called "Hippocrates' plane tree," and it is at least the same KIND of tree as he taught medicine under in his day, but as the guide pointed out a plane tree only lives about 500 years, this could not possibly be the original.

I had been to <u>Pella</u> (capital of Macedonia in Alexander the Great's day) and <u>Thessaloniki</u> before and in any case there are only ordinary houses' mosaic floors as yet uncovered at Pella. But the treasures dug up from the tomb at Vergina believed to be that of Philip of Macedon last year are now on display at the museum in Thessaloniki, along with things from various other Macedonian tombs, and this was a really exciting exhibit for us to see. As of the time we were there the archaeologist had still not found any written proof that this was Philip's tomb, but all the circumstantial evidence indicates almost positively that it is. The small marble portraits of Philip, Olympias and Alexander, the metal greaves, one shorter and thinner than the other as would be necessary for Philip with his lame leg, the royal emblem on the gold coffers, the beautifully worked gold crowns, purple robe, and other family items, plus the carbon-dating to the period when Philip was the only King it could have been at the time, all make it fairly certain that this was Philip's grave. There is also an iron helmet and cuirass, the only examples from this period ever found.

I had a few days in London before and after the Greek trip, but not enough time to see all my friends or all the exhibits and plays I would have liked, which was quite frustrating, but nevertheless the cruise was marvelous and I can't complain, after having two vacations in one year...!

Best wishes for a Merry Christmas and Happy New Year!

1980

Greetings!

I have no foreign travels to report this year, but perhaps my domestic ones will sound sufficiently foreign to overseas readers.

Looking back over the year, I seem to have spent a good deal of time taking evening or weekend classes, the most noteworthy being one on Wagnerian opera, at the instructor's house in Berkeley. This culminated in a "Ring Weekend," wherein from 0800 hours on a Saturday and running straight through till 0630 hours on Sunday, we listened to the best selected recordings of the entire Ring Cycle of operas. We had one-hour intervals between acts and between operas, during which we ate prodigious amounts of food, each participant having brought all sorts of things for the whole group to eat. I managed to stay up till about 1:00 AM, retreating to a back bedroom to sleep awhile, re-emerging at dawn for the end of "Gotterdammerung. Nobody but a real Wagner fan of course would endure such a program. It was MARVELOUS.

I made a weekend trip to Los Angeles at the end of March to see a special exhibition of American Impressionist paintings and to hear a symposium presented on the subject by several top New York experts in the field, which was excellent, and very stimulating. I was pleased to discover a painting in the exhibit by one of my father's New York teachers, which added a nice feeling of 'continuity' for me.

I stayed at the old Ambassador Hotel, which with its spacious grounds, subtropical plants, attractive pool area and terrace bar seems to epitomize what one thinks California ought to be like. When returning to the hotel one evening I discovered a film was being made on the doorstep, literally, so I hung around and watched the proceedings a few hours, with great interest. I'd never seen movie-making before so this was a splendid surprise. The film was the life story of Jayne Mansfield (America's Diana Dors, of the 1950's). Not exactly the most urgent subject matter today, but the flamboyant costuming, hair styles, etc. were most amusing, as was the fact that the role of her husband was being played by Arnold Schwarzenegger, the former world champion bodybuilder, whose excessive arm and chest muscle development makes his head appear the size of a pin. I have subsequently seen this film on television (October), and very little of the episode I had watched being made was actually used. But think of all the actor "extras" who managed to work all evening and get paid, even though their part was cut out!

Last year I won a prize at the San Francisco Opera raffle, which was luncheon for four at one of California's better wineries up in the Napa Valley (north of S.F.). I waited until the warm weather of summer to take advantage of this prize, and went up there in August with three friends who are both opera buffs and wine buffs. We had our own private tour of the winery and private wine tasting on the veranda of a 130-year old house on the grounds, followed by a superb 6-course luncheon (catered by a Continental chef) with appropriate wines for each course. The hostess and the Winemaker were charming, and we had a marvelous day. It was all so gracious it was like something out of Tolstoy-- lunching on one's country estate.

My principal vacation this year consisted of two weeks on the East Coast (July) spent mainly in seeing friends. (I did not have to be a tourist, since I'd seen it all before! In any case, the frightful humid heat was so debilitating that really heavy tourism would have been impossible). I was in Baltimore briefly (landing just after a tornado, finding trees and branches lying all over the roads), then spent a few days in Washington, where I went to a very beautiful and "international" wedding (American/Chinese/Belgian, with lots of government/political/diplomatic types), and took in the exhibition of Post-Impressionists at the National Gallery (one which had previously been shown in London).

I spent most of the time in New York, where I saw the Picasso exhibit at the Museum of Modern Art (staggering, too much to digest on one afternoon), and also the revival of Richard Burton's "Camelot." The play is a load of rubbish to my mind, but I wanted to see him making a comeback in the theatre. I read that he sees this run as a period of getting in training to tackle "King Lear" later on, and I certainly hope he will do that--something much more worthy of his talents.

I made brief forays into Connecticut and Vermont (Burlington), and in the latter, with the help of friends, I found my father's boyhood home, a Victorian house still in use.

(Other ancient relics such as schools and church, had been demolished and rebuilt.) The day-long bus ride from New York gave a good view of the lovely Vermont countryside, rolling hills and quaint villages which I had thought were either a thing of the past or from imaginary Christmas card illustrations! But they really ARE like that.

I spent a couple of weekends in the Carmel/Monterey area, which is always enjoyable--this is the cold, windswept, leaning-cypress-and-pine-tree aspect of the California coast... very different from the south. A bit too many tourists now, however...

Our San Francisco opera season has been rather disappointing (fewer "big stars" which seems to be needed to generate more excitement into the performances), but as of this writing the season is not yet finished so I'll hope for better things yet to come.

Best wishes for a Merry Christmas and Happy New Year!!

1982

Greetings!

I failed to finish writing my Christmas cards last year (my apologies!!), but since there were no foreign travels to report, you didn't miss a thing. This year, however, I managed to get a decent holiday, and covered quite a bit of ground. Since I'm late getting this written, and rushed, this may be pretty un-polished writing, so bear with me. (Not to mention very cramped typing, to get more onto each page.)

The main event was a 2-week tour with a small group of 13 people entitled "Russia of the Great Writers," designed to track down places associated with the major 19th century Russian authors, Tolstoy, Chekhov, Turgenev, Lermontov and Pushkin. (No, the tour did not include Leningrad/St. Petersburg, hence no Dostoyevsky.) We had a guest lecturer (son of a former British Ambassador to Moscow) to give us talks on the various writers and their work as we went along, and some other members of the group contributed to the success of the trip with readings, translations and personal historical information (notably a retired British diplomat who writes poetry and has done fine translations of some of the Russian literature, whose wife (not with us) is a Georgian Princess; and a Russian Princess who had escaped the Bolshevik Revolution as a small child and now lives in Germany; our British courier was the daughter of the last Ambassador of the Tsars to England). Except for myself and one other "colonial" (New Zealander), the rest of the groups were British. Moscow was our starting and finishing point, and long bus rides as well as 3 domestic flights enabled us to cover vast distances and a considerable variety of landscape and sites in 2 weeks' time (end May/early June).

Soget out your atlases, and here we go. The international political tensions vis-a-vis US/USSR give one slightly cold feet to start with. Then on arriving at <u>MOSCOW AIRPORT</u>, the blood runs cold as well when you find the entire airport, immigration and customs formalities are in charge of the ARMY. (Technically, "frontier guards.") Now you know you are in the grip of an arbitrary police state. This is it. This highly intimidating set-up takes on another aspect, however, when Russian inefficiency starts to show; the "London" aircraft luggage all comes off the "Belgrade" carrousel; a young soldier/immigration clerk is thrown into consternation when he finds one lady's visa had not been signed at the point of origin; after consultation with another soldier, he carefully copies the signature from someone else's visa onto the blank spot. We stumble round rather helplessly through all the proceedings - X-rays of selves, X-rays and searching of luggage, careful scrutiny of all books & papers. (My paperback edition of the film script of the 1930's French film "La Grande Illusion" with Erich Von Stroheim in WWI German military uniform and moocole on the cover really threw them. But they let me keep it).

After several hours of this airport hassle and further confusion as to time and place of our own bus into town, we take off for the hotel. Passing some birch-forests and seeing some peasants languidly strolling or picnicking in meadows, we are relieved to see these innocuous reminders one expected from the old literature.

The HOTEL METROPOL is a large place with some vestiges of its pre-Revolutionary grandeur left but it was designed in a mish-mash of styles even then. Now it seems dismal with the Communists' lack of grandeur. Exhausted by the long day of travelling and the unsettling airport scene, I seek out some tea, having read that Russian hotels have to provide you free tea on demand at any time of day or night, on each floor. (N.B. The first word I learn in any country is for "tea.") I make my request to the "dragon-lady" on the landing (from whom one gets one's key), and return to my room. Eventually a cheerful, warm-hearted old "babushka" type peasantry woman appears with an electric kettle of hot water in one hand, the cord dragging along the floor, a little jar of sugar and two drinking glasses containing tea leaves in the other. From this homely array she makes two glasses of inordinately sweet tea, which, along with her amiable and bumbling preparations like a scene from a Chekhov play, cheers me considerably.

My bathroom is also a source of amusement, like several others on the trip; with its coating of ceramic tiles extending about 6 feet up the sides of the walls, it is like standing in the deep end of an empty swimming pool. I am also cheered by the splendidly old-fashioned 1930's array of real cotton hand towels, starched and ironed*. The Turkish towels, though, were not as thick and sumptuous as those in the West. (*For benefit of my overseas readers, not many Americans will iron a towel these days--all Turkish and fluff-dried in an automatic drier.)

During a stroll around Red Square and the main part of town after dinner our lecturer pointed out some of the non-literary sights such as Lubianka Prison where dissenters are "Dealt with," the private chauffeured little black limousines for use of Communist Party/Govt. Hierarchy, and the medical clinics for exclusive use of each agency's hierarchy.

Itineraries to the USSR always contain the warning "subject to change by Intourist" - the only way one can travel there is under the auspices of this State tourist agency - and to be sure, "changes" are one thing you definitely count on. However, when the Intourist guide assigned to accompany our entire tour (who fit the stereotype mold of the uptight Communist female one sees in comedy shows) announced that we could not see the Pushkin Museum because it was closed on Mondays, our distinguished lecturer phoned the museum director who opened it specially just for us (he knew our lecturer and the poet/translator member of the group and was thrilled to have us pay a visit). This put our guide's nose out of joint and it was certain she would try to get her own back later on. The Pushkin Museum is not the poet's own house, but it contains the country's main collection of pictures and memorabilia, MSS, etc. Pushkin is just about universally loved in Russia today - in fact, they have a "Pushkin cult." We also toured around the city to see sites associated with various writers, their statues, and a house which Tolstoy used as a model for the "Rostov house" in War and Peace, which is now used as the offices of the Writers' Union.

65

An evening visit to the theatre to see Chekhov's "The Three Sisters" was arranged, and having seen it twice before I was not concerned about the language barrier. However, a few minutes beforehand we discovered the program had been changed on short notice to a contemporary play called "The Thirteenth President." The Russian audience arrived without even knowing the program had been changed - not pleased, but apparently accustomed to such arbitrary disappointments in life. Knowing no Russian, I could only try to absorb what was going on by observing facial expressions, emotions etc. of the actors. The play turned out to be a courtroom drama. The strange thing about it was that the defendant and all the witnesses (mixed bag of tpes) were presented as the sympathetic, lively, active, positive characters, while the judges and prosecutors were flat, expressionless, empty, devoid of any emotion - "dead." All the audience response (including that of some Army officers sitting a few rows in front of us) of loud laughter, applause, approval etc. was for the defendant and his witnesses, throughout. The play ended with the judges leaving the stage, presumably to render a verdict against the defendant and one assumes he and maybe the others would go to jail. After the play was over our lecturer explained the thing to me: the defendant was the president of some collective industry who was on trial for making illegal arrangements for his workers' holidays. All the witnesses were there on his behalf to say what a great manager he was and what a great production record they had achieved at the factory, etc. I wondered how the govt. could allow this sort of play to be shown, with the govt. side of things presented in such a non-favorable light. Lecturer said no doubt so that the govt. could say "look how liberal we are, allowing this kind of thing to be shown."

A very long bus ride took us to the provincial city of OREL (pronounced "ariyoll" in Moscow but on the spot, as "oreyell." The pronunciation of the word for "tea" changed on me, too! My one and only word, down the drain, transformed from something like "chai" to "chay" as I recall.) This is a pleasant sort of place with tree-lined streets and 19th century bldgs. & houses mostly in the shade of yellow found so much in East Germany, Austria etc. It had been quite a "literary town" in its day with a publishing house and various writers were born there or lived there at some time. Tolstoy visited the prison described in his <u>Resurrection</u>. Pushkin had come out of his way to visit General Yermolov, hero of the 1812 Napoleonic War. We visited the Turgenev Museum and looked at a house that may have been the model for the one in his <u>A Nest of the Gentry</u>. Our dull provincial hotel surprised us by providing a lovely dinner, and with flower and Union Jack flags decorating our table. We had little miniature creme puffs in the shape of swans for desert. I had not expected such niceties in a utilitarian State. (Things seemed to be better out in the country than in Moscow - further from the seat of Power.) Breakfast was especially nice here, too, which included our first sampling of "sour milk" (A sort of liquid version of yogurt, drunk from a glass) and blinis filled with apples.

Rain next morning, but we press on to <u>SPASSKOYE-LUTOVINOVO, TURGENEV'S</u> country estate. Only one wing left after a fire during his day, not rebuilt. Shuffle around in oversize "museum slippers" looking at interesting furniture, (some made of Russian birch in odd designs), pictures and memorabilia etc. Portrait of Turgenev's father on the wall--extremely handsome man in his Napoleonic War uniform with medal from Battle of Borodino. He married wife for her money and vast estate (she owned 5,000 serfs to whom she was a cruel taskmaster; cruel also to her offspring; apparently a warped, neglected wife, since husband was noted for his various love-affairs with others). Tile furnaces, floor-to-ceiling height in the every room, which we also found in other houses we visited. We strolled through the grounds of the estate on winding paths through the lacy trees, the rain having given way to a fine mist, past a lovely lake - an idyllic poetic "Corot-like" setting. The raucous cawing of crows and chattering of other birds reminds us that Turgenev ought to be coming home for a bit of his favorite sport of shooting.

On to <u>TOLSTOY's</u> country estate, <u>YASNAYA POLYANA</u> (trans: "bright meadow"). But there seem to be more trees than meadows, and we approach by walking down a long lane of birch trees, then past a rather unkempt apple-orchard (has this been turned into a collective farm, I wonder?) and the houses where various of Tolstoy's relatives had lived. His own house, further on, is of very simple design - just a white wooden "country house" with a covered verandah and apparently no door at the front - entry being from what seemed like the back. Among the various portraits and memorabilia, we see the green couch on which he was born.

Another walk along a curving wooded path leads us to Tolstoy's grave. The house guide to us that he had wanted to be buried in "the place of the Greek Stick," a spot on the property where according to legend a green stick was buried which held the secret of how to make people happy. (Owing to her accent I'm not sure if she said "old people" or "all people.") At any rate this is the most beautiful spot in a small clearing under tall trees, with a curving hedge of small evergreens along the pathway. Instead of a stone the grave is marked with a sort of thicket-hedge trimmed in the shape of a coffin. Several large bouquets brought by the steady stream of visitors lie nearby. It is a great satisfaction to pay respects to the great writer stream of visitors lie nearby. It is a great satisfaction to pay respects to all the great writer stream of visitors lie nearby. It is a great satisfaction to pay respects to the great writer who had "grabbed me" at the romantic age of 18 with his <u>Anna Karenina</u>. All these years I've wanted to see the home of the man who could write such a book, and at last I've reached this place. And how marvelous that he has just about the most beautiful burial site I've seen.

Another long bus ride back to <u>MOSCOW</u>. (N.B. USSR has "concealed unemployment" -- several people to do the work of one man. We have two bus drivers, one for the outward journey, another who rides along and then drives us back while the first one just sits.) This time we're lodged at the <u>NATIONAL HOTEL</u>. Full of Communist propaganda leaflets etc. displayed in all the rooms, lobbies, etc. This place has many smaller separate dining rooms, which is handy for segregating all the different foreign groups--Chinese, Africans, etc., as well as the actual Russians, who have an orchestra and singer in their dining room. I found an antique torch in one of the hallways that the Reds apparently failed to loot or destroy at the time of the Revolution, made of carved wood with handpainted porcelain Napoleonic War scene.

Next we leave cold Moscow for the sunny south, taking off from the domestic airport. Long wait, but VIP treatment, VIP lounge, no one else there but us. This is merely because we are foreigners and they want us to get a good impression of the country, as well as to keep their own citizens away from us, and vice versa. We board first: then swarm of Russians surges round the loading ramp and onto the plane (no such nonsense as standing in line). Fairly smooth flight to the Crimea, despite horror stories I'd heard about Russian planes & pilots. Terribly ear-splitting music plays on takeoff & landing, though. Three hours, "no frills" (i.e. no food or drink but water).

Land at SIMFEROPOL**, admin. & industrial capital of the CRIMEA. Smallish airport. Luncheon in unprepossessing-looking cafe in town, 1930's type booths. But voila, an astonishingly delicious meal. The soups are "real" everywhere, but this one is the best--very rich, full of vegetables, broth, and sour cream, and the meat course is equally delicious, the gravy being likewise laced with sour cream. In distant past the Crimean area was the Greek TAURIS, associated with various old friends such as Iphigenia, Orestes, & so on.   We take a winding mountainous drive to the seacoast resort of YALTA through very dramatic scenery. Stay at huge YALTA HOTEL, a dreadful thing of about 2500 rooms, totally impersonal--I would describe it as a "guest factory," filled with a horrendous babel of many nationalities, a not very fashionable collection, mostly from the Eastern Bloc, or budget-tour people from the West. This coast strikes one as a cross between Russia, Greece, and Mallorca, with its very sunny Mediterranean climate and plants such as cypress, pines, oleanders, etc., but still some of the Russian plants as well. Bright and sunny - like summer.

**Later I read that one of the places the USSR trains foreign terrorists is located in the Simferopol area--horrors! Obviously nowhere near the tourists.

Touring, we start off with the Nikitinsky Botanical Gardens (18th c.) and a drive to Gurzu village, passing a huge road sign "USSR Bulwark of Peace" (!!) and a "Pioneer Camp." "Pioneers" are the Communist equivalent of a sort of Hitler Youth group, who wear a uniform consisting of light blue short-shorts, white shirts and red neckerchiefs. A squad passed us shouting in unison "Good morning to all of you from all of us!" (In Russian, of course.) We climbed up the ruins of "Pushkin Grotto" (a place with great views from tower on a cliff something like that at Lindos on Rhodes (Greece). Russian speakers in our group chatted with some of the "Pioneer" kids, who said they were preparing a play on Pushkin. It seems that if you speak Russian and if you are a Pushkin fan, you have an instant link anywhere you go in this country.

Back to <u>Yalta</u> for luncheon at the old <u>Tavrida</u> <u>Hotel</u> (under renovation, not in use as hotel at the moment), where many famous writers, musicians etc. stayed in the old days, such as Chekov, Stanislavsky, Moussorgsky, Rimsky-Korsakov, et al. Luncheon was served in one of two lovely courtyards with a fountain in the center, palms, and the galleries of rooms ranging above--something like the courtyards in some New Orleans hotels, and probably for the same climatic reason. Very pleasant luncheon, peaceful, unlike the mob scenes in our dreadful modern Yalta Hotel.

We visit <u>CHEKHOV'S HOUSE</u>, where he wrote "The Cherry Orchard" and "The Lady with the Little dog," the quay here at Yalta being the setting of that story. Afternoon free, I inspect the "beach" just below our hotel, reached by an industrial-looking elevator and dark tunnel out on the cement, "promenade" where oiled, sunburning bodies bulge out of inadequate bathing suits on wooden grills, and bathers must pick their way across about a 16-ft. expanse of rocks and huge gravel to get to the water. UGH! Absolutely awful, at any rate from the point of view of a Californian accustomed to vast beaches of real sand with hardly any people on them.

After dinner we see a film show of Chekhov's "The Hunting Accident." Gorgeous actor in the leading role, with right touch of cynicism for the part; ask guide who he is - Oleg Jankowsky. Hotel also provides so-called Ukrainian dance entertainment in the dining room later, which is not very good, probably not real Ukrainians anyway, all female, and screeching.

Next day, another "one up" for our side over Intourist. Our British diplomat/poet/translator persuaded guide to arrange an unscheduled visit for us to what had once been the summer palace of his Georgian Princess wife's uncle (!) (a Grand Duke).   Now, as the result of the Revolution, it is a rest-home for the Soviet Army (!)   Place   built   in pseudo-Turkish style on splendid cliff site overlooking the sea. All inmates had been cleared out for our visit, presumably went down cliff to the beach. Deputy Director, a military type but not in uniform, showed us around, rather proudly I would say, and our Russian Princess said that he was very well educated, well-spoken and easy to talk to, and that there was "no gap to bridge" when talking with him. He asked for an old pre-Revolutionary photo of the place. All the rooms were filled with small cot-type beds, something like a child's boarding school dormitory, and with the sparsest furnishing--little room for possessions, which I presume they hadn't much of anyway. I have subsequently read that the Soviets send their war-wounded (i.e. from places where they are fighting like Afghanistan) to the Crimean rest-homes for convalescence so that the people on the home front are more or less kept relatively unaware of their wars). Depressing to think of someone's lovely private home being confiscated in a revolution and ending up being used like this. It looks all wrong. I daydream about how nice it would have been to have summer holidays in such a spot in its heyday.

Resuming our regular itinerary, we come to ALUPKA, summer palace of the 19th century Court Vorontsov, a very handsome man, judging from his portrait, and the richest man in all Russia in his day, owning 80,000 serfs as well as nearly all the Crimea. Positively puts the U.S. Southern slaveholders in the shade. His palace is built in pseudo-Scottish baronial style by an English architect. (Russians consistently deny anything having been done by foreigners, insisting on claiming credit for everything themselves.) Churchill stayed here at time of Yalta Conference. The Music Room has an usual wall treatment, blue background with white moulded plaster floral ornament "appliqué" all over the walls, like Wedgewood pottery. It is inf act called the "Wedgewood Room." Haven't run across anything quite like this in my travel before. The grounds have a park with pools, swans, peacocks etc. But the public "toilets" are just as vile as those everywhere else.

Then on to LIVADIA PALACE, the summer palace of the Tsars, now a sanatorium for treatment of lung & circulatory diseases. It was the scene of the Yalta Conference at end of WWII. Gorgeous location on cliff overlooking sea, stunning views, beautifully landscaped, particularly on the ocean side.

We wind up our Crimean stay with a visit (inland) to the remains of rock-hewn monastery in the side of a cliff and then the PALACE OF THE GREAT TARTAR KHAN at BAKSCHISERAI. This village sits in a low-slung valley situation and the palace is in a Turkish-Persian style with minarets, etc. which seems odd considering these were descendents of the Mongol invaders--the last descendent of Genghis Khan in fact. Inside it is much like places one sees in the Middle East. The outstanding thing here is a small exterior wall-fountain, the "Fountain of Tears," designed by a Persian architect as a memorial to the Khan's grief over the death of a favorite wife.

Another domestic flight from Simferopol to TBILISI (formerly Tiflis), capital of the "Republic" of GEORGIA. Large city

Resuming our regular itinerary, we come to ALUPKA, summer palace of the 19th century Count Vorontsov, a very handsome man, judging from his portrait, and the richest man in all Russia in his day, owning 80,000 serfs as well as nearly all the Crimea. Positively puts the U.S. Southern slaveholders in the shade. His palace is built in pseudo-Scottish baronial style by an English architect. (Russians consistently deny anything having been done by foreigners, insisting on claiming credit for everything themselves.) Churchill stayed here at time of Yalta Conference. Another domestic flight from Simferopol to <u>TBILISI</u> (formerly Tiflis), capital of the "Republic" of <u>GEORGIA</u>. Large city with river running through it and mountains all around. The old quarter of town with small houses having a variety of.interesting balconies & grille-work well worth a look. Sioni Church has frescoes of saints with serene, benign expressions, all Georgian facial types. The resemble their neighbors the Armenians in physiognomy). Astonished to find our uptight Communist courier is quietly lighting a candle in the church. We are baffled but say nothing. Have read that Christianity is making a comeback in USSR but since Intourist employees would have to new the govt. line *we don't quite know what to make of this event. We see the outside of a house where Lermontov stayed, rather attractive, light blue with white grille-work balcony. (*i.e. atheistic govt.)

We win our battle against the local Tbilisi female guide who tries to prevent our seeing the Turkish Baths on pretext they are being renovated, closed, etc. We press on and find not only are they open, they are in use at this very moment, and we sail in, just interrupting some men about to go in for their baths. Pushkin had bathed here, so everyone had to see <u>his</u> bath. Everything all quite handsomely tiled inside and out. Princess tells young man bather that if he bathes in Pushkin's bath he should be very popular. (Pushkin having been a great womanizer).

On top of one of the hills there is a huge armored female statue made of riveted-aluminum segment something like an aircraft body, holding a sword in one hand and a bowl of wine in the other. This we are told is to symbolize how Georgia greets its enemies and friends simultaneously. Stroll round some shops in town with a chap from our group. We experience a bit of enthusiastic Georgian hospitality when some young women students hearing us speak English come over to practice their English, helping us with our postcard selection and then buying some for us as presents.

The Art Museum has a fantastic collection of medieval church art—icons, crosses, etc. with lovely expressive figures and some particularly fine enamel work, much more colorful than that found in Greece. I particularly liked St. George spearing a "dragon of many colors," with each scale a different color. This museum is in a building which was formerly the monastery where Stalin studied for the priesthood (!!) The History Museum has sane interesting pre-Christian gold jewelry and artifacts, their "granular" technique being noteworthy.

We attended a ballet in the handsome old opera house. Not many people in audience, so ushers indicate we can just wander around and sit anywhere there is a seat, regardless or what price category of tickets we've bought! I take this to be a bit of casual indifference and inefficiency on the part or the ushers but it seems to be standard practice. Ballet is third-rate with several really clumsy performers, but most of them are at least enthusiastic and trying hard.

Leaving Tbilisi, we start off on the GEORGIAN MILITARY HIGHWAY, built early 19th c. as part of Russian conquest and "pacification" of the fierce mountain tribes in the Caucasus. It is apparently the only road to Tbilisi. We visit the CATHEDRAL OF SVETI-TSKHOVELI in MTSKHETA (ancient capital of Georgia) where we find graves of former ruling family including father-in law of our diplomat/poet/translator. Also visit ruins of Ananuri Church overlooking riven Luncheon is in a rustic garden grape-arbor setting at PASANAURI, several tables; happen to be this time with New Zealand chap, Moscow courier, Tbilisi guide & driver, who buys us wine. Knowing Georgians detest Russians, I offer toast "To Georgia!" which pleases him.* He shows picture of little blonde, blue-eyed fair-skinned daughter. Guide says that used to be typical Georgian coloring. Apparently the inroads of Persians, Turks, etc. resulted in different ethnic mix. (*Georgians get very angry if you call them "Russian." They're very proud of their own nation. Their language and alphabet are their own and I'm not sure if they relate to any other. The Tbilisi road signs would no doubt throw any Russian driver into a tailspin not knowing which way to turn; I wondered if they did that on purpose.)

As we proceed along the Highway into the CAUCASUS MOUNTAINS we encounter more and more flocks of overwhelmingly woolly sheep which swamp us each time, but our driver ploughs right through them, blowing the horn madly. The Highway gets more and more dramatic as we ascend higher and higher. Prometheus was bound on one of these mountains. They're mostly capped with snow and we feel the cold. Sheep increasing on us. Shepherds wear splendid shaggy sheepskin hats, Driver blows horn more and more furiously. Each flock presents just another challenge to his determination. MOUNT KAZBEK (5333 metres elev.) is in clouds, can't see the top. Stop at small museum, formerly house of a local Prince and of the Turkish Bey of Kazbek. Place called "Kazbagi." In addition to historic-type exhibits we see local fauna such as enormous stuffed eagle, wolves, huge owl, misc. cats, boar, ibex, etc. which live in the mountains.

Entering the DARIALI GORGE, driver plunges us into an impossible traffic jam, bus face-to- face with a truck, and a thousand sheep and shepherds milling around trying to get by, all on the edge of a narrow road hanging on the side of a huge mountain. Your basic Macho scene, everyone yelling angrily, blowing horns, and each driver trying to make the other back up. We could all fall over the cliff but we must preserve face and tough it out. Eventually we get through this ridiculous mess and pass the site of "Tamara's Rock" featured in a Lermontov poem. Reaching the end of the Gorge, we now enter the OSSETIAN REPUBLIC. Another ethnic group here. Driver halted by police for-some traffic violation as we come into the town of ORDZHONIKIDZE. He makes a bit of a scene, yelling "Damned Osset!" (Georgians & Ossetians apparently hate each other.)

As an aside on the subject of ethnic groups and dissidents, I should mention that a local Communist official who cadged a ride on our bus in the mountains, sat next to Princess and told her about how a couple of local tribes which had been exiled to Siberia during the Stalin era had been allowed to come home during the 1960's. However, one of those tribes refused to settle into the Communist collective farm mold, being determined to maintain its own traditional way of life and farming. He said "So we dealt with than." She said "How?" He said "We dampened than down." She asked "With what?" Answer: "With flame throwers." End of tribe.

ORDZHONIKIDZE (formerly VLADIKAVKAZ, "Mistress of the Caucasus" but renamed after some prominent

Communist) is our overnight stop, not a bad little town, hotel modern and relatively pleasant. Loud rock band and singers—American-type music—drown out dinner conversation, but we have a nicely-decorated table and a delicious little beef & potato stew affair in sort of a miniature bean-pot, with a pastry lid. Princess asks what it's called. "Stew with a pastry top." Not very imaginative name, but we jot down ingredients for future reference.

On to PYATAGORSK ("Five Mountains"), stay in old pre-Revolutionary hotel, handsome and probably gradious in its day; Communist furnishings dreary & ill-coordinated. English flag on dinner table again. I wonder if other foreign groups get their national flags, or are we special. Much of Lermontov's Hero of Our Time takes place in this area, and he himself was killed in a stupid duel nearby. We visit cottage which was his military quarters, another house where the argument precipitating the duel took place, and the duel site itself, which now has a monument to him. One or the military cottages is now a Lermontov museum, has portraits of the "duelling seconds," one of whom was our Princess' great uncle. She says.they were not actually "seconds" but just friends who were all trying to talk the two quarrelling men out of duelling. This news was surprise to Museum Director.

Pyatagorsk is a spa town, with many mineral springs and baths, used for health purposes. It had been the headquarters for the Russian military in the 19th c. as base of operations and also for "rest & recreation" during their long warfare against the mountain tribes of the Caucasus. It was then fashionable for mamas to bring young daughters they wished to try and marry off to suitable young officers. Today, under the Communist regime, we see dejected, glum-looking peasants and factory workers roaming aimlessly or sitting around, looking thoroughly miserable, having been sent to this vacation spot for "medical" treatment in the mineral baths, in order to make them work better when they get home again. 200,000 people are sent here yearly for treatment.

I strolled around the town in the afternoon and climbed up a hillside with one of the people from our group. We go a better view of the town, and also a bout of fright when we saw two policemen climbing up behind us.

CLUTCH! What have we done? Was this view worth going to the Gulag? No. Whew, they pass right by, ignoring us. Apparently just out on a routine patrol. Great sighs of relief.

We attend a concert in the evening given by a group from the Northern Fleet of the Soviet Navy (!) Scrubbed and polished, energetic young men sing various set pieces which I understand from Russian speakers in our group were standard propaganda-type numbers against their enemies (guess who). Then they launch into livelier traditional peasant songs and dances with great vigor and enthusiasm. Various members of audience take bouquets of flowers to the performers at the end of the show.

Strolling around a bit after the concert, I hear trilling, singing noises coming from one of the ornamental pool areas near the hotel; go back to hotel for flashlight to investigate. No birds anywhere in sight. Singing stops when I get close to pool. Examine pool with flashlight and find two large frogs in it who must be the songsters. Hope spies are following me; this would drive than crazy. Don't see any spies. Too bad.

On our excursion to <u>KISLOVODSK</u>, another pleasant spa town not far away, we stop en route to climb up a sort of sandy cliff to some caves, where the character Pechorin took Princess Mary in Lermontov's <u>Hero of Our Time</u> "Princess Mary" story. But in the town, we are at last foiled by Intourist—they have eliminated our scheduled excursion to the country site of a duel in that story, and they make us visit the Yaroshenko Art Museum instead. The painter Yaroshenko with a few other late 19th c. artists broke with academic painting to paint "common people" etc. This gives them some cachet with the current regime, even though it just reflected an art trend that took place in other countries at the time too. At any rate, the Museum Director was obviously pleased to have an English group come to visit, and I'm glad we saw the place.

Our lecturer got into a big row with the Intourist guides in trying to continue to the site we had intended to see. They used all sorts of phoney arguments about why we could not do so. He topped all their arguments with facts, but nevertheless we lost this round. After several feeble excuses their "ultimate argument" was "It is forbidden to foreigners to go there!" "No it is not, I was there myself 10 years ago! There is nothing there but Nature!" "Well if it is just Nature, you can see Nature all around you and you don't have to go there!". Finally, they insisted the bus driver had to be back by a certain hour so therefore we couldn't possibly go to the site.

We didn't get tg see a famous stud farm in this area either, although since it was not on our program in the first place at least we did ret have that element of frustration, and the reason "They are too busy preparing for the horse auctions" was at least logical, whereas arguments regarding the fictional duel site were patently absurd.   A   stud   in Corraumst parlance is a "horse factory." We did get a glimpse of it off in the distance; it once belonged to the Stroganoff family estates. Princess takes long-distance photo for book she is writing on Stroganoffs.

The morning of our departure from Pyatagorsk we had to turn in our keys early so that bags could be taken down (why don't they have extra keys themselves for this purpose?). I then retrieved my key in order to go back and brush my teeth. Door would not open, and it was the right key. Baffled, and suspecting something sinister, I at least decided to try and get the maid to open the door. Maid knocked and called out to someone inside the room. (Heavens, what's going on here?) Then someone opened the door from inside, and a very embarrassed and scared looking young girl rushed out with a towel on her head and arms full of toilet articles. She was apparently a hotel employee in.there taking a bath and washing her hair in this "luxurious" bathroom with hot water. Realizing the low standard of living and probable shortage of such amenities for the population one could hardly blame the girl for her efforts at cleanliness.

Later, while we were assembling outside and getting onto the bus, two young girl students came along, and hearing us speak. English, asked if they could ride out to the carport with us on the bus in order to practice their English, which they did. (WHY are people studying English in this country, if they are never allowed to travel abroad and use it, and their access to foreign publications is controlled?!)

We depart from <u>Mineraliyevody Airport</u> (refers to the mineral-water spas of the area) & return to the National Hotel at <u>MOSCOW.</u> I try to find picture of movie actor at shops on Gorky St. with no luck. Investigate grocery store, find less variety and quantity of foods in the capital city of this so-called "Great Power" than in sleazy small shops in poor districts of any American city. (The situation was the same in a grocery store I visited in Tbilisi, also a largencity.) After dinner, stroll thru Red Square with one of my fellow-passengers and sit chatting on a park bench near the Kremlin for awhile. (I can't believe this. "What am I doing here?!") Is the man next to us holding his head in his hands really stoned out of his mind in a total drunken stupor, or is he spying on us? One is constantly paranoid about being watched and eavesdropped on, which of course gives a sharper edge or excitement and enjoyment to the whole trip: cryptic and veiled conversations on sensitive topics, especially in places assumed to be bugged such as these major hotels, etc. Well, if this drunk is spying, he will be bored with our touristic-type conversation. However, I think he really was just a drunk, especially since we read so much about the regime trying to combat drunkenness in the population these days.

On our last morning we wind up the tour with a drive round Moscow seeing a few more writers' statues, such as <u>Gribqyedoff's</u> with characters from his novel sculpted all around the base (as were those on <u>Gogol's</u> statue seen previously). We visit <u>Tolstoy's town house</u> now, which is a very ordinary "bourgeois" wooden house, ugly brown on the outside, but homey in a Victorian sort of way inside, furnished just as if they were still living in it. He was keen on "simplicity" as a matter of principle and deliberately sought a country-ish type of house rather than the grander sort of place a man of his noble rank would usually have had. All sorts of memorabilia here, bearskin rug which he had shot, also stuffed bear on stair landing, holding an ashtray! There are shoes he himself had made, and the bicycle he learned to ride in his old age, etc. All these Russian houses have a dining table and chairs in what we could call the "living room" or "sitting room." On inquiring why, I was told that they have them for drinking tea with guests.

On leaving for the Airport we passed crowds gathered round the <u>Pushkin statue,</u> where they had came to bring flowers and read poems on the poet's birthday.

Our last Airport scene is not unlike our entry—military set-up, many hurdles to get through (currency exchange at two-thirds loss, <u>ergo,</u> change only the smallest amounts of currency each time as you go along, and spend it all before you leave, since you'll lose most of what you have left at the airport); exit-customs form, baggage inspection, passport control and interrogation (icy, baleful stare; studying passport—"—Is this your picture?" "What is your name?" etc.) Endless waiting, delays. One never feels one will ever really escape from this country until the plane is (a) off the ground, and (b) no longer over Soviet soil. Finally get aboard British Airways plane, where cool, level-headed, staff's voices soothe the nerves, an, tons of.free British newspapers help bring us up to date with the outside world. Heave great sigh of relief. On

arrival back in a FREE COUNTRY / (England) one would like to flop down and kiss the ground. However, at airports there isn't any "soil" and anyway one is too busy trying to get out of the airport and back to one's hotel etc.

I should mention a few miscellaneous items of interest about the trip not described above. Abacuses are used almost everywhere instead of adding machines except the big hotels. The hotels have real tablecloths and napkins. The women's clothing is somewhat old-fashioned looking and very modest. We learned that more fashionable items and other sought-after consumer goods are available only to certain categories of people in the regime, including Intourist staff, in special shops— which gives something of an incentive, but we never saw anyone "smart" or "stylish"- in the western sense. Food was in general monotonous (I have only commented on the more interesting surprise items we encountered) -"meat and potatoes',' soup, heavy (lard?) pastries, lots of cucumbers, but practically NO fruit or greens other than sprigs of a parsley-type plant. One develops a terrific craving for fruit and lettuces. There is lots of bread which is quite good. American wheat (I'm sure their citizens don't know that), baked to Russian recipes. The two grocery stores I visited in major cities had very little in both quantity and quality of foods, and judging from the paucity and shabbiness of the vegetables, and the scarcity of meat, I deduced we were being much better fed in the hotels than the local citizens in their homes, particularly as to quantity of meat.

The "dragon lady" on each floor of a hotel from whom you must get your key and turn it in each time you go out (surveillance as well as convenience) is called a "Dezhumaya" (not sure of Russian spelling, but it derives from the pre-Revolutionary days, from the French "du jour" - person on duty for the day, or as one would say in the military, '"officer of the day" etc. This is annoying since they all look more like police surveillance types than helpful servants, but since this is the place to order your tea any time of day or night, the system has at least one advantage in your favor. Usually the tea is from a samovar kept going all the time, but sometimes it is made up to order. These women are thrown into, embarrassed consternation if you happen to get up before dawn and catch them ASLEEP on their sofas in the hall.

There is another surveillance feature in the lobbies - usually a man or men standing around watching everybody - mostly to keep Russians from caning in, I think, but they generally look more like idle loafers than proper security staff. Phones in the hotel rooms never seem to work; one assumes this is to force you to go downstairs to some other phone that they can monitor. On the other hand it may just be one more thing that doesn't really work properly in this country. Our retired British diplomat managed to make calls to the British Embassy in Moscow regularly to find out what was happening in the outside world, such as the course of the Falklands.

The hotel bathrooms were more or less European in nature although a bit shabby looking and there was usually something that didn't work properly. Public toilets, on the other hand, were unbelievably ghastly. In theory they were the "Eastern": stand-up type, hole-in-the-ground with some sort of cement base to stand on. But since the hole was small and nobody seemed to care about either hygiene or aesthetics, one had to walk in a mass of excrement. This is the worst I have encountered in my travels, even worse than North

Africa and Middle East. My apologies for bringing up a distasteful matter, but if anyone is thinking of a trip to the USSR they can at least go with a realistic idea of what one must contend with.

Directors and other functionaries of the little museums we visited were obviously thrilled and honored to be visited by our distinguished little British group, and they were all dressed stiffly and starchily in their best suits, looking a little old-fashioned and frayed around the edges, giving us a very warm welcome. Our diplomat/poet/translator presented them with volumes of his translations, which delighted them.

Since I could not speak the language, as I mentioned, I was particularly watching expressions and emotions. In a couple of places we arrived at, our own (British) courier would introduce us to the new local guides, indicating where we were from. They would beam with pleasure on hearing "England" but when I was introduced as from "America," their faces would cloud over immediately with mixed distaste and, I believe, fear. I am sure they are fed a steady diet of propaganda about how terrible the U.S. is, and it may be their public thinks we will attack them any minute. Since their country has a long history of being invaded by various other countries, most recently and devastatingly the Germans (now designated the "Fascists" instead of "Germans" for political purposes), the regime can play upon any national paranoia with its propaganda quite well. Since the Soviet govt. can freely pour everything into building up a vast military machine for international political ends, -- and the U.S. govt has an endless struggle trying to convince its legislature and public of the need to maintain some sort of parity, it is probably just as well if the Russians are afraid of us.

Along these lines, the various inefficiencies one observes (nothing seems to work right, nothing is on time, everything is slow and a bit bumbling) are perhaps somewhat reassuring. You wonder -- maybe if they make a war they will mess it up. Or on the other hand, is that an even worse prospect???!!! But even if higher echelon officers are intelligent, they have to depend on some rather "klutzy" people to do the work. Then again one must not underestimate the innate toughness and endurance of these people. They are <u>hard</u>, and they <u>lie</u> with no compunctions whatever. And Power is for the sake of Power.

The whole economy is run bureaucratically, by and for the State. The political/economic system allows no real free enterprise other than minor things like selling surplus backyard vegetables etc. The country needs what they frankly call "hard currency" (admitting their own is not!) and they have "hard currency shops" and "hard currency bars" in hotels, where they sell only to foreigners. But it doesn't occur to them to produce much that foreigners would really want, such as lots of good quality picture postcards. There are very few of those & of poor quality. They could make heaps of money on that alone if they used their heads. Most of the souvenir items are not worth bothering with.

In sum, it was a fascinating trip, we saw many wonderful things from the standpoint of history, art and literature, from the past, but it is NOT a pleasant country to visit -- not "fun" -- because you are constantly aware of the arbitrary regime, where people can be locked up with no redress, & you must be constantly on guard as to what you say. In short, you are not FREE. We take our freedom for granted in the West, but an experience like this gives a real appreciation of how fortunate we are.

****

At the end of this trip I spent a few days in <u>WEST BERLIN</u> (which I'd seen only very briefly a few years ago) and enjoyed all the wonderful museums, elegant restaurants, charming cafes and smart boutiques immensely. A defiant outpost of freedom and free enterprise, surrounded by the Communist East German wall, it is nevertheless a relaxed and enjoyable place to visit. The 1 1/2-hr. long protest parade against President Reagan's visit cast a sour note (assorted left-wingers, anti-American, anti-Defense, anti-Nuclear. types, etc, with misc. Iranians, Turks and PLO thrown in), but the disapproving looks and blase attitude of the rest of the public (who continued eating their ice creams and cakes in the sidewalk cafes which line the main street) kept things in perspective. Demonstrators thick in numbers, but not very energetic looking. Next day we saw a spirited petite elderly lady angrily shaking her fist telling off some scuffling demonstrators in the street.

I also had a bit of time in <u>LONDON</u>, seeing a few friends and a few plays, but was quite frustrated in not having enough time to see EVERYONE. The major highlight was getting in to see Churchill's wartime bunker at the end of its '"open" period (since it was shortly thereafter closed down for a year of "renovation" into a public museum). It was a real thrill to clamber around the grubby cement underground rooms full of pipes, debris, etc and odds and ends of furnishings left from WWII, the war maps and reconnaissance photos, Churchill's bed, and the table where the cabinet meetings took place; we were allowed to sit in their seats (each place had a cabinet member's name on the table). Everyone wanted to sit in Churchill's chair after we'd sat for the explanatory talk. It turned out that nearly everyone in the small group I toured the place with was from a U.S. Air Force base out in the country, and that made this tour the more realistic somehow, since their mission in England is much the same as that of all the historic materials were looking, at, and they could appreciate all the technical matters involved.

The guide, an enthusiastic ex-Royal Navy officer (WWII), gave a marvelous tour; he said 90% of all the visitors they had had over the years were American. The British people were unaware that it could be visited (it had not been publicised in England). Americans knew about it from travel articles or word of mouth. I was most fortunate to get in because they were fully booked up and I got a "cancellation." The place won't be quite the same when glass walls are put in and it gets cleaned up.

****

Not much to report from the home front other than an occasional trip to Santa Barbara or Carmel & Monterey, and doing the splendid San Francisco Opera season this fall. We have a new director and he's doing wonders for the pace, artistically and financially. (Fund raising for the endowment.)

If you haven't gone completely blind trying to read this squashed-up typing, MERRY
CHRISTMAS AND HAPPY NEW YEAR!

1984

Greetings, and a belated "Merry Christmas!"

This lateness is largely owing to the year's main news-
-I quit my job at Stanford Medical Center and moved back to
Morro Bay (Oct. 1), and find that the entire contents of my
Palo Alto apartment does not fit into my father's already-full
house (which my parents bought in 1928). Trying to cope with
household painting, renovations, plumbers, electricians, etc.,
and the winnowing of "things," while surrounded
by/stumbling over/bumping into/knocking down hundreds
of boxes and mountains of excess furniture seems to create
more and more mess rather than reducing it. Then I
discovered that one is allowed (by city ordinance) two garage
sales per year, so I felt I must rush to get one in under the wire
for 1984, which I did on Dec. 15-16. It was more work than I
expected, preparing for it, but worthwhile in the end and
rather fun. Then I had to brush up for and take a batch of
exams for the German language class I've been trying to keep
up with (doing my final Sunday the 23rd!). So no Christmas
cards got done at all before I went to Santa Barbara to spend
Christmas with friends there.

After many years at Stanford I miss my friends in the
Bay Area, but salaries were inadequate for the rent levels of
Palo Alto (53% of take-home pay!!!) so I cut my losses by
leaving and will have an interlude here to concentrate on the
family house, which has been somewhat neglected since my
father's death 7 years ago. I shall probably rent another
segment of the property when I get things sorted out and into
shape. (Up to now only the garage has been rented).

I am trying to go up to the S.F. Bay Area about once a
month or so to see old friends and keep up with operas, art
exhibits, weekend seminars etc. so that I won't feel cut off

from everything I'm interested in. (Note to out-of-state readers: Morro Bay is about 200 miles south of Palo Alto, 240 s. from San Francisco; in fact it's halfway between San Francisco and Los Angeles).

No overseas travel to report for 1984, unfortunately. I did take two trips to Los Angeles where I saw the J. Alden Weir (an "American Impressionist") art exhibit, as well as the "A Day in the Country" French Impressionists exhibit (marvelous!), and two stage shows. "The Detective with Charlton Heston and Mariette Hartley, and the high-energy musical show "42nd Street," both good. Also had a few trips to Carmel & Monterey and the usual batch of operas and art exhibits in San Francisco including the Grant Wood show, which gave one a wider view of his whole career and was very enjoyable. "The American View of Venice" is also a good show I hope to see again.

Never having had the slightest interest in soccer, but being caught up in the "Olympic Fever" which swept the state last summer, I decided I must get in on it, so I went to see two Olympic soccer matches at the Stanford Stadium--Brazil vs. Germany, and the semi-final, Brazil vs. Italy. It turned out to be quite fun despite my not knowing beans about the subject, and the zest of the players plus the wild enthusiasm of the spectators, who were a whole show in themselves, made for very entertaining evenings (combined with our picnic supper on the grounds outside beforehand, amidst a very international crowd).

I was sorry then that I had not had the sense to book up for some of the Olympic events in Los Angeles, since this was the first time the games had come here for 52 years and L.A. put on such a marvelous show of the whole thing.

Since Santa Claus has not given me my fond wish for a neat, tidy, spruced-up, sparsely furnished house, I must return to my mountain of work on this place...meanwhile, sorry for the delay, and thanks for your cards which are being forwarded here by the P.O. Please make note of my change of address since I have left Palo Alto, and will be here for an indefinite time.

Happy New Year!

1987

Annual (Christmas/New Year's/Easter) Greetings!

My apologies for not keeping up with my Christmas cards very well the last few years, and thanks to all of you who keep sending me yours, in spite of my lapses. A friend loaned me a computer right after Christmas to try and get my address lists into order and to produce some mailing labels, which took about two weeks (not completely finished yet). But I had to drop that project and spend many more weeks getting financial records ready for the accountant to do my income tax. So now I'm hoping to get these notes off by Easter!

To summarize events of recent years, having resigned from my work at Stanford Medical Center in 1984, I have been back in my family's house in Morro Bay, where I'm STILL trying to sort out and dispose of endless "things" and do renovations on the property. The work goes very slowly, since I'm doing so much of it myself, on top of my full-time job at the local high school library. I escape on occasional weekends by going up to San Francisco and environs to see old friends and catch up on movies, operas, art exhibits, etc. I've also made a few trips to Los Angeles and Santa Barbara. But I haven't had a "real" (i.e. overseas) vacation since the literary tour of Russia in 1982.

Last summer the Carmel Art Association borrowed four landscape paintings by my father (A. Harold Knott, 1883-1977) for its special 60th Anniversary Exhibit, since he had lived there during the 1920s and was one of the original members when that organization was formed in 1927. (For non-Californian readers, Carmel is about 100 miles north of here, on the coast, a "picturesque" village originally founded as an art colony around the turn of the century, and now much frequented by tourists and vacationers.) The exhibition comprised works by members from the Association's first 10 years, 1927-1937, and was a wonderful show, enthusiastically received by members and public. I was so pleased to see my father's work shown again among that of many of his old friends. And it is gratifying too to see the work of this particular generation of painters enjoying a resurgence of interest. The CAA held a lovely reception to launch the show, with music by a string quartet adding to the happy ambiance. The highlight of the summer.

In October an abandoned cat insisted on taking me over. Starving, shabby and dirty, but with a cheerful, eager and determined little spirit, he ingratiated himself into my household. Barely past the kitten stage, he was quite unprepossessing in his looks, tabby-colored with assymetrical white trim, his only distinguishing feature a huge set of white whiskers and eyebrows, so I named him "Whiskers." After several weeks of good food, he began to flourish and drew two neighbors into his orbit. From a starving homeless waif he became a success with two houses and an apartment, a luxurious fur coat, free medical care, and three human beings to cater to his needs. His long fur expanded out to the dimension of his whiskers for the cold winter. But he is now shedding down to a lightweight sports coat for spring.

A childhood friend and her husband came to visit at Christmas who have been living in the Midwest for years, so they were keen to look at the ocean and for mountains as much as possible during their stay. Christmas Eve we drove along a lonely road on the rugged coast south of the Bay to watch the sun set over the sea from the Montana de Oro State Park. Southern California was having its coldest winter since 1883, so it seemed bleak and chill as we watched the golden-orange sun sink into the ocean's horizon, and we turned to drive back on the deserted, rugged winding road in the dusk between mountains and the waves crashing on the rocky coastal inlets below.

Suddenly we were startled to come upon SANTA CLAUS in full costume, getting out of his car. He waved, we laughed and waved back, and a DEER bounded across the road just in front of us. It felt like Christmas Eve in the "Twilight Zone" - and what a delightful surprise! A perfect evening was completed with roast Christmas goose at an Inn directly over the quiet Bay, where herons nest in the Eucalyptus groves and small boats rest at anchor.

A replica of the "Golden Hinde," ship of the 16th century English privateer Francis Drake, sailed into our port last week, and I just dropped by to have a look. Swarms of tourists and school children have been going through it steadily, as it sits berthed between the U.S. Coast Guard cutters, large fishing boats and smaller pleasure craft.

BEST WISHES FOR WHAT'S LEFT OF THIS "NEW" YEAR--AND HAPPY EASTER!

1990

Greetings!

Not knowing if I'll finish my cards in time for the holidays, I'd better call this my "sporadic 'annual' summary letter."

As I look back on this year's events, art and opera seem to predominate. I made a couple of trips to Santa Barbara. The first included visits to two fine private collections of California art (of my father's "period"). One of the hosts keeps his paintings in an immaculate garage with his collection of vintage Mercedes cars. During the second trip, I heard the opera singer Marilyn Horne give a master class at the Music Academy. Most interesting--and they have some promising young singers there.

I made the first trip to Los Angeles mainly to visit a private collection of the 19th century American art (this and the Santa Barbara tour were both sponsored by a museum group I'm a member of). For this one we were instructed to leave everything in the cars--including purses-since the host's rooms were small in relation to the crowd of visitors. Aghast at the idea of leaving my bag in the car in Los Angeles, Crime Capital of the World, I stuffed my money, identification and credit cards into my pockets. But as it turned out, nothing could have been safer than this neighborhood--every house bristling with private security firms' "instant armed response" signs!"

The second L.A. trip was a wild dash down and back all in one day (ca. 200+ mi. Each way) to see the Annenberg Collection (Impressionist/Post Impressionist paintings). Fearing we might be late for our scheduled 1:00 museum ticket entrance, we couldn't take time to make our way down onto the sand and ended up eating our picnic lunch in the car on a service road behind the beach houses of Mailu--garbage cans and all--lunching "in the backyard of the Stars," as it were. I told my companions next time we should leave early enough so we could eat in their front yard (i.e. on the beach).

The major vacation event of the year was the San Francisco Opera presentation of Wagner's Ring--in fact, four complete cycles (Der Ring des Nibelungen, 4 operas in each cycle, to those of you not familiar with this, though how could you not be after the Metropolitan's televised production?) There were masses of peripheral Ring-related programs going on in S.F. for months--lectures, exhibits, concerts, films, etc. and even a Pocket Opera Co. production of the first opera Wagner ever composed as a very young man, "Das Liebesverbot." (Before he had developed his own distinct style.) I saw this, and I also travelled up for a long weekend early in June before my own 4th cycle tickets, in order to attend the University of California Medical School's 2-day symposium on medical aspects of Wagner's Ring (!) Fantastic!

Then during my 11-day stay for the 4th cycle at the end of June, I helped in hostessing at some programs sponsored by the Wagner Society of which I'm a member. I was a ticket-seller for a Syberberg-directed film about King Ludwig of Bavaria, and for a recital by young singers doing lieder by Wagner and other composers influenced by him. I was a ticket-taker at a lecture/symposium. And at our piece de résistance event, held at the ballet building, I acted as one of the hostesses for the opera singer guests at the big reception we sponsored in their honor. This involved meeting them at the entrance, escorting them to the room where the party was taking place, getting them drinks and making a bit of conversation and/or introductions, and then going back to fetch someone else. In this fashion I escorted one

Rhinemaiden (Wellgunde, one Valkyrie (Waltraute--and husband), one Alberich (the villain--in real life a continental charmer), one of the three Brunnhildes of the season (Gwyneth Jones), and the General Director of S.F. Opera, Lotfi Mansouri--a jolly, delightful chap. The party was a huge success, much enjoyed by members, singers, and public guests. (over 200 people).

In between this busy festival-like schedule I managed to do the round of art galleries, stores, etc. and see a few old friends in the Bay Area.

This fall I have only been up to the opera for one weekend, seeing "Fledermaus" and "Capriccio" (R. Strauss). The surprise guest cast member in the ball scene of Fledermaus was Bobby McFerrin of the cranberry-juice commercials on cable TC, who led both cast and audience in his own special brand of improvised mouth-music for a few minutes. Warm "vibes" and laughter all around.

On the domestic front, I have reported previously on the cat "Whiskers" who runs my household to suit his extravagant and heedless tastes. He is now all fluffed out for winter, presumably to predict cold weather. Questioned as to the possibility of rain to end the severe 5-year drought, he says nothing, and assumes the traditional mysterious poker-faced stare. The lawn has not grown for over a year and is one-third dead, not responding well to the poor quality and small quantity of water permitted under mandatory restrictions here. The so-called drought-resistant plants are not looking any too hot either. The drought has also resulted in another creature's taking up residence: a small frog, Fred by name, whom I found sitting in the cat's outdoor water dish. (This is sheltered from wind by a wooden crate.) Fearing for little Fred's life, I put out another dish of water behind the box and admonished him to move, lest he end up just a passing hors d'oeuvre. He has agreed now to sit in his own dish, retreating to the woodpile by day.

Hurrah! I managed to squash all this onto one page after all.

Best wishes for a happy Christmas and New Year!

1991

Greetings!

Time for the annual report again. Incidentally, some of my correspondents may have had the impression that I do absolutely nothing but chase around to cultural events. Wrong. It's just that I don't think you really want to hear about my job, my housework, yardwork, plumbing repair, sewer roto-rooters, termites, mold, rust, corrosion, dry rot, moths, laundry, marketing, cooking, dishwashing, housepainting, vacuuming/squishing/fumigating spiders out of the garage, etc. etc., do you? Let's focus on more interesting matters.

Took a couple of trips to Los Angeles last winter to attend some art exhibits and also saw a wonderful performance of "Love Letters," the two-person show that ran for over a year and has recently been brought back again, in which different pairs of actors take part each week. Since there are so many actors running around Los Angeles who find it easy to fit in a week somewhere between their other assignments, if you lived there you could see just about anyone you ever heard of in this play The night I went we had Ben Gazzara & Gena Rowlands, who were perfect in this beautifully-written piece of work.

Speaking of actors, I had forgotten to mention that the previous year I had arrived in L.A. one night on the train, finding everything to a blaze of intense light, and picked my way into the station through a snakepit of big black electric cables all over the floor. People were bustling around in 1940s--vintage clothes, including men in various WWII uniforms. I'd done it again for my second time--stumbled into a film set. I was preoccupied (and sleepy) trying to retrieve my checked bag so I never found out what show was being filmed--probably some TV program.

My own show biz career came to a halt at an early stage, in elementary school, to be exact. (Credits: Humpty

Dumpty, in a stiff, scratchy white buckram shell (age about 5 or 6); and Ghost, draped in the limp grey gauze, assuming what the director called "grotesque positions" around a graveyard to the tune of "Danse Macabre" in a Hallowe'en tableau (age about 10). So I do enjoy these occasional brushes with the Real Thing, Hollywood-style, from time to time.

I haven't been running a car of my own for some time, but had to rent one to haul one of my father's paintings down to the L.A. area for a small museum exhibit at the beginning of March, and then go back to fetch it at the end of the month (Easter weekend). Driving the maze of 6 to 12-lane freeways down there is an adrenaline-churning adventure of the first magnitude, especially trying to remain on the designated route without finding oneself channelled off the right-hand lane at the wrong place. (I was proud of myself not having come off in the wrong place more than 3 times per trip!) The museum group had a nice little buffet luncheon for the lenders on both the hanging and taking-down days, and the painting was well received.

In the spring I was one of the "volunteers" hostessing on a garden tour sponsored by the American Association of University Women. The place I was assigned to was very small, the display consisting of assorted rosebushes at the front. At the back of the house the owner had 80 plastic trash-barrels filled with rainwater he had collected during the short but heavy period of rainfall we'd had in March. He exulted over the fact that the rainwater was "free," but he must have spent at least $1200 on the barrels, not to mention getting up in the night and all hours of the day to move them to and from the drain spouts.

(I myself had bought "only" 3 metal garbage cans to save rainwater, a lot of which I had then transferred into plastic gallon jugs. For my non-California readers--we are now in the 6th year of drought here--bad news for gardens, and water is rationed--and expensive.)

In the fall I volunteered again for the AAUW, which this time was one of many groups involved with the town's "Harbor Festival," a sort of Breughel-by-the-Sea affair which raises funds for the groups sponsoring it and other charities. All kinds of seafood being sold and consumed on the spot (cooked in every conceivable way), and vendors selling all sorts of artsy craftsy goods, etc. I was assigned to collect the admission fees at the main gate. Swaddled head to toe to keep off the sun, including wearing the biggest straw cartwheel hat I own, I attracted a newspaper photographer who, my dentist later informed me, had to put my picture in one of the local papers. (I subsequently obtained some copies, of course.)

In August I spent a few days in San Francisco going to museums and art galleries and then went to Carmel for their Art Association's annual anniversary show, which this year featured work by six of their early women artists. I had loaned a small etching (by M. DeNeale Morgan)* to the exhibit. The CAA held a lovely reception for the lenders and members, and I also enjoyed seeing a few friends there as well. (*Miss Morgan was a friend of my parents when they all lived in Carmel in the 1920s.)

Sprinkled through the year were a few short jaunts to Santa Barbara, and I also heard a performance of Mozart's Requiem in a splendid setting, the old 18th c. Spanish mission church in San Luis Obispo.

In September I went to San Francisco again for a couple of operas (Traviata and Don Giovanni, and to a small reunion party of college friends. (The hostess then went abroad on vacation for a few weeks, returning to find her house had just burned down in the massive Oakland fire in October. Major shock!) Colossal disasters, California's specialty--

Some of my correspondents have inquired after Fred, the frog of whom I wrote last Christmas. I regret to say that he was only with us a few weeks. This engaging little fellow disappeared, and I fear the worst--that he must have perished in the digestive tract of Whiskers, the cat. I felt terrible. I should have moved Fred's water dish deep into the interior of the hedge. Neighbors tried to console me--"He probably just moved away," or "Frogs dig themselves holes in the ground in winter, don't they?" etc. -- But he is gone, and I feel a special sorrow for the only frog I ever had.

Whiskers is doing reasonably well, despite his allergies (it seems there's no real advantage being a cat, if you get all the ailments that people get). Lately he has taken to perching on the ridge of the garage roof, alternating with the house roof, like a furred weather vane into the wind, grooming himself busily the while. From there he also keeps an eye on his territory, plus all passersby on both streets. He still declines to function as a Working Predator, despite my daily requests that he "Get out there and catch those gophers who are undermining my yard!" He continues in the pampered and fey dilettante role he prefers. In addition, he prefers to drink out of my saucepans, mugs etc. instead of his own water dish painted "Cool Cat," or even the one painted with "Cat" in four different languages.

I look forward to hearing your news--in any language. Merry Christmas and Happy New Year!

1994

Greetings! Surprise!!

My apologies to everyone I didn't write to last Christmas. I was unable to do many cards or to write a summary letter owing to a thoroughly unpleasant holiday season devoted to "arthroscopic knee surgery," its preliminaries and aftermath. My Christmas "vacation" was spent lying around in pain or hobbling around on crutches, trying to feed myself, etc. It was, you might say, a "Tiny Tim" Christmas. Knee cartilage had mysteriously torn a year previously (no fall, no bump, no specific event I could identify), and after a year of limping I had decided to try the surgery. So far I seem to have merely traded knee pain for a whole lot more pain in more places--from foot to waist--and after months of gruelling physical therapy exercises (which in themselves cause pain) I've regained only about 40% of the atrophied quadriceps muscle. I had been able to return to work (am still at the local high school library) only a few weeks after the surgery, but the rehabilitation of the leg is taking FOREVER!

Apart from that, and a severe, virulent kind of flu in the spring of 1993, most of the news for the past two years is more positive...

There was the usual sprinkling of trips to art exhibits and/or tours of private collections in San Francisco, San Diego, Irvine, Malibu, Santa Barbara, Los Angeles and Pasadena (notably the "Arroyo Seco" area for a combined architecture/art tour of the "Craftsman Period" houses and studios of various late 19th-early 20th century artists and craftsmen* with exhibits of paintings hanging in several, which was wonderful). In Monterey, I attended the opening of the Art Museum's new wing at the "La Mirada" satellite building, which is dedicated mainly to showing California and Oriental art.

*Including the Judson stained glass studios, whose business has surged in replacing earthquake-smashed windows in churches, etc.

The main event for 1993 (April 18-July 18) however, was a solo exhibit of paintings by my late father (A. Harold Knott), at the Ontario Museum of History and Art (Ontario, Calif.--in the greater Los Angeles area). This was most gratifying, as it was the first one-man show of his work since the 1960s, and it made a handsome exhibit: 39 oil paintings (both landscapes and marines) arranged in three galleries in the Museum's old Spanish-style building. I had to take up a new career field as "lady truck driver" in order to ferry the paintings down there and back in a rented cargo van--! I also wrote up a biographical piece about my father which was printed as part of the Museum's flyer announcing the exhibit. The show was warmly received by curator, board members and public. I was very pleased about the whole thing.

Other 1993 activities included some time in Carmel doing library research on my father's career (old newspaper microfilms), since he had lived there during the 1920s. In San Francisco I saw the opera "Meistersinger" and attended a panel program sponsored by my Wagner Society featuring various singers and others from that production. We also had a silent auction of Wagner-themed pictures by one of our members as a fundraiser for our very own production of "Das Rheingold."

So in 1994, after months of struggle to rehabilitate my leg and myself after the surgery, I had progressed enough to be able to act as a volunteer usher when our "Das Rheingold" was produced in the Palace of Fine Arts Theatre in San Francisco on Wagner's Birthday, May 22. Our members all pitched in doing various volunteer jobs in connection with the production. We had a young professional conductor and singers, and the orchestra was primarily made up of students from San Jose State University, with a few professionals included. Everyone was very keen to do this opera, since there are so few opportunities for musicians and singers to do Wagner. In concept this was a modern-dress version, with minimal props (e.g. Rheinmaidens in bathing suits, sunglasses, etc. on beach, Alberich as a beach bum with a metal detector after the gold, Wotan and Fricka (King and Queen of the Gods) in sleek dress-mythological or stylized/abstract approach to costuming and sets, as modern-dress versions go, this was well thought out and workable. I was amazed at what a good production it turned out to be, considering how small our organization is and how small its budget! We were all very proud of ourselves for our collective success.

In April and July I had a couple more visits to Carmel to continue the library research, and made a short trip to Santa Barbara in August. There I heard an interesting lecture by a film composer on how music is composed and/or selected and produced for movies. As a long-time film buff, I found this fascinating.

We had a major fright at the end of summer when a massive brush fire (arson) at the north end of our town spread out of control over a large part of the county. On its second night I could see a huge wall of flame coming over the mountains toward us about 2-4 miles to the north and another about 5-7 miles to the east. We are hemmed in on 3 sides by mountains. I packed up as many important items as I could into my luggage, tote bags, etc. in readiness to evacuate if necessary via a friend's car and my things in a neighbor's truck. I felt we could survive by going to the widest part of the beach and standing in the ocean. Fortunately a cool fog and change of wind developed overnight and by morning the fire had burned out on this end, but continued heading east. It took several days for firefighters from all over the state to put it out.

In September I went on a one-night trip to Hollywood with friends to hear a concert at the Hollywood Bowl. The British Hallé Orchestra was performing under its conductor, Kent Nagano, who is the only world-famous person ever to emerge from this little town of Morro Bay, or from this whole county, as far as I know. It was a "family program," with Britten's "Young Person's Guide to the Orchestra" narrated by Lynn Redgrave; "Peter and the Wolf" narrated by Timothy Dalton (who did a great job with the different animal voices--better than he has done as Mr. Rochester, James Bond or Rhett Butler, in my view!), and Holst's "The Planets," which included a lovely laser light show adding a touch of magic to the scene.

We stayed at the 1927-vintage Hollywood Roosevelt Hotel nearby, and the next day I put my feet in the movie stars' cement-based footprints at Graumann's Chinese Theatre across the street. Again, for an old movie buff, this was great fun. I particularly enjoyed Humphrey Bogart's inscription to the owner Sid Graumann: "Sid, may you never die till I kill you" (1946) The biggest feet I could find were Victor McLagen's and Harrison Ford's--much bigger than mine!

In November I went to San Francisco for a long weekend and saw the opera "Hérodiade" (Massenet) which had been hauled out of well-deserved oblivion. Placido Domingo had inexplicably accepted a tiny and unattractive part as John the Baptist. King Herod had the only big part, and gorgeous costumes. Basically it was an inspit, gutless piece, and not the usual hard-nosed Salome tale we are accustomed to via Oscar Wilde & Richard Strauss. But with Domingo in it, they had no trouble selling all the tickets. "SRO" (and I was in the "S" group).

As of November I can report my leg is getting stronger, even though not pain free. I'm in a dilemma of exercising to rehabilitate muscle vs. not exercising, to reduce pain!

The cat Whiskers, 7, whose Human Being I am, still rules to the household, charging around knocking things off tables and shelves, and demanding fine delicacies such as breast of roast chicken and baked rainbow trout. When the telephone rings he comes running, as if he were expecting a call. However, it usually turns out he just knows he can get some quality lap time when I'm pinned down in phone conversation. Likewise he comes running when he hears the typewriter, but not always to dictate a letter. Again it's a chance to curl up for a lap snooze. As for our amphibian friends, Fred's dynasty lives: three frogs spend part of each day in my rain-barrels, so I have to keep the lids slightly ajar for them. They then hop back into the salt-bush hedge when their ablutions are completed We also have a possum-in-residence, whom I have encountered just before dawn in the back yard, and who scuttles into the hedge at daybreak. I don't know where the raccoons hang out in the daytime but I know they're out there at night, from the empty and muddied water dishes and the footprints I find in the morning. Squirrels continue to gnaw off the growing tips of the pine boughs and shred the green cones all over the grounds. No one can say I am not Involved in the Ecology.

Now must begin the massive clerical effort of getting these letters and cards underway. Look forward to hearing your news. Merry Christmas and Happy New Year!

*Speaking of Herod--did I ever regale you with my hilarious adventure fending off a grabby, amorous "guide" at the Herod family tomb in Jerusalem? (On a Middle East/Holy Land trip years ago....)

1995

Greetings!

This should set a new lateness record for the generic Christmas letter. My apologies! I had to schedule jaw surgery for my 2-week Christmas vacation, and all the preliminary appointments, tests, hospitalization, convalescence, frequent post-op doctor appointments and general low energy levels turned the early winter into a Black Hole. [All for nothing, as it turned out; an alleged problem of the salivary gland turned out to be merely an enlarged muscle!] Thank you for all your Christmas cards and letters, which provided a bright spot in an otherwise dismal holiday season.

Now that I'm on "summer vacation" from the school library job, I'm trying to catch up on the backlog of my own work, including this letter.

Activities for 1995 were as usual highlighted with musical or art events. I've also been involved with the small, struggling local historical society and its newsletter. (Very few people want to do any work, hence the struggle.) But I was able to organize a roster of people to man our display table in the "Maritime Pavilion" (AKA the "history tent") at the Harbor Festival, and I loaned a charcoal portrait my father had drawn during the 1930s of a grizzled old fisherman called "Johnny off the Whaler" for this exhibit. (It seems there was still whaling activity along this coast during the '30s, and the artists apparently talked this fellow into posing for their sketch club.)

I attended a Monet exhibit in San Francisco--works from his WORST years, when cataracts had ruined his vision; a very poor idea for an exhibit, in my opinion. But there were a couple of lovely paintings from his earlier period that made it worthwhile.

It was most gratifying, on the other hand, to see some of the BEST works by my father (A. Harold Knott) in exhibits at the Monterey Museum. Two ("The Sand Bar" and "The Golden Shore" are still on display, as the Lure of the Sea exhibit has been extended (at the Museum's La Mirada satellite building).

I was asked to give a talk to the Morro Bay chapter of the American Association of University Women about my father's career, and I showed a number of his paintings at this event. The presentation was warmly received, and spurred a few members to trek up to Monterey to have a look at the Museum exhibit.

I also loaned one of my father's paintings. "Deserted Church, Cayucos," for the Morro Bay Presbyterian Church's centennial celebrations. The church in nearby Cayucos had been abandoned for some years owing to changing demographics, and within two years after my father did his painting (1928 or 29) the church was totally dismantled and a school subsequently built on the site.

San Francisco proudly celebrated the 50th anniversary of the United Nations with an array of events, the festive and joyous mood of which was all out of synch with the near-uselessness of the UN's "peacekeeping" in the Balkans. But one could enjoy the events for their own sake, at any rate. I saw the Gluck version of Orphée at the opera house in May, and by June things were really hotting up both musically and meteorologically. The Opera de Lyon (France) - the orchestra of which is directed by Morro Bay's Kent Nagano--performed The Love for Three Oranges, a first rate, hilarious production. Noye's Fludde, performed in an old church by a troupe of Canadian youngsters in animal costumes and a few adult professionals was also delightful. At the symphony hall a concert version of Fidelio, directed by a peppery, brisk conductor (Eschenbach) and with Hildegard Behrens as the lead singer, was as rousing and exhilarating as Beethoven could have hoped for.

The temperature had reached about 100° (or was it 103°?) by the time of the open air concert in Stern Grove with the Opera de Lyon Orchestra in shirtsleeves but with both Maestro Nagano and soloist (Van Damme, singing Wotan's Farewell--hopefully not prophetic, given the temperature) stoically enduring their tailcoats throughout.

Later in the summer I saw La Périchole in a full production by young trainee singers in the same spot, with the temperature then only in the mere 90-ish range.

During the regular fall season, Madama Butterfly was pretty humdrum.

I spent two 1-week sessions (Easter and August) continuing my research on my father's career in old newspaper microfilms in the Carmel and Monterey libraries. (He lived there during the 1920s.) I also spent several days in Santa Barbara.

As usual I attended a number of programs put on by our Wagner Society in San Francisco, a cluster of which were arranged around the date of a performance of Die Walküre. We had a symposium on this opera featuring several cast members and the conductor discussing their approach to the work, and we also had a lecture and a reception (jointly with the Performing Arts Library & Museum) honoring the 100th anniversary of Kirsten Flagstad's birth (one of the all-time great Wagnerian sopranos).

But our piece de résistance came in early December (before my having to deal with the surgery issue). This was what the Wagner Society calls its "Cosima Birthday Party," celebrating the birthday of Wagner's wife (Cosima Liszt Von Bulow Wagner). Since she was born on Christmas day, this December event also serves as a Christmas party. We met at the gracious old Century Club. After a glass of wine and conversation with other members and guests, we gathered in the foyer, where a tall decorated tree stood in the stairwell, and we were treated to a reenactment of Christmas morning in Wagner's villa, "Triebschen," in Lausanne, on Cosima's 34th birthday in 1875. On that occasion, she awoke to hear musicians on their staircase playing what is now known as the "Siegfried Idyll," which Wagner had composed as a birthday present for her. (Wagner himself called it the "Trieebschen Idyll.") Two of our members in costume enacted the parts of Wagner and Cosima (in mime), and a string quartet positioned on the stairs (and piano on the second floor) played the music. It was most moving; an outstanding occasion. Afterwards we dined upstairs (with more music from the quartet).

I was asked to write up the event for our quarterly journal, Leitmotive. Since the evening had been a perfect episode of time travel, I wrote it up in a time-travel format, and the article was published in our spring edition. (Gratifying to see oneself in print, even if no pay. However, copies are sent to Wagner Societies worldwide--and to the Library of Congress--so I can say I have an "international audience," at any rate.)

Other activities of '95 included a small college reunion party at a classmate's home in Oakland. I opted out of the gigantic, multi-class reunion activities on the campus (Stanford). And a full-scale high school class reunion in San Luis Obispo. The school having been pretty small by modern standards, this is a very manageable-sized gathering. (In my teen years there was no high school in Morro Bay and we rode a bus to SLO every day, 14 miles each way.) It was fun to discover that one classmate has been appearing in TV commercials from Los Angeles as one of the wry, irreverent "old geezers" advertising Rice Krispies cereal. He says doing commercials is much more lucrative than his former career. He also says they made them EAT the Rice Krispies. (I won't quote the effect on his insides.)

Now for more mundane matters--how about re-roofing the house last fall, after serious leaks the previous winter. This involved flinging two layers of old cedar shingles onto the ground in two huge piles on either side of the house (which drove the cat crazy when I let him out to inspect things at night), and massive debris fallout into the attic and service porch inside, which drove me crazy, plus three weeks of chaos (and noise) to complete what the contractor had thought would be a three-day job. On top of that, my aesthetic sense was offended by the city's requiring <u>fake</u> fireproof roofing materials instead of real wood as specified by the original architect's design. But California being one vast tinderbox, aflame regularly every summer and fall, one can hardly argue the point, and who has energy to fight city hall?

And underneath the house--another problem. By wintertime, my insurance carrier was demanding certification that the house was bolted to its foundation in order to continue my usual earthquake coverage. What do you know? Contractor went down to have a look--no bolts! Furthermore, this so-called "crawl space" was not sufficiently crawlable for him to get in and do the bolting work, owing to massive earth mounds thrown up by gophers over the last several years. [Note to non-Californians: many houses, if not most, do not have basements--just "crawl spaces." Gophers are mole-like rodents who burrow underground eating roots of every plant you really want or pay a lot of money for. They construct a network of tunnels and throw the earth up onto the surface in huge piles.] Since there are no plants under the house, why are they so busy down there? Do they find the earth warmer and cozier for their sleeping quarters? Is it that the dry ground is preferable to hang out in when the outdoor earth is soaked with rain? Or are they just doing this deliberately to sabotage my house? If so, they are pretty successful.

At any rate, in order to meet the insurance company's deadline, I had to have all this work done during the rainy weather, hiring a number of stalwart Cal Poly students to dig out the excess earth, at well-above-average wages (otherwise, who would do it?) I provided dust masks (changing the filters twice daily), sundry tools, and an old rug on which to load and haul out the dirt. The work was so difficult, dirty and exhausting I felt compelled to also ply the lads with Coca Colas and substantial sandwich lunches. The boys would hack and dig their way into the dirt under the house, maneuver it onto the rug (tied like a hammock on each end) and drag it out. They emerged each time from the crawl-hole covered in a thick coating of dust, looking like grotesque space-aliens. Then, outdoors, the pouring rain quickly turned their dust coatings to mud, which streamed down their faces and clothing like a variation on the old "fire in the wax museum" movies.

All this dirt brought out had to be piled elsewhere on the property, and with the rain and the insurance deadline there wasn't time to have it nearly spread around, so I still have to decide what to do with the pile. Anyway... after several weeks of this digging/hauling activity, the boys had carved out enough space for the contractor and assistant to get under the house and bolt it down, just in the nick of time to send off the insurance certification. One more hurdle in the joys of home maintenance and bureaucratic demands surmounted.

Now let's get back to those gophers. Most of their activity is outdoors where you can see it--that's part of their fun. They love to throw up piles in pathways and bury the lawn in dirt mounds, not to mention piling dirt against wooden fences and walls so that the termites have easier access to good eating. (The Conspiracy Theory.) And I regret to say that my famous cat Whiskers is no help at all, indifferent to the whole problem, considering himself essentially a "people cat," or "lap cat," and not a hunter. I even carried him to a gopher hole where the rodent had just peered out; old Whiskers just turned and walked away. Lovable as he is, he is not a professional cat. He only catches prey when he's in the mood.

Most of this season I've had just one frog hanging out in the rain barrel (which is actually a dark green plastic garbage can full of rainwater, with a lid which I keep slightly ajar for his benefit. I don't know if this is one of my original Fred's descendants or relatives, but he definitely feels this is his home. He doesn't say much, though. While a whole frog chorus sings out when rain fills an abandoned fishpond down the block, I rarely hear a solo number from this little amphibian friend. Just this very morning of writing, however, I found a small frog just inside the kitchen door trying to camouflage his skin to match the floor covering, so I took him out to put him in the rain barrel. He leaped out of my hand before I got the lid open, but then I discovered two additional frogs in the barrel--so this makes a total of FOUR frogs as of mid-July! Hurrah! I'm doing my part in keeping the species alive (since I've read that frogs world-wide are dwindling severely in numbers--baffling scientists; but one of the leading theories is ultraviolet radiation owing to the thin "ozone layer" problem in the skies...)

Another species turned up last year on the lawn, which I took to be a dead bat. However, as I tried gingerly to maneuver it into a bag for disposal, it raised its head, and -- EEK!.No, it didn't turn into Bela Lugosi in a black cape lunging for my throat--but it did hiss menacingly, repeatedly. I backed off, realizing it must be a sick bat, since it didn't fly away. I covered it with a flower pot and called the County Animal Regulation Dept. to come and fetch it. (More bureaucracy; they require a written request pinned to your door authorizing them to enter the property and remove the animal.) As I was anxious to have a potential rabies-carrier removed, compliance was no problem.

Well, so long, bat, wherever you are; perhaps among the eternally Undead characters in those old Dracula movies.

I'm cutting this off with "winter" more or less, in the interest of space, and assuming I can get the Christmas letter off in timely fashion will save the bulk of 1996 reporting for that. It's too late for Merry Christmas/Happy New Year/4th of July etc., but here's wishing you a good summer, and I'll look forward to hearing your news around Christmas.

1996 - 1997

Greetings!

My card-sending the past two years has been incomplete, owing to jaw surgery Christmas 1995 and 'flu in December 1996. I tried to catch up with "generic letters" during vacation last July,but didn't get the task finished then either. Now, as of December 17, as I was completing the final draft on this letter, the computer destroyed the whole thing while I was at lunch. WHY? And I'd carefully "saved" it, too. So much for technology. I'm just a low-tech person trying to cope with the high-tech world...sigh...

So this letter will be even later than I thought. I'll recreate it from an earlier draft. It will just be highlights of 1996 and '97. I may never catch up with 1995!

BOTH YEARS:--Assorted museum and art exhibits, musical or lecture events, etc., and continuing researches (during short vacations) in old newspaper microfilms at the Carmel and Monterey libraries, looking for info about my father's art career when he had lived there. I organized exhibits and teams of volunteers for the local Historical Society's display at the October Harbor Festival, on a fishing pier! This October ('97), when we were packing up the displays at the end, a fisherman came up and asked if we wanted to buy a whole albacore [this is the "solid white meat tuna" when it's in cans] for $10.00. They were huge, and frozen, from the hold of the boat. I said "Why not?" So this creature lay in my fridge thawing for three days. It was like finding Moby Dick in there every time I opened the fridge. He was baked then, providing steaks, sandwiches, salads, etc. for me, and fabulous snacks for Whiskers the Cat.

1996: During the summer I heard a lecture and concert rather out of the ordinary at the 18th century Spanish mission church in San Luis Obispo--with both recordings and live performances of 18th century Spanish colonial church music. Spain used to send court composers out to create original music for the cathedrals and churches in its vast empire, of which California was part. The speaker had delved into some old long-lost compositions in a cathedral archive in Mexico. The music was lovely!

Since my high school days were spent two years each in two different classes, I went to another "class reunion" in 1996 (having been to the other one the year before). It is a shock to walk into a room thinking of the teenagers you remembered--and finding something altogether different at this stage! But it was fun to see them anyway, and find out how everyone's lives had turned out.

The outstanding event of 1996, however, was a brief trip to PARIS on rather short notice during Thanksgiving week in November. This was precipitated by my interest in seeing film actor Alain Delon in his first stage play in many years (*"Variations Enigmatiques"*), plus my discovery of a cheap airline fare (via Frankfurt, thus affording a couple of hours of German ambiance each way). I also got to see another old favorite film actor Jean-Paul Belmondo on stage in a 19th century Feydeau farce (*"La Puce à l'Oreille"*). I visited two museums that had not existed when I was there 100 years ago, the d'Orsay and the Pompidou. And I made a little literary pilgrimage to the site of one of my favorite poems, "Pont Mirabeau"--riding the *Métro* to the other side of the river so I could walk back across the bridge, clutching plastic-encased poetry book under an umbrella in the pouring rain!--then going back down into the *Métro* on the other side to return to my base of operations.

I loved exploring my St. Germain *quartier* in the rain, with all its historic literary and artistic associations, bookshops, galleries, restaurants and boutiques. Walking across the pedestrian bridge at night in the rain was great too, with all those handsome buildings cleaned and lighted up on both sides of the river. And just staying in a 17th century hotel which Louis XIV's architect (who established the Institute of Architecture) had built for his own home, was a treat in itself for an architecture buff!

I was pleased to see that a small street (one block long) was named after the poet referred to above, Apollinaire.

It was gratifying to find that all the years of French class and continuing to read a French magazine enabled me to cope reasonably well in the language, even though I haven't had much oral practice lately. It was a short trip--but most satisfying.

Not long after returning home I caught a bad case of the 'flu, so my winter was blah. No energy.

<u>1997:</u> But, energy or no, I had to stir myself northward for a few days, as I'd been asked to take some photos and memorabilia of my father (A. Harold Knott) on New Year's Day, to be displayed in the Carmel Library (Park Branch) foyer through the whole of 1997. This was to tie in with at alk I was scheduled to give about him in April. They arranged the materials handsomely in a glass display case: some 1920's photos, a portable paint box for oils, a set of water colors, palette brushes, etc., and his folding stool, for use in painting out of doors, plus a small oil painting he had done of Point Lobos in the '20's.

My talk was on April 28. In honor of the 70th anniversary of the Carmel Art Association, the former President of the Association spoke on its history, and I spoke about my father's life and career, as one of its founding members [1927!]. Our theme was "Enduring Vision"--perfect for art, so I took that and ran with it, and it worked out very well. I showed several of my father's paintings "live" along with the talk. We had to give our talks twice in the same day because there wasn't enough seating to accommodate all the eager history buffs at once. We had fun doing this, and our "show" was warmly received.

In August I was back in Carmel, delivering some of my father's paintings to the Carmel Art Association's 70th Anniversary Exhibit. The space allocated for past members' work was limited, but they hung <u>two</u> of my father's water colors, plus a portrait photograph of him, so I was very pleased.

As for matters Wagnerian, I saw the David Hockney production of *Tristan und Isolde* in Los Angeles in February. In October, a UC Berkeley professor lectured to the Wagner Society on Tristan and Schopenhauer (!) It seems that we are so overwhelmed by the music and the love story in the opera that we scarcely realize that Wagner has used the text to reflect Schopenhauer's philosophy. Pretty heavy stuff!)

By way of a sideline, in Los Angeles I stumbled into another filmmaking situation while climbing up the hill to my hotel after breakfast. Found some women cowering under small sidewalk trees who told me to take shelter because a parachutist was about to come down upon us. I went on and asked a man who seemed to be part of the crew; he said yes, I should get into a doorway. I looked up and spotted someone floating around on an orange 'chute, so I sheltered against a building for a few moments. He disappeared, so I assumed he'd landed elsewhere, and I started out to the sidewalk again. Applause from unseen hands broke out behind me; I looked around and saw that the parachutist had plopped into the street a few yards back. Now I wondered--is my long-delayed film career taking off at last? Will I be the unpaid co-star in an Indonesian TV commercial? Or will I wind up on the traditional cutting-room floor?

In March the Wagner Society sponsored a concert in San Francisco by young singers (some of whom were recipients of grants from us towards their musical training). They were all good, and two extremely so, Pamela Hicks and Richard Liszt, who got a standing ovation for their Siegmund and Sieglinde scene.

For our Wagner Society's annual "Cosima Birthday Party this year (which amounts to a Christmas party because Wagner's wife was born on Christmas day), we were the guests of the German Consulate in San Francisco. (The Consul and his wife are members.) The event included a concert by a wonderful young Australian tenor who was with the SF Opera this season, Stuart Skelton. We predict a big future for him! A lovely party in gracious surroundings with magnificent views of the Bay. It's some time since I swam in semi-diplomatic circles (long ago and far away in London...the U.S. Air Attaché's Office of the American Embassy, to be precise)--fun to experience a bit of that again but on this side of the pond.

Afterwards I went on to a concert by an *a capella* male chorus ("Slavyanka") of Russian and Slavic music. So it was quite an international evening.

Now for the most important part of my "annual" report: an update on the feline and amphibian members of my household. Whiskers the Cat (aka "Furball') is nows 11, "middle aged," but he thinks young, and acts it too when he is feeling in good form and not half sick with seasonal allergies. He doesn't seem to get up onto the gate lintels or the roof anymore, (neither do I) --but he can still spring from bathtub edge to window sill, or from floor to chair to kitchen counter-top (and I can't). When he's feeling wonderful he races around the house like a kitten, playing like mad, and practices his predator skills on <u>me</u>. I wear a lot of iodine and band-aids. (A suit of medieval armor might be a good thing.)

He has recently taken to attacking the wallpaper in the hallway, either to emphasize an ignored demand for attention, food, etc.--or to annoy/punish me for dereliction in this regard. (He succeeds; this wallpaper pattern can't be replaced.) I hasten to add though, he's a devotedly affectionate little cat.

Fred the Frog and/or his descendants and collateral relations still hang out from time to time inside the lid (kept ajar for them) of my plastic garbage can which holds rainwater. The original point of saving water was for plants because of our usual drought situation. But I feel responsible for keeping the frog species afloat, as it were, so I have to leave the barrel about ⅓ full for their sake. They register their gratitude by singing me an occasional solo. The weekend of John Denver's funeral, a recording of one of his songs was being played over the radio in my kitchen. Suddenly Fred joined in to sing along with him. John Denver would have liked that.

Now with our respective musical and vocal greetings--("MEOWWW!" Purr, purr..." "CROAK! Ribet, Ribet!" and "Compliments of the Season,")-- we wish you all a Merry Christmas and Happy New Year!

1998

Greetings!

Time for the annual massive clerical effort that is Christmas! Even if I have only one year's worth of news to report! (And I must kill your eyes with small, crowded print, in order to fit this on one piece of paper.)

Nature provided a dramatic highlight in February with a violent "El Niño" storm that took out the electricity, telephone and TV cable service in many parts of town including mine, and gave us a day off work. Because of the lack of electricity and so many fallen trees blocking the roads, they had to close the schools. Staying home for a day by candlelight and firelight was not too bad, since I have a wood fire and gas heat and gas cooking which were in working order. None of my trees crashed, including a dead one, although many branches and tgs came down. Two healthy trees crashed only a block away!

During the April Easter vacation I went to Carmel and continued my researches and catching up on the art galleries and museum, etc.

At the end of May I took some time off from work and went to Arizona, staying one night outside Phoenix in a delightful inn once the home of a famed cowboy artist (Lon Megargee). The heat was just about overpowering (about 101°) so my sightseeing and art gallery viewing was rather a chore. Then I left this hot, flat cactus-dotted landscape and headed north in a rental car to a high-altitude, pine-dotted hilly region, to stay in Flagstaff, and take in Arizona Opera's production of Wagner's *Der Ring des Nibelungen* cycle, as well as to see the Grand Canyon and other features of this region, where I'd never been.

The combination of four heavy-duty Wagnerian operas plus all this Wild West surrounding made for a schizophrenic vacation. My hotel in itself was almost more entertaining than the operas. I'd chosen the 101-year-old Weatherford, because (a) it had been the "grandest thing of its day" there, and (b) Theodore Roosevelt, one of my favorite people in history, had stayed in it. It had gone downhill, turning into a youth hostel for a time, but was now being renovated and upgraded back into a regular hotel. A real period-piece: creaking floors, heavy, darkly-stained woodwork, small rooms with high, high ceilings, TRANSOMS over the doors!-and real sash windows you could open and close! A tiny, shallow clothes closet, for which I had to REQUEST some clothes hangers--and a tiny but modern bathroom. There was a huge Victorian bar ("The Zane Grey Ballroom" on my floor, [Zane Grey also used to stay at this hotel.] In addition, there was another bar/poolroom downstairs, and a "bar & grill" restaurant with fabulous food. Most American hotels have a Gideon Bible in every room--but in my room here, there were instead four Zane Grey paperbacks and one Louis L'Amour!.

There never seemed to be anyone on duty at the reception desk, so one wondered "Who's minding the store?" There were always lots of young men shooting pool at the bar/poolroom beyond the reception area, which added to the rugged western atmosphere, but on closer scrutiny they all looked pretty clean-cut, probably college students.

Flagstaff and environs are at about 8000 ft altitude, which means less oxygen (huff, puff up those hotel stairs, for me--and oxygen tanks for the opera singers backstage between scenes and some hidden onstage as well, we were told). The acoustics of the theatre (belonging to the Northern Arizona University) were wonderful, as were many of the singers.

I attended an opening reception gathering, where I teamed up with an old opera buddy from the east coast, whom I'd met on the horse-carriage tour in Bavaria before going on to Bayreuth for Wagnerian opera in 1988. Another highlight organized by the opera festival was a ride on a restored old train to the Grand Canyon, with two cars reserved for the operagoers and singers. Since this train trip is a regular Wild West tourist feature every day anyway, they have "colorful local characters" in appropriate costume and exagerrated picturesqueness of manner, story-telling and singing cowboy songs to entertain the passengers. So our opera singers were tossed into this milieu to walk up and down the aisles talking to passengers about the opera. Duelling genres, you might say--statuesque Valkyries up against grizzled cowpokes and vintage railway conductors. Freia meets Walter Brennan, so to speak. The gods were there too, Wotan, Donner, Froh, Loge--and none under 6ft4in., the latter being made to feel "short." "Mimosa" drinks served with the brunch added to the jollity of the ride.

We were then taken by bus to a very "casual" barbecue picnic lunch, in a rustic forest-clearing area. Lunching with the gods and goddesses, we all grow mellow, awash in wine. Not your usual opera type meal.

Then we were taken to the Grand Canyon to view this flabbergasting ancient gorge on our own--some just strolling a few hundred yards peering over the edge (like me), some clambering down into it. I have to say this site is even bigger and more beautiful and more ancient and awesome than all the photographs one has ever seen. I was duly impressed.

I took several other tours of the region on my own, seeing things like the Painted Desert, a huge meteor crater, a beautiful wooded canyon, and the overrated tourist trap village of Sedona (horrible, thanks to gross commercialism), and in Flagstaff itself, the old Lowell Observatory, where the planet Pluto was discovered many years ago. There are several kinds of huge telescopes used over its lifetime, showing the evolution of this technology.

The American astronauts were taken to the meteor crater to learn how to identify various geological and meteoric specimens in preparation for their trip to the moon, and also visited this planetarium to expand their knowledge of the universe, they were about to explore.

A segment of what's left of the famous former U.S. transcontinental highway "Route 66" goes right through the middle of the town (remember the old song "Get your kicks on Route 66")--and every year they have a Route 66 Festival;

I went over to look at a display of vintage cars from various "Route 66 Auto Clubs." The prettiest one that caught my fancy was being watched over by a couple of young men, one <u>wearing guns</u>--not a policeman, not a uniformed security guard; in fact I'd seen him in my hotel at breakfast, with guns. I asked him if he was the owner of this beautiful car. "No, we're the hired goons," he said, adding that it belonged to the owner of my hotel, and then, "Would you like to sit in it, Ma'am?" Faced with guns at such close range, I circumspectly declined. (If I had inadvertently scratched the car, would he have shot me?)

After my return to California and winding up the school job for summer vacation I spent a week in San Francisco for a bit of recreation, including an opera performance of Alban Berg's *Lulu*. This was disappointing. Based on the story of the 1920's German films (*Pandora's Box* etc.) featuring Louise Brooks as the amoral sexpot who comes to a sticky end, it could hardly compete with the old films, especially with such slow, insipid music. None of the hard edge and darkness of the films.

Much of my spring and summer was taken up nursing my sick cat "Whiskers" through the extremes of hyperthyroidism, thyroidectomy, severe post-op anemia, hypothyroidism, and his usual severe skin allergies. Many trips to the veterinarian, tests, medications, home-cooking and hand-feeding, changing of "bedsheets," etc. Poor little fellow. He was pretty well shut down for some time. But by October he began to seem more like his old self, and by December about 95% in shape, though he hasn't got his winter fluff coat fully in place yet, nor his handsome ruff. He needs this to look like "a lot more cat,"-- and to insulate him from winter's cold.

At the end of August I went to Carmel and Monterey for a few days, cramming a week's worth of galleries/museums etc. into about 2 ½ days, including a visit to the new Steinbeck Center in salinas, not far away. A comprehensive "multimedia/interactive" museum plus gallery for rotating exhibits (on this occasion, paintings of the Depression and WWII era, reflecting some of the poverty and despair elements found in his books, though not so harshly depicted). The exhibits for each book are intriguing and especially attention-grabbing for youngsters. A large blow-up photo of him receiving the Nobel Prize is accompanied by a recording of his acceptance speech. The book & gift shop sells not only the usual themed gift items and all his writings, it sells all the classics he loved to read when he was young as well.

He was despised and resented in his home town when he started publishing his gritty novels, but after all these years of literary pilgrims coming through the area from all over the world, the younger generations has glommed onto him as a veritable gold mine. The Center is unique and should do very well in drawing even more visitors.

I had a day in Santa Barbara and saw the exhibit of the Chinese artifacts and the lifelike clay sculptures of soldiers dug up from an early emperor's grave site (buried with replicas of his entire army, it seems). I was intrigued by the unusual "saddle" on a cavalryman's horse, covered with round button-like bumps on what may have been leather, or wool--which looked extremely uncomfortable to sit on! And of course no stirrups in those days.

The only operas I've seen this Fall were *Tristan und Isolde* (somewhat disappointing--the orchestra didn't "blow you away" the way you expected to be blown away). *Norma* (beautiful music, Carol Vanness not bad--but no one can live up to Joan Sutherland *cum* Marilyn Horne in that opera, so far, anyway! And *A Streetcar Named Desire*--newly commissioned just for the San Francisco Opera. Well done, music (by Andre Previn) suits the story and characters for the most part--but no tuneful numbers to stay with you or to be sung in the shower. The old Marlon Brando/Vivien Leigh/Karl Malden film can hardly be improved upon, with or without music!

Attended a Wagner Society lecture by the President of the Barcelona Wagner Society! (He's even named his children Tristan and Freia!) His lecture subject was the career and a work of a Spanish artist who did traditional paintings and stage designs for the Barcelona Opera.

On the home front, sadly I lost my aesthetically-most-important tree, which succumbed to a disease decimating the

Monterey Pines of California, and it had to be cut down. Cleaning up the ensuing mess of small debris and rehabilitating the Vinca and Mesembryanthemum ground covers will take a long time. So far 5 truckloads to the dump and about 12 garbage cans full to the "green waste recycling." Probably many more cans to be filled, at the present rate. Am researching to try and find another type of pine to plant that can resist this disease.

I continue to shelter a few small frogs in my "rain barrels" (plastic garbage cans full of rainwater), and they continue to favor me with an occasional song. No, I flatter myself. Actually they sing to attract other frogs as mates. One seems to have come into the house and hidden under the water heater and I haven't been able to lure him out. I'm worried that the bursts of gas flames may be too hot for him whenever the heater kicks on!

That's about it for the year, up to early December, at any rate. Look forward to hearing YOUR news. Meanwhile best wishes for a happy Christmas and New Year!

1999

Greetings!

The holiday season (gasp!) is at our throats again: will I get all these mailings out in time??

I felt like Mrs. Dalloway in February, helping to hostess at a series of teas given by a friend (four, over three weekends): standing near the entrance in a pseudo-1930's style outfit, as the guests arrived at the top of the stairs, and then "pouring." These parties were gatherings of the progeny of some of the 1930's "English colony" here plus some members of the local Episcopal church. Services had been held in my friend's house (formerly his grandmother's) in the days before a church was built. He managed to do this the year the church was about to celebrate its 50th anniversary.

Two other people helped (the wife wearing a 1920's drawn-work linen dress belonging to the host's aunt). Then after the guests had gone we changed clothes, transforming ourselves into scullery maids; I washed thousands of dishes while the couple dried them, and the host hand-washed all the Irish lines. One misses the era of household staff! Nevertheless it was a lot of fun and the guests enjoyed being spoiled with all the home-made and imported goodies.

In March I went to San Francisco to see the "Impressionists in Winter" art exhibit, which was wonderful. And I was very lucky to get a last-minute cancellation ticket for the sold-out stage play "Indian Ink," by Tom Stoppard. I'm not a fan of Stoppard's. But the point was to see the actor Art Malik "live," whom we were familiar with in the part of Hari Kumar in "The Jewel in the Crown" TV series some years ago. He still has his looks and charisma, despite some balding.

The "Van Gogh's Van Goghs" exhibit drew me and millions of others to Los Angeles in May. I got there during the exhibit's last few days when the museum kept the show open literally round the clock. Fortunately my ticket was for the afternoon. (The paintings were on loan from the Netherlands while the home museum was being renovated.) I loved the exhibit, especially the pot of chives and the crab at a skewed angle on its back--I have some respect for the species through experience catching lots of them in home-made nets in our bay as a teenager.

I also took in an exhibit of elegant calligraphy from the heyday of the Turkish Ottoman Empire--both religious and secular documents.

By a stroke of serendipity, an American production of the French play I'd seen in Paris in 1996 was underway, *Enigma Variations*, starring Donald Sutherland in the role originated by Alain Delon. Interesting contrast: the French production was dead serious, sad and cruel; the American take, 180° different, was one of wry humor with constant bursts of laughter from the audience.

[NOTE: If you attend anything at the performing arts center in LA, you get a substantial discount on your room at the Intercontinental Hotel, only 2 blocks from the center.]

Making it a really busy long weekend, I also went on an all-day tour of some private collections of California art with an enthusiastic museum group I belong to in Orange County.

As you know, I can't really get through a year without a Wagner fix. So after my summer vacation had begun I went to San Francisco for a week filled with the *Ring* (4th orchestra I'd heard, live, doing this work. Singers pretty good too. But I must say even if she is now the world's "leading Wagnerian soprano," Jane Eaglen's 400-500 lb. body works against the aesthetic.

I had volunteered to assist at our Wagner's Society peripheral events, and I was told I'd be selling T-shirts (!) at the opening reception. Fortunately, when I got there they said I would be hostessing at the champagne table instead. A decided improvement. I definitely prefer a Mrs. Dalloway role any time. (And with catering staff to open the bottles.) It was great fun greeting guests literally from all around the world as well as the rest of the U.S. and introducing some of them to our president so she could welcome them as well. They held a reception before each of the four cycles, so the world-wide Wagnerians could attend a welcoming party and meet their local kindred spirits.

The Society also sponsored a screening of a novice-filmmaker's movie (*Valhalla*) about some young men in LA staging their own amateur *Ring* for their house-bound father who'd become too ill to travel to see a real one in Bayreuth. It was both funny and moving.

My usual gallery and museum crawling and visiting friends rounded out the SF week, as well as a week in Carmel at Easter and a few days in Santa Barbara in August. And I organized a batch of volunteers to sit at local history display table at the Harbor Festival in October.

The most unusual event of the year was a quick trip to Cincinnati, Ohio, in early November. I had worked in the Cardiology Division at Stanford Medical Center for some years. Our former chief left there in 1986 and has been building up the University of Cincinnati Medical School ever since. Partly to celebrate his birthday and partly to take advantage of the fact that many of our former post-doctoral fellows would be traveling to the American Heart Association meeting not far away in Atlanta, he decided to set up a 2 ½ day reunion gathering for the former fellows whom he'd mentored early in their careers.

I turned out to be the only "civilian" in the crowd other than our former business manager. The program included a tour of the new hospital there and the new Center for Molecular Studies (designed by Frank Gehry, whose art museum in Bilbao, Spain, has created something of a stir internationally), and presentations of scientific papers and personal comments. As the most unscientifically-minded person on the planet, I of course opted for the latter. I, who struggled hopelessly with high school chemistry and found it hard to take college biology seriously. So there I was, standing at the lectern of a Frank Gehry auditorium, reading my "Reflections of a Cardiology Civilian," sandwiched in among some of the best medical brains in four countries speaking on such topics as "The Rationale for Using Beta Blockers in Heart Failure," "The Impact of Clinical Trials on the Treatment of Ventricular Arrhythmias," "Neutrophil Mediated Mechanisms of Myocardial Reperfusion Injury," and "Reduced Event Rates with Use of Coronary Stents."

Dinner parties and more personal comments rounded off the social aspect of the gathering. It was great fun seeing so many of the old gang and catching up on their subsequent careers. Rather like an "old home week," but in a distant setting.

After everyone had left on the Saturday I went to the Taft House Museum and Cincinnati Art Museum on my own-handsome buildings with wonderful art collections! And walked down to the river's edge to get a close look at Roebling's pre-Brooklyn Bridge! But I was unable to find anyone around to sell it to me.

There are a lot of other interesting things to see in the Cincinnati area, but I had to return to California on the Sunday. My cat Whiskers had insisted on it. As he sprang onto my shoulder and purred madly, a frog sang out a loud welcoming croak from his perch on the rain barrel.

Earlier in the year I had peered into the barrel and discovered I was godmother to about 150 tadpoles. But on subsequent inspection I found they'd grown up and left home. About four adults have remained to keep the Fred Dynasty going. Hope this "La Niña" weather continues as predicted to provide adequate rain for the tribe.

Whiskers, who suffered horrible skin allergies and infections all his life, has been transformed into a picture of health by starting on a home-made diet last February, thanks to a book by a veterinarian (Dr. Pitcairn), *Natural Health for Dogs and Cats*. There are several recipes but Whiskers prefers the "Beefy Oats." A mouth-watering mix of various vitamins, bone meal, lecithin, yeast, kelp, eggs, salad oil, oatmeal-and ground-up raw beef liver.

The preparation of this once a week is quite a job, and an unparalleled aesthetic experience. In expendable costume and big plastic apron I poke large slices of liver into an old 1930's meat grinder and crank away as the bloody pulp extrudes out into the bowl containing the other ingredients. Blood oozes and drips all over the counter, the floor, and me. The cat sits on a nearby stool, watching with great interest. It's surreal: "The Bride of Dracula Cooks!" (Watch for my upcoming TV culinary show.) Then when everything is mixed, Whiskers gobbles up a liberal serving-with fresh parsley garnish, of course.

So think about that as you whip up your elegant cakes, pies and cookies for the holidays!

Meanwhile, I look forward to hearing your news. Merry Christmas and Happy New Year!

2001

Greetings--

It's been a sad year-my beloved cat "Whiskers" (age 14 ½) died in July after a few months of serious medical problems. Then the horrible terrorist attacks on our country in September brought an added and nation-wide bereavement. So Christmas is not so "Merry."

Ironically I had just been to an air show in nearby Paso Robles September 9th, particularly admiring the wonderful Navy "Hornet" fighter plane--and the fine young men piloting it. Military aircraft always made me feel so "protected." Then two days later it became apparent that we are not protected at all against insidious terrorist horrors. A new kind of war. (On the whole I prefer the old.) And now our fighter planes can be forced to shoot down our own passenger aircraft if they are again hijacked by terrorists.

****

I was heartbroken at losing Whiskers, my feline "best friend" of so many years. At the end of summer I didn't feel ready to get a new cat, since no one can take his place. But I accompanied a neighbor (who does volunteer work for an animal rescue group and takes in "foster kittens") to the pound at the end of August. The pound in this area is called "Animal Regulation" and comes under the County Sheriff's jurisdiction--in the same building as the JAIL. The place is a jarring array of armed, uniformed deputies, teenagers fetching their criminal pals being released from stir, and a cacophony of barking dogs. The cats don't make much sound, and t heir cages are small and depressing. Animal-loving volunteers post written notes of appeal on each cage: "My name is _____," with a description of his/her endearing qualities, in hope of attracting human adoptive parents.

As I walked along the row of feline inmates and read their labels one frail little kitten ("Hello! My name is Jazz! I'm four months old, and I love humans!") kept reaching both front paws out through the bars of his cage and grabbing my arm. I think he was telling me something: "Get me out of here!" I asked to hold him, and he cuddled happily purring in my arms. I just couldn't leave such a cute little kitten there in that awful place on Death Row, so I went through the bureaucratic paperwork process and adopted him.

At my house, little Jazz-for whom I couldn't think of another name, though jazz is not my favorite music-was forlorn and obviously lonely every day when I left him for work. He craved someone to play with and I didn't have much time for that even when I came home. Also, his being reduced to practicing feline fighting skills on my ankles and hands was not much fun for me. So I took in another kitten a couple months later, whom my neighbor had been fostering- a feral one, who oddly enough likes humans. This is "Butterball," aka Butterfield, Butterscotch, Buttercup, Butterfingers and Butterface. He's orange marmalade in coloring, younger and smaller than Jazz. After a couple of weeks they got used to each other and became pals, having play fights and noisy gallops around the house, then nestling together for naps. So things seem to be working out satisfactorily. And Jazz has stopped attacking my legs. They both climb aboard for lap time after dinner and they're already snoozing on my bed when I turn in. This puts me into the role of pseudo-mother cat.

Jazz, being black with a white bib, eyebrows, whiskers and tummy--and white paws with black pads--looks like something created by Walt Disney. (His personality as well. When I come home in the afternoon, he lies over on his back and waves those paws in the air, then does a deft barrel roll after his tummy has been rubbed.)

There is less to report on my frog friends; there were usually three or four encamped on the rims of the "rain barrels" all summer, but not much song. Now that we have a bit of a rainy season I haven't seen much of them. Where do they go in the meantime?

Human activities this past year comprise the usual trips to Carmel, Santa Barbara and San Francisco, various concerts and movies, etc. The favorite movies that provided respite from these trying times were "The Closet" (French), "Bread and Tulips" (Italian), and "Greenfingers" (English). Lots of laughs and some heartwarming aspects which we sorely need these days. If you haven't seen them in the theatres, try to get the videos!

As for movies from the production angle--I again stumbled into a film shoot. This time in nearby San Luis Obispo. (Normally this just happens to me in Los Angeles.) Walking along minding my own business I saw all the masses of huge black electric cables, trucks and film crew chaps flailing about with walkie-talkies. But a sign on the sidewalk said "Shops open for business," so I kept going. A civilian crew fellow tried to stop me, but another one, evidently higher in authority (he had the walkie-talkie) held out his arm with a grand gesture and said "NO! LET HER PASS!" (Dazzled by my great beauty, or just my beautiful red hat?)

So I marched on, in what I hoped was a regal manner, in case any cameras should focus on me. But I could see no cameras anywhere, no director. There were two "cherry-picker" trucks aiming strong lights into the windows of a room above one of the shops on a corner, and I heard a director shout "Roll it!" but saw nothing. All the action must have been inside that room above. Then the director's voice again, "CUT!"

I went along to do my errands in a drugstore, where I learned that the movie was to be called "Foolproof," starring Sandra Bullock. I went back the same way and started to turn left at the filming corner. A crew member barred my crossing the street: "Please wait one moment…" Then we heard a voice yelling "CUT!" and he said, "OK, you can go now," and off I went, to the reality of my prosaic errands.

It remains to be seen whether my 10 to 15 seconds of fame are in the works. My show biz career has been unduly slow coming into full bloom, but one always hopes.

However, an erstwhile neighbor has had great success in his screenwriting career. After some years of making a living at it but never seeing his work actually produced, he finally has a real live movie, which premiered Sept. 28: "Don't Say a Word." Starring Michael Douglas. The local theatre luckily opened the film the same date (normally it would be weeks later), and he bought up 175 seats for all his friends. (This left only 150 seats for the rest of the public.). It was exciting, with everyone greeting and congratulating him out in front of the theatre, and he bursting out of his skin with joy. Then when we were all seated and the credits began to roll, his name came up on the screen and we yelled and cheered and applauded (which continued again after we came out at the end). His name is Tony Peckham (on the screen it says "Anthony"), andhe's from South Africa, but has lived here a few years after fleeing the crowded L.A. scene.

In October I curated an exhibit of 1930's and 40's photos of the town and its waterfront activities for the local Historical Society's display at the Harbor Festival. They were from the collection of the woman who owned the first photo shop cum art gallery in the town, and included some really stunning shots. This was a ton of work (the woman's nephew enlarged & printed the photos from his computer and I did all the rest) but it was a great success and the Harbormaster particularly complimented me on it, which was gratifying.

****

Look forward to your news, and hope you and yours are OK. Best wishes for Christmas and the New Year.

2002

Greetings!

To get the bad news out of the way first, half my year was taken up with the gruesome experience of total knee replacement surgery (right knee, August), and the subsequent recuperation therefrom. It was a real horror, weeks of severe round-the-clock pain. Daily physical therapy exercises too, which are in themselves a source of pain. So-called painkillers do not kill pain, they merely lower it a few degrees. What they do do, however, is kill the appetite, so I could call that a fringe benefit in that I lost 22 excess pounds. (Added bonus: I can now get into some clothes I'd had to put away for the last couple of years owing to the combined results of dietary indiscretion and inability to do all the walking I used to do before the knee got so bad.)

The physical therapy sessions have continued till this month and I still have to continue doing the exercises at home; I'm also going to to try to do some at the gym. (Trying to strengthen atrophied and tightened muscles after years of limping.)

Even this unpleasant surgery experience had its moments of humor:

*Hospital staff write the word "NO" in big black letters on your good knee so that the doctor doesn't cut off the wrong one.

*The visiting nurse was coming to my house the first few weeks after I got home from the hospital to test blood coagulation with a small portable machine. One day she forgot her glasses and couldn't read the figures on the machine. So I, who must be at least 20 to 30 years older than she, and who needs no glasses, had to read the figures to her.

*And since I am now composed partly of metal (as well as plastic) I suppose I can look forward to creating havoc going through airport metal detectors in future.

****

On the brighter side of the year's events, I made my Easter vacation trip to Carmel again, still researching old newspaper microfilms for items about my artist father, who lived there during the 1920's. I also went back there one day in August shortly before the surgery to attend the opening of the Carmel Art Association's 75th Anniversary Exhibit. One of my father's paintings (A. HAROLD KNOTT) was included in the show, since he was one of its founding members (1927!) It was particularly pleasing to see that (because of the size of the painting I had loaned) it was displayed in a glass case at the center of the gallery, together with a photo of him painting on the Carmel shore--along with another small painting by one of his best buddies during those years (Myron Oliver). That made it very special. Artists have their immortality in exhibitions through the years, where they come together again with old friends.

I made a brief trip to Santa Barbara (shopping), and San Francisco/Palo Alto (appointments and Wagner Society and an opera working rehearsal). (Listening to the old director trying to correct the cast and crew's endless blunders.)

We had quite a few good movies at the "art theatre" in San Luis Obispo, thank goodness. And I also saw a regional theatre performance of "Holly Dolly" -- a very old show, but the first time I'd seen it.

In February I gave a talk to the local chapter of the American Association of University Women about my mother, which they had asked me to do since she did all the groundwork in getting this chapter organized and launched in the 1950's.

In March a cousin I'd never met but with whom I've corresponded about family history matters came through briefly and it was fun to discuss these things in person. Both of us trying to see family resemblances in each other's faces, etc.

During my recuperation months this fall I heard a talk about Walt Disney's involvement with small-scale trains and railroads, sponsored by the group who are organizing a railroad museum in San Luis Obispo. That was fun--Walt having such a part in our childhoods with his movies--

Even more entertaining was an old film shown by the Friends of the Library at the nearby little town of Cayucos (7 miles north of here), as a fundraiser. This so-called "horror" movie, "The Monster of Piedras Blancas," was filmed there and at the disused Piedras Blancas Lighthouse further up the coast in 1958. It is one of those "B" movies that is meant to be scary but is so badly written it becomes hilariously funny instead. The monster (a fellow in a reptilian rubber suit, something like the "Creature from the Black Lagoon," lives in a coastal cave near the lighthouse and his mission is to terrorize the local citizens by slicing off their heads as cleanly as if with a guillotine.) (No explanation of how he does it with nothing but those reptile claws to work with.) The script was so ridiculous that the audience roared with laughter the whole time. It was better than any comedy. (This is unlikely to be available on video, but if it turns up in your neighborhood as a "cult" film," rush out and see it for an evening of laughs.)

In between the two showings of the film (at the veterans' hall) some of the local citizens who'd appeared as extras in the film were to take part in a panel for discussion along with the star, Jeanne Carmen. Jeanne, who must be at least in her early 60's by now, looked ageless, totally groomed and glamorous in the best Hollywood manner, carrying herself in a regal manner like a true star.

My young cats (now approx. ½ years old) are still very playful and energetic, and they've been good company during my convalescence. Jazz, (black with white trim -- long, soft fluffy coat) and Butterball (orange marmalade, short hair), still have play fights and then curl up and nap together, sometimes with their arms around each other. Jazz sheds his fluff all over the house, and Butterball sheds wiry short orange hairs onto all my clothes--very hard to get off.

Butterball is hazardous in other ways. His idea of play is still to bite my hands, and he loves to shred anything made of paper. I could rent him out to some of those crooked corporations we keep reading about in the news. Newspapers, books, magazines--he can chew a hole through about ten pages' thickness from the center of an open book (difficult for me to reconstruct, if not impossible). He's also an absolute whiz at catching birds, which causes me some distress, since I love birds too. He brought a young hummingbird into my bedroom while I was doing my exercises; when I realized what it was I managed to rescue him and set him outside on a fence ledge, with a dish of water. When I went back later he had rallied from the shock and flew away, so apparently he had not had vital organs pierced by feline fangs (I hope) The next bird BB brought into the bedroom was bigger, and BB was smarter -- when he saw me get up to rescue it he snatched it and ran outdoors again.

Although he came from a feral setting, BB is extravagantly affectionate, demanding lots of lap time (or stomach time, if I'm lying down during exercises. Jazz is a bit more independent; he announces his arrival in a room with a loud purr motor, touches base--visits the lap for a moment, then settles nearby.

Now for the wildlife. I found a lot of tadpoles in my rain barrel in late July but don't know when or whether they matured and made it out to wherever frogs hide in the dry season. An even more dramatic discovery in late July was a group of odd-looking big birds which I was told were wild turkeys. (I'd never seen one before.) A mother with six babies, the babies being about the size of a bantam hen, evidently came out of the State Park (nature reserve) a few blocks east. They were having great fun scratching for bugs and seeds in the soft soil. A few days later there were only four babies. Oh dear! Cats must have gotten two of them. And then I saw my cats stalking them. Horrors! I must have made an interesting spectacle out on the lawn--lame lady, limping frantically around chasing the cats who were chasing the turkeys.

It would have made a great photo. (You can never find a cameraman when you need one.

The turkeys worked their way around my yard and others in the neighborhood and kept everyone entertained. They were still here when I got home from the hospital, but the babies had grown to about the same size as the mother. I haven't seen them for some weeks now, and my veterinarian--I mean, my <u>cats'</u> veterinarian!--tells me he's seen them on the golf course (a few blocks south) and that a father turkey has joined the family. A nice place for a family reunion, with its grand panoramic view of the bay, sand bar and ocean beyond --

****

Hope all goes well with you and I look forward to your news. Best wishes for Christmas and the new year!

2006

Greetings!

Christmas is creeping up on us, and I'm no speedier at getting cards done. Hope this isn't unduly late.

It's been a fairly tame year, but punctuated with the usual round of plumbing disasters and suddenly-defunct old appliances, plus having a bit of exterior paint work done, hoping extra caulking everywhere will stop the leaks that sprouted last winter.

Took a few trips to Santa Barbara on the Nordstrom's shopping bus--a cheap and easy way to spend a day down there, for shopping, lunching, museum-going, etc. I also took a one-day down and back train trip there with some women from the school where I used to work. The train route gives one great views, going through the vast undeveloped land of

Vandenberg Air Force Base where the public can't go--the railroad tracks having been in place before Vandenberg came into existence. Miles of wild shrubs and flowers, and a spectacular ride along the edge of cliffs by the sea (a bit scary--one enjoys the view while praying the train doesn't tip over).

On another occasion I actually stayed in Santa Barbara a few days with a friend who lives there. A highlight of that visit was an exciting polo match with the top-rated players (the highest-rated being from Argentina). What a fabulous game! Gorgeous horses galloping at full speed up and down the huge field and maneuvering deftly around while equally gorgeous hunks smack the ball hither and thither.

My March trip to San Francisco and Palo Alto, timed to see my tax preparer, also gave me a chance to lunch with a few pals from my Cardiology Dept. days. On this occasion we were saddened by the passing of Dr. Norman Shumway, famed heart surgeon, a few weeks before. By a coincidence, his memorial service was scheduled for the same day as our lunch date, so I was able to attend. The Stanford church (huge) was packed; people had come from all over the country and even from Europe to attend. A distinguished career, improving and saving many lives, and a good buddy. R.I.P.

July 4th -- I hadn't bothered to go down to the waterfront to watch fireworks for years. This year a friend was in town and we watched from his vacation house on the street behind mine, on the edge of the State Park. We had a spectacular view of the Bay, and the stunning fireworks display, viewed in comfort from indoors, with no crowds and no shivering in the damp night air!

In August I spent a few days in San Francisco and saw a few friends as well as a museum exhibit of "Monet in Normandy" (paintings mostly done in his early period before he embarked on what became known as the Impressionist style, though there were a few paintings from that phase also included. Museums continue to batten on trundling Monet around the globe and peddling all kinds of souvenirs with reproductions of his pictures emblazoned on them. What would he think of that?

In October I made another trip to SF to see the opera *Tristan und Isolde* and attend some related events sponsored by the Wagner Society, including an all-day symposium with distinguished speakers and a reception. They also sponsored an evening tribute to the late singer Birgitt Nilsson. In addition I went to a bookstore "CD signing" which drew an intimate group of opera buffs: Maestro Donald Runnicles (Scottish conductor of SF Opera) and Isolde soprano Christine Brewer each spoke, chatted, answered questions and signed copies of the CD they'd made together with the Atlanta Symphony. (Plug: Wagner, Prelude & Liebestod from *Tristan und Isolde,* and Richard Strauss, Four Last Songs, and Death and Transfiguration.) An enjoyable session--they were both very friendly and personable.

And of course I enjoyed a visit to the newly-opened Bloomingdale's store--very large, grant, light and spacious (whole south wall of plate glass windows), with miles and miles of elegant clothes in uncrowded arrangements, and lots of sales personnel being cordial and helpful all over the place. (A rarity nowadays!)

I went to an exhibit of work by an apparently well-known German artist at the Museum of Modern Art -- Anselm Kiefer--who, having been born at the end of WWII, seemed still to be depicting war-torn-rubble type material in both his paintings and sculptures, all in dank gray, charcoal and black tones. This made for a bleak museum experience. I wonder how many people buy this sort of thing for their homes.

Now for **Nature Notes**. My cats, Jazz (black and white, longhair) and Butterball/Butterfield/BB/Beebs (orange stripes, short hair), both now aged five, continue to thrive. And why wouldn't they, being spoiled with spoonfuls of canned salmon for their morning and evening treats? As for their dry food, Jazz, despite his macho posturing and John Wayne gait, caves in every time to BB's aggressive determination to be Top Cat (coming from a rough and tumble world in his feral kittenhood youth). So Jazz stands aside and waits until BB gets first crack at the dry-food bowl. (I serve their salmon treats on separate plates, and stand guard, however, in an attempt to be an Equal Opportunity Cat Person.)

Sometimes they have play fights that deteriorate into real screaming, biting, clawing matches. I try to intervene, throwing cushions and towels at them and shouting "STOP! CATS!! STOP THAT!!" They ignore me. At other times, though, they cuddle up together for a cozy, peaceful snooze on the bed.

BB is an ace hunter, catching quite a few gophers (underground rodent, a root-eating pest), which he may deposit at the door or sometimes bring inside. He is fast as lightning and catches a lot of birds, too, to my dismay, sometimes gobbling them up on the spot, sometimes leaving them in the house (oh dear!). I try to have a decent burial for each dead bird I find, with a little bird-prayer.

However, one day I looked out the kitchen door and saw BB heading toward me with a huge dove in his mouth! Horrors! I couldn't bear it, so I shut the door and went back inside. A little later when I thought the carnage would be over, I looked out the window and saw the dove shoot straight up in the air and fly off in triumph, leaving BB looking embarrassed on the ground. He slunk off into his cave in the saltbush hedge.

Doves   1
Cats   0

Let's hear it for the dove! I was so relieved. The mourning dove is such a beautiful bird, with his lovely sad song. That day he could rejoice.

Another time I looked out the back door and saw BB having tennis practice with himself, using a freshly killed gopher as the ball. He leapt up, flung the gopher thru the air with one paw, then leapt up a couple of feet away and batted it with the other paw, hitting it back and forth to himself. A fabulous feline athlete!

As for my **Frog Saga**, I'd seen no frogs last year and worried that the fungus that thrives on global warming and is decimating the world's frog population had wiped out all my frogs. But this year I've seen several--never sure if it's one or two frogs multiple times, or multiple frogs once. At any rate, there has been one wearing grayish-tan and another in green, at least. I'm not sure if they change color to match what they're sitting on, namely my "rain barrels," (plastic trash bins, one green and one brown, with lids slightly ajar to accommodate the amphibians). I marvel at how the frogs survive and wonder if they hide in the hedge, possibly digging holes. And I hope they continue to avoid being caught by BB as they rek from the hedge to the barrels. I like to think these are descendents of my original Fred.

Another species to report on: Thanksgiving day around noon I went out in the back yard and found a flock of wild turkeys browsing around, scratching for bugs and seeds in the soft earth among some bushes. (A similar flock had moved to the nearby golf course a few years ago.) What a timely surprise. A mother and four almost-grown youngsters. All so graceful and friendly -- they seem to think they are people, (or else that I am a turkey). I enjoyed watching them for a while. Later I came out again and they were lying around resting on the lawn, enjoying their post-prandial snooze. A delightful visit arranged by Mother Nature for Thanksgiving Day (when we eat only domestic turkeys).

On December 3rd the Episcopal Church put on its annual Lessons and Carols service (à la King's College, Cambridge, in England), and while not so grand a choir or such grand architecture, it was a creditable program for a small town. This normally gets one into the mood for Christmas, but the hot, Santa Ana winds that day were counter-Christmassy.

I hope all is well with you, and I look forward to your news. Best wishes for Christmas and the New Year!

2007

Greetings!

Christmas is creeping up fast! If this is late, my apologies!

No earth-shaking news (fortunately, in earthquake country)--just the usual array of jaunts within California.

A San Francisco trip in March included a visit to the Oakland Museum's exhibit on the art and craft work of Arthur and Lucia Mathew (Arts & Crafts period), and the Legion of Honor Museum's show of French design, with a lot of fantastic jewelry. (Naturally, I was most impressed with a small cat figurine wearing a collar made of tiny diamonds.) The DeYoung Museum had a puny show of American Modernism (hardly any paintings!), and a display of bizarre fashions by the designer Vivienne Westwood.

An August trip to San Francisco yielded the Legion of Honor Museum's "Works on Paper," encompassing small pieces by just about every artist from the Renaissance to the present--not what you would call a "focused" show, but interesting. The Museum of Modern Art displayed various items illustrating the reciprocal influences between Matisse and other artists of his period.

Back to SF in September for a Wagner Society symposium on *Tannhäuser*, and a performance of it at the Opera House. The décor-- a heavy layer of dirt, a tree, and piles of brush all over the Wartburg Castle floor! The opera incorporates two different legends, so it doesn't work very well for me in the first place--but the music was good.

Samson and Delilah was playing that weekend too, so I took that in. A Biblical tale of sex and violence. Delilah is supposed to be an ace seductress. Imagine how sexy this is going to be with very overweight singers--thus paying minimal close attention to one another.

Southward travel--just a couple of one-day excursions to Santa Barbara on Nordstrom's "shopping bus" -- an opportunity to browse around the town, galleries and shops.

I attended the Carmel Art Association's 80th Anniversary celebration in August. My father (A. Harold Knott) was one of its founding members, and I'd loaned a painting for the show of past members' work. The emphasis for this anniversary was on throwing a huge block party for the community, with music, dancing, entertainment, a birthday cake, and the street closed off for displays by many other nonprofit organizations.

The actual exhibit of past members' paintings was small, and ran for only three days instead of the normal three or four weeks (they said because of "security concerns"). The ladies working in the gallery told me all the visitors loved my father's painting -- "Little House of River Winds," which depicts our home when my parents first bought it so long ago -- so that was gratifying.

During the Carmel visit I went to dinner one evening with friends at a restaurant further down the coast, right on the edge of a cliff, with the sea swirling and crashing on the rocks far below. A dramatic spot for dinner! And it was the kind of rocky coastal scene my father had depicted in many of his paintings from the years he lived in Carmel, and later when he'd moved to Morro Bay.

Locally--entertainment is mostly movies in San Luis Obispo, where thankfully there is an art theatre with three screens for a goodly selection of independent and foreign films, (as well as two mainstream theatres). A special place for live theatre is the Pewter Plough in Cambria (about a half-hour's drive north of here) is an old building that must once have been a house or place of business. It's small and intimate, with directors' chairs (nicely padded!) for seats, each with the name of some legendary actor or actress on it, instead of seat numbers. Audience members love to see whose chair their ticket will put them in. Cambria also has the Tea Cozy, for an English tearoom type of luncheon or afternoon tea, which suits my nostalgia for the years I lived in London.

I've spent a good deal of time and energy this year gathering things out of the attic that I'd collected over the globe, and donating them to various worthy bodies' fundraisers. This is an ongoing task (decisions, decisions!), and serves me right for having treated the family home as a storage depot all the years I was living and traveling elsewhere!

****

Now for the <u>NATURE NOTES</u>:

The major <u>FELINE</u> news of the year occurred at about 7:30 am one morning in May, when a transformer blew out with a loud explosion on the power pole on the Kern Street side of the property (the house is on a corner). Right by the saltbush hedge, bottlebrush shrubs and vinca beds which comprised BB's favorite hangout--his little jungle, so to speak. The horrendous noise of the explosion shattered his nerves. Terrified, he dashed back into the house, just as I was also coming in the back door after putting something in the trash bin. And he would not budge out of the house again for <u>four months</u>.

(BB, you may recall, is the shorthair orange-striped number who came from a feral background as a youngster.)

So this poor little fellow has been suffering from shell shock, or "post-traumatic stress syndrome," in current parlance.

BB had hitherto been a mighty hunter, and although since the end of September he's begun venturing outdoors under cover of darkness, in the early morning and evening, his catch of prey has been greatly diminished. But as of early December he's started occasionally popping out for one or two minutes during daylight, so I'm hoping he will continue to recover his composure and regain his former bravado.

The other cat, Jazz, (he of the long hair, black with white trim), being of a more mellow temperament, was only freaked out for one day by the explosion, and was ready for his usual outings the next day. His coat has thickened and fluffed out for winter, so he now looks like a whole lot of cat in this outfit. However, this, and BB's stress notwithstanding, has not stopped BB from continuing to assert himself as Top Cat. Even if BB has just eaten, or seems not at all interested in eating-- the moment Jazz hits the dry food bowl, BB springs up, pushes him aside, and starts eating as a matter of principle. (It's not fair--Jazz came here first, and by rights should have seniority.)

As for <u>FROGS</u>--so far I've only heard one calling out on a couple of occasions (not really "singing,") in what sounds like a hoarse (I hope not "elderly") voice, which I believe they do when seeking a mate. I don't hear any answering calls. I've only seen one frog in the rain barrel a few times (perhaps more than one, separately?) I worry about the frogs, having read that the diminishing numbers of all varieties worldwide is due to global warming, which causes certain virus(es) and / or bacteria to thrive and overwhelm the frogs. I hope it stays cool enough here for frogs to hold out.

The many Southern California fires were all at least 150 to 200 or more miles away. We did have the hot Santa Ana winds, and the smoke from down south did reach us (cough, cough, sniffle, sniffle) -- irritating to the eyes, nose and throat.

Only a fraction of an inch of rain so far--and we <u>need</u> it. Pray for rain! (I also have an antique clay figurine of an Indian Rain God here--hedging my bets).

Hope life goes well with you and yours. All best wishes for Christmas and the New Year!!

P.S. The computer's spellchecker thinks "Matisse" should read "mantises" !!

2008

Greetings!

I'm late in composing this letter, so if the card is late, my apologies!

Looking over the calendar, I find the year's highlights involved, as usual, music and art.

San Francisco in March--the annual visit to the tax preparer was ameliorated by seeing various friends and a visit to the Legion of Honor Museum. I didn't care for the Annie Liebowitz photography exhibit--the portraits were so ordinary, so superficial--not the slightest reflection of character in each person. But being a keen archaeology nut, especially regarding places I've traveled, I found the exhibit of artifacts from the Holy Land (on loan from Israel) more my cup of tea...

In April it was great fun visiting with a cousin from Toronto and his wife during their tour of California. I hadn't seen him since my trip to Canada when he was only four years old! We had a great time discussing our various genealogical / ancestral matters. His grandfather was one of my father's cousins.

In May, a wonderful male choral group based in San Francisco, "Chanticleer," gave a concert of Spanish colonial-era sacred music in the 18th century Spanish mission church in San Luis Obispo (our country seat, 14 miles east)--part of their tour of many California's old Spanish churches. It included both music from the Mass in Latin, and other sacred music in Spanish. It was exquisite music--giving one a real spiritual uplift.

Another trip to San Francisco in May-- our Wagner Society threw a big bash to combine celebrating Wagner's birthday and the 25th anniversary of our Society. A concert at the SF Conservatory featured a small orchestra of its advanced students playing the "Triebschen Idyll" (aka "Siegfried Idyll"), and two young singers to whom we had given grants to advance their training sang selections from Wagner's operas. There was also a pianist who played piano transcriptions of some Wagner music. Then a slap-up reception. A wonderful day.

Back to SF in early June for a Wagner Society symposium on the opera *Rheingold*, a reception (in the museum part of the Veterans' Building), and an opera performance of *Rheingold*. This was the first installment of a so-called "American Ring" (*Der Ring des Nibelungen*) to be presented one opera each year and then the whole Ring all together). I disliked the production intensely--they turned the Gods into vapid Noel-Coward twits, listless and blah. I could see nothing good in the producers' taking such liberties with the script, going against everything in the story and characterization. When I grumbled to a friend in the Society, she tried to defend it, saying, "Oh it's supposed to be an American Ring." I said, "Not a whole lot of Americans are Noel Coward twits!" So she said, "But they're supposed to be robber barons." I countered that robber barons were even <u>less</u> likely to be twits.

For a very un-twitty American program, the little Pewter Plough theatre in the town of Cambria a few miles up the coast from here, produced a one-woman show, "The Belle of Amherst." A lively young actress portrayed the reclusive 19th century poet Emily Dickinson, who you might expect would have been a twit, but evidently wasn't, judging from this script, at any rate. Quite a spirited woman, even if reclusive.

In early September I spent a few days in Santa Barbara, and again took in a wonderful polo match by the highest rated teams the season. Gorgeous!! What fabulous horses, and superb horsemen-hunks.

In late September, back to San Francisco to see a rather oddball opera, *Die Tote Stadt*, composed by Erich Korngold while still in Germany, before he came to Hollywood to do film scores. The story was weird, but the music OK, and featuring one very lovely aria.

In early November I went to Los Angeles and out to Laguna Beach for the opening of a retrospective exhibit of William Wendt paintings--an artist friend of my father's, and whose works today are greatly sought after. I also inspected two buildings that had sprung up in Los Angeles since I was there some years ago. The Disney concert hall, made up of various curved sheets of silvery metal (similar to the Bilbao museum in Spain, and by the same architect, Gehry) was interesting on the outside (closed, so I didn't go in). They had had to sandblast the metal because its intense reflected glare had been frying people in their nearby apartments.

The new R.C. Cathedral is a massive fortress-like structure, huge chunks of ochre-colored stone, and inside--a vast emptiness. Pews, altar cross, bishop's chair etc. dwarfed and almost lost in it. As an architecture buff, I was so disappointed, since the Spanish architect (Moneo) had done some interesting buildings in Europe. This building just did not generate anything like a spiritual experience, which should be the architectural purpose.

This Fall, had a lovely surprise when I heard that the National Steinbeck Center in Salinas had borrowed one of the paintings by my father (A. Harold Knott, 1883-1977) from a gallery in Pacific Grove (as well as works by various other artists from his period) for a special exhibit juxtaposing writings of John Steinbeck, and the Carmel poet Robinson Jeffers with paintings and photographs reflecting these writers' celebration of California landscapes. And it was even more exciting to learn that my father's painting, "ROCKY INLET," was placed right at the entrance to the exhibit--the first thing visitors would see! What a splendid venue, since the Steinbeck Center has visitors from all over the world.

Everyone is familiar with Steinbeck's novels; many of his works are assigned reading in our schools, and many have been made into movies. The poet Jeffers is nowadays less well known than in his heyday of the 1920's-30's. His poems celebrated the grandeur of Nature--the rugged coast and mountains, of California.

As the curators wrote in the Steinbeck Center's Newsletter,

> "The words written by both Robinson Jeffers and John Steinbeck echo a deep response to the landscape of California's Central Coast. The rich soil. The quiet valleys. The howling surf. The timeless granite. The skeletal cypress, majestic oaks, and sentinel pines. And the delicate lupine and fragrant sage. Artists of the time were recording responses to the coastland's natural beauty in paintings. Jeffers and Steinbeck, too, were artists creating enduring images, their work in word and thought rather than pigment...Both writers shared an intense intimacy with the landscape. For Steinbeck his native surroundings served as a microcosm for the human experience...For Jeffers the natural world offered a tangible source for exploring the vastness of intangible thought--mortality, eternity, meaning."

> (D. Silguero and Dr. L. Staples, Guest Curator)

Now for a few less-grand aspects of Nature on the home front. My famous longhair tuxedo cat, Jazz, disappeared in February. I put out flyers (with his picture) on telephone poles all around the neighborhood, phoned all the friends and neighbors, police, veterinarians, and listed him on the animal shelter's "lost and found" website. I looked in every nook and cranny of the house, garage and studio. I was distraught. A couple days later, having just about given up in despair, I had to settle down and do some paperwork. I opened a drawer in the metal filing cabinet--and there was Jazz, curled up at the back of the drawer! "JAZZ! You're HERE!!" What a relief. I hauled him out, none the worse for wear, apart from hunger and thirst (he rushed into the kitchen to drink and eat too much, promptly throwing it all up). Evidently I'd left that half-filled drawer open, and he'd climbed in and gone to sleep at the back, where I didn't see him when I subsequently closed the drawer.

Of course when I called everyone back to say that the lost was found, I heard a lot of jokes, such as "Was he filed under "C" for "Cat?" etc. Well, not exactly. But I later noticed that he had chewed up a lot of the material at the edges of folders under "B" for Bank."

Recently when I too-vigorously pushed the seed out of an avocado, I sent it flying across the kitchen and rolling along the floor. My orange-striped shorthair cat, BB, flew after it and had a great time chasing it about. A new and inexpensive cat toy! (But the trouble with cat toys is that they disappear under beds or other furniture, reappearing months later in unexpected places.)

On the Amphibian front, I saw only ONE frog all year, flopping into the rain barrel when I lifted the lid. And I heard only ONE frog sing, calling from the saltbush hedge in an attempt to find a mate. If there is really one one frog out there, what about the future? Or are there actually two frogs, who do manage to get together? As I've mentioned before, I'd read that global warming has increased the viral or bacterial population, which is in turn killing off frogs everywhere. I just hope my tiny frog population here can hang on.

Now to get this printed up and on its way. Best wishes to everyone for a happy Christmas and New Year!

2009

Greetings!

Where did the summer go?

I must put part of the blame on the fact that since buying a Mac laptop in April (switching from the olD Dell and Microsoft Windows system), and taking the weekly one on one training sessions in the Apple Store in San Luis Obispo, I've been embroiled in a Big Learning Curve-- learning the different terminology used by this company, and how to cope with some of the many things the machine can do. Although basically I like the machine and all its possibilities, I still say all computers make simple clerical tasks complex and difficult to learn. Hence, just the process of feeding everyone's addresses into the machine's "address book," producing the annual generic letter, and, hopefully, some sticky mailing address labels, has eaten up a great deal of time. I probably could have done it all much faster by hand.

The year's activities included, as usual, a couple of visits to Santa Barbara (another wonderful polo match!), and several trips to San Francisco, seeing friends, museum and art gallery exhibits, and attending a few Wagner Society events.

One of the latter was an internal fundraiser in which members donated some of their books and Cd's, etc., for others to buy. But the big event of our year was the annual "Cosima Birthday Party" (early December). Wagner's wife Cosima Liszt Von Bulow having been born on Christmas, this also becomes our Christmas party, as it were. This year we were fortunate to have the nationally-acclaimed Wagnerian soprano Jane Eaglen, and a young heldentenor, Gregory Carroll, give us a concert: scenes from *Walkfire* (in the roles of Siegmund and Sieglinde) and *Der Fliegende Holländer* (The Flying Dutchman) in the Crystal Ballroom of the real elegant Marines' Memorial Club, followed by a late luncheon. A splendid dress-up occasion, and Ms Eaglen's great voice gave a real "Wagnerian fix," so to speak.

The most notable museum exhibits I saw in SF were ones of the Yves St. Laurent's many years of fashions, and one of Fabergé, Lalique and Tiffany objects and designs.

On the home front, I had cataract surgery in November on my "other eye." another roaring success (the first one having been done a year ago). I'm impressed with the speed and efficiency and relative lack of discomfort or inconvenience this procedure involves. Let's hear it for modern ophthalmological surgery!

I saw a couple of plays at the charming Pewter Plough Theatre in Cambria (and luncheons at the aptly named Tea Cosy Restaurant, emphasizing English dishes and teas).

I've heard several Christmas carol concerts already, including the Festival of Lessons and Carols at the local Episcopal Church (modeled on the program originated at Kings College, Cambridge, in England).

An exhibit of about 350 small-scale (table top) crèche scenes at the Lutheran church was fascinating. Many carved wooden ones, the kind we're accustomed to from Germany, Italy and the Holy Land, plus some in ceramics and other materials. But the most interesting and unusual ones were made by various African tribes, some utilizing seeds, pods, leaves and plant materials I'd never seen before.

Incidentally, at the Monterey Museum of Art opening, some ladies came up to tell me I look like Julia Child. Since this also happened when I went to the Laguna Art Museum retrospective of William Wendt's paintings last year, and has happened to me at several other times and places over the years, I'm beginning to feel as if Julia's ghost is trying to take over my body. I always insist that I don't look like her (or cook like her), it's just that we're both tall. And I also point out that Julia was in fact several inches taller than I.

****

In keeping with the Christmas and midwinter emphasis on lights (Winter Solstice!), the neighborhood I live in, from my corner west and south, went all out and organised to display hundreds of *luminarias* the evening of December 13. These are little brown paper bags filled with a base of cement-sand and a votive candle lit inside each one, and they were arranged about two or three feet apart all along the roadside of each house. Their flicking lights made a charming and cheerful sight, and drew many visitors on foot or by car.

By the time I'd returned from the Lessons and Carols and its refreshments, a short cloudburst had extinguished about a fourth of my lights, so I went out with a long candle to re-light those, although the visitor traffic had abated by that time.

****

Another noteworthy recent event was seeing the new movie *Invictus*. The screenplay was written by Anthony (Tony) Peckham, who lives here--formerly about a block from me, now out on the rural edge of town. He is from South Africa, and the film is about Nelson Mandela's effort to unite blacks and whites through sport--in support of the Springbok Rugby team, winning the World Cup against New Zealand's team. An exciting--and moving film--Bravo, Tony!

****

Now for NATURE NOTES. I saw only two frogs in my rain barrels this year--and even noted them on my calendar: a grey-ish tan one on Aug. 6 and a green one on Aug. 15. I don't know if it's the same frog changing his color to match the bins, or two different frogs. But in any case, it's a lonely life for him/them. I wonder how they keep their species going at all. I wish they could make a big comeback--I've grown fond of the little creatures, and I miss their choral songs of yore.

The cats, Jazz and BB, are in fine form, even though, as the veterinarian puts it, they are now "middle-aged"--8 years! They continue to catch a few gophers (burrowing rodents -- garden pests), which they bring indoors to devour, and/or offer up to me for the family larder (thanks, cats!). Of course they leave the messy remains and blood for me to clean up.

Alas, small birds are also pretty--one of which escaped Jazz's jaws to fly briefly around my living room before Jazz leapt over the back of the sofa and caught him again. (I had to leave the room: I wasn't fast enough to save the bird.) Butterflies, unfortunately, are also occasional victims--evidently just for the thrill of the chase, because they hardly qualify as "food."

Another species gave me a big surprise when I was out for my exercise walk one morning. Suddenly a plump brown rabbit came from behind, hopping in a circle around me, about two feet from me. I thought I was hallucinating. I turned around to see if there really was a rabbit, and sure enough, there he was. I said "Good Morning," and started to continue on my way, but he followed me. I feared he would get lost or run over by a car, so I needed to try to find his home. He was obviously tame, somebody's escaped pet, and not the kind of rabbits that are found in the wild here. The nearest house seemed to have no pathway to the front door from the street I was on, but while I tried to make my way in, a woman emerged from the house. "Is this your rabbit?" I asked. She said no, he belonged to a little girl in a house farther back up the road, and she picked him up to take him home. He was a cuddlesome, adorable little creature. She said he lives in his owner's house and is so domesticated he uses a cat-litter box for toilet purposes!

****

That's about all for now. Hope all goes well with you and yours. I look forward to your news. Meanwhile, best wishes for Christmas and the New Year!

2010

Greetings!

I'm still writing this as of Dec. 19 -- so, my apologies if the card is late!!

A look back over the calendar shows the usual mix of art and music. The March trip to San Francisco included an exhibit of Cartier diamond jewelry at the Legion of Honor Museum-- a blinding display of opulent designs past and present. And a Wagner Society talk by Wm. Klingelhoffer (Co-Principal Horn Player with the San Francisco Opera) on "The Bel Canto and Wagnerian Horn Player," was illustrated by performance and recorded selections.

In June, I attended the Society's symposium on *Die Walküre*. (I didn't attend the actual opera, since I disliked the current SF *Ring* approach, 180° off Wagner's story and characterizations, in *Rheingold* the previous year.) We also had a festive banquet at the Marines' Memorial Club, an elegant venue, and we were entertained with a recital by two young sopranos.

During that trip I went over to Oakland to see the new (opened 2008) R.C. Cathedral, Christ the Light, with unique, impressive architecture, the design based not on the traditional cruciform shape, but the fish symbol used by the earliest Christians. This makes for an unusual-looking exterior (tall, but with the fish footprint-shape).

The interior is most interesting, with a huge curved glass ceiling covered with natural wood louvers to filter the natural sunlight. More natural wood is used in a "woven" appearance for the road screen, and a large granite baptismal pool is near the entrance, big enough for a full-body-dip adult baptism.

Contemporary art is used for Stations of the Cross. One or two pieces of older art were salvaged from an earthquake-destroyed church that had previously served as the cathedral. In the crypt they have burial vaults for coffins, and small glass-doored niches to hold cremation urns and small memorabilia or photos of the deceased.

(Architecture buffs, take note: This is worth a trip. After all the ancient churches and cathedrals I've trudged through round the world, I was intrigued by this fresh design approach.) (Architect: Craig Hartman, of Skidmore, Owings & Merrill.)

In October a traveling group of singers from Russia (the Petersburg Chorus) gave a concert at our local Episcopal

Church. Russian throats seem to achieve a unique type of vocalization in both sacred and folk music! A musical treat.

Good news for this Central Coast area -- the Performing Arts Center at the Cal Poly campus in San Luis Obispo began showing the "Met Live in HD" series of opera simulcasts this Fall (from the Metropolitan Opera, New York). I was thrilled to see the Met's new production of *Das Rheingold*, which followed Wagner's story and characterizations properly, yet used a lot of fantastic modern technology to achieve the effects. A knockout performance. What bliss to have access to those operas, here in the "remote provinces." We will have several more of their operas up through May, when they'll do *Die Walküre* --hurrah!

I became a tourist in my own count in October, for a hair-rising trolley ride up a winding mountain road on a cliff near the town of Avila south of here to tour the recently-restored buildings of the old San Luis Lighthouse, now an "historic site." [It dates back to the late 19th century and ceased operation in the 1950s. Previous railroad tracks had been removed for their metal to be used for the war effort in WWII]. A volunteer group has been lovingly restoring the old lighthouse keepers' quarters, etc. in period styles. Terrific view from a high cliff of the seacoast. What a lonely outpost it must have been for the keepers.

As for Sports (spectator, that is)-- I attended The Bombardier Pacific Coast Open final Polo match in Santa Barbara (end of August) -- terrific game! They had induced the Argentine "superstar" player to come this year -- Adolfo Cambiaso -- considered "the world's greatest polo player." A 10-goal rated man. He was fantastic, and another Argentine, Hilario Ulloa, a 9-goal man, who came in to replace an injured player, was pretty impressive too. What a gorgeous, fast-paced, exciting game!!

I also opted to watch most of the World Cup matches from South Africa on TV, trying to figure out why the whole world gets so excited over this game. It seemed to me frustrating to watch, since so little scoring is achieved, but the palpable excitement of the players and the crowds -- including royalty and celebrities -- infectious.

A major event of the year was my college class reunion/homecoming (Stanford University) in October. These are held every five years for each batch of classes (this year, they honored, e.g., 1935, 1940, 1945, 1950, 1955, 1960, etc up through 2010). This meant there were over 8,000 alumni running around the campus for four days! When my class met ten, and even five years ago, a lot of people I knew were there. This year only two people I'd known in my freshman dorm corridor attended. Some had other commitments, some (or their spouses) had health problems, and a few had passed on. That was saddening, but on the other hand it made me all the more determined to attend -- for myself, and also on their behalf, as it were. And I could touch base with people I'd known just by sight.

I stayed in my usual "bargain" motel in San Francisco (unwilling to pay exorbitant Palo Alto hotel rates). On the second day of the reunion, the friend who lives in Oakland and no longer drives, hired a chauffeured limo to take her and me (at 06:30 am!) -- so we arrived on the campus in grand style. The other classmate from our freshman dorm corridor came out from New York with her husband for the event. (See photo at right.)

My chauffeured friend attended only on the second day, so for the other three days I became a Silicon Valley commuter, riding back and forth on the train to Palo Alto, surrounded by people engrossed in their laptops, iPhones, iPods, Blackberrys, iPads and cell phones, while I sat in my quaint, old-fashioned way reading a print newspaper, or (gasp!) a book!

Addendum to 2010 Christmas Generic Letter for the "Roble 1-C Girls"

The very idea of a "60th reunion" is mind-boggling. How can it be that long since we graduated? Instead of still wondering "What do you want to be when you grow up?" we face the fact that we're old.   [I prefer denial!] Going back to the college campus at this stage becomes a pilgrimage into the past, a time for moments of reflection. What have we done, where have we been? Where are we going?

The first day, Thursday, started with 10:00 registration, deciding which of the 46 "classes without quizzes" to attend, and getting oriented on the detailed map to find my way around the campus, now so jam-packed with buildings that didn't exist when we were students. A few old familiar ones, like Mem Aud, Hoover Tower, Encina, etc., served as reference points so that I didn't feel totally as if I'd come from outer space to a strange planet.

That day I attended the "students' experience" panel (several students telling of their diverse backgrounds and experiences at Stanford) and the "Why the West Rules" class and its following reception in the Humanities Center, which I loved.) (This Center is in what was once Bowman Alumni House, opposite the ancient Fire House.)

The second day, Friday, I had a very early-morning start with Barbie Judson, who came over from Oakland and picked me up at my motel in the City in her chauffeured limo, and we had a good visit in the car.

Most of the reunion/homecoming events were attended by members of all the 5-year-interval classes from 1935 on up through 2010--a huge number of alumni all over the place! Our own Class of '50 has dwindled in numbers, some of our friends having headed into that Great Beyond. Others were absent because of health issues.   And so at our own Class of '50 Panel meeting, on the Friday, we were "family"--but a smaller family. I would estimate about 100 to 150 people attended this.

Our most famous classmate on the panel, Sandra Day O'Connor, told us how she'd been appointed the first woman Justice on the Supreme Court: called from a very short list of eligible women to meet with President Reagan--never having been to Washington. They got on well with their mutual interest in horses and ranching (she having grown up on horseback on a huge cattle ranch). She also told us of a current project she's into, called iCivics. Appalled by present-day young people's lack of knowledge of our Declaration of Independence and Constitution, etc., she is promoting the reinstatement of the teaching of Civics in public schools. So she says to our assembled class, "I want YOU to go out there and help me with this!" (So get out there, classmates, and do it! See the website iCivics.org for more info.)

After the panel speeches, some of us were making a point of seeking out and talking with people we may not have known well, but with whom we'd had a nodding acquaintance in our living groups, classes or other campus activities. A feeling of survivors "circling the wagons." An upbeat greeting and brief reminiscence - with a strong attitude of "Hang in there!" either spoken - or understood without words. Not yet the Last Man Standing--and determined to hang in as long as possible.

Someone came up from behind to greet me with an arm around my shoulders--I was so astonished I blurted out, "Oh, that tall handsome man from my Western Civ class!" I was just **floored.** (When were **in** that class, 64 years ago-- well, you know how we used to make sidelong glances around the room at the dishy guys--I'd thought this splendid specimen would barely have noticed me at the time.)

I made a point to remind another chap of how we'd stood next to each other for 11 ¾ hours in the registration line that first day as new freshmen, in blazing heat (the hottest day on record?), and how his humorous banter with his buddy had entertained me through that ordeal. He'd forgotten all about it. (He and his friend were looking over the course catalog at engineering classes, and came across one on Sewerage. He'd said, "Henry, I bet this course stinks!" I've been telling this anecdote all these years, and he didn't even remember it. His wife, who'd never heard it, had a good laugh.)

Barbie Judson had not opted for the class dinner and left in her limo in mid-afternoon. I went to my class ("Barriers to Conflict Resolution: The Israeli-Palestinian Conflict"), then grabbed one of the golf carts Stanford was furnishing (with drivers) to help people get around the campus. Rode merrily down Palm Drive in the golf cart, walked over to the train station, under the underpass to Alma Street, and headed north along the sidewalk to the Stanford Park Hotel (about a 20-min. walk). This hotel, venue for our own class dinner, is just over the border in Menlo Park.

(I'd packed a lightweight red silk outfit plus some suede shoes and an evening bag into the tote I'd carried around all day, so I could change when I got to the hotel.)

Changed clothes in the ladies' room, and waited in the lobby till the check-in for 6:00 party time. That check-in table was located in a sort of passageway between the lobby, the bar and the patio, and I sat in that area with my glass of wine, where I could keep an eye on people as they arrived, to see if there was anyone I knew. Sure enough, here came the only other Roble corridor 1-C girl, Ronee Herrmann and her husband, Norman Bank! (I knew she was attending the reunion from the list we'd received in our registration packets, and I'd left a message on her cell phone, hoping I'd see her.) So the three of us had a lively conversation, "after all these years." I hadn't seen her since the 50th reunion. We stayed there in the warm indoor spot because the cocktail party area on the patio-terrace was cold, even with overhead heaters.

When it was time for dinner in a upstairs dining room, we managed to get seats at the same table and continued our spirited conversation. A very enjoyable time, over a good dinner. I think the word was that there were 163 people at the dinner (?) - which would include some spouses of classmates.

Afterwards I walked back to the train station and commuted back to the City - not getting into bed till around midnight. (A long day, with a lot of walking, fueled mainly on determination and adrenaline) from about 5:00 am till midnight!)

So the next morning, Saturday, I was not exactly bursting with energy. Since the earliest Saturday train would not get me to campus in time for the Roundtable (see letter, and list at end of this addendum), I'd arranged to meet other friends (ten years behind me at Stanford) for breakfast. When they dropped me off on campus I spent a quiet time in the Arrellaga Alumni Center (VERY nice facility!) reading the papers in their little library - a nice peaceful retreat - until it was time for the "tailgate" luncheon. Since it was raining by now, this tailgate was in fact food served at an indoor location--hamburgers, hot dogs, etc., salads, dessert.

(Fortunately, Stanford had already designated

alternative rain sites for everything, listed on one of our registration materials.) After the lunch I went to the string quartet class, -- yes, ignoring the football match! (I lost interest in football after graduation.) And thence back to SF - hitting the stores!

Sunday, last day of homecoming, the day I called "Golf Cart Central" to ask for a golf cart ride up to Palm Drive, it was rainy again. I went to my "Boston Tea Party" history class, and it was raining even more when we emerged from the basement site of its building next to the Art Museum.

Stanford had arranged a nondenominational service-cum-memorial for deceased alumni in Memorial Church, (which was held at the same time as my class. (I would otherwise have liked to attend the service.)

In a reflective mood deepened by the grey skies and steady rain, I sloshed over from the class to the Quad. How many times had we walked around or through there during college? Rough earth and a weed or two in those days, now tidily paved over.

I went into the church. Inside, acolytes were just snuffing out an array of votive candles on a high table that people had lit in memory of deceased friends. I got hold of a fresh candle and asked if I could light it, even if only for such a short time. I lit it from one of the tall tapers nearby, recalling our now-deceased Roble 1-C girls as they looked when we first knew them. (By maiden names, alphabetically--Jane Bush, Joan Maxwell, Marjorie "Tex" Miller, Betty Rahn, Sally Smith, and Elaine Walton. And a Lagunita classmate, Ann Thomas.)

There are some 1-C girls we'd lost track of completely, either since graduation, or since our 50th reunion, so I don't know if any others have already left us as well.......

Sitting there, I also sent up some positive thoughts for those of us whose health problems and/or those of their spouses prevented their coming to this reunion.

A swarm of tourists, mostly Asian, was already starting to mill around the church, snapping pictures. I sat there quietly for a while, before heading to the rain site for the homecoming's farewell lunch in a restaurant under the "new" Grad School of Business. Didn't see anyone I knew there.

And so I wound up this busy four-day homecoming, laced with moments of nostalgia, hitched my "farewell golf cart ride" down Palm Drive, and rejoined commuters on the train back to the City, and the world of Today.

2011

Greetings!

The holiday season sneaked up fast, and because I was away the first week of December, I'm even further behind than usual.....sorry!!

I briefly became a tourist in my local area in March for a walking tour of the salt marshes and mudflats of Morro Bay--which I'd always taken for granted, thinking of the marshes as just a blanket of "weeds," and the mudflats as just "mud." This tour is led by a professional marine biologist, (under the auspices of the State Park system). I was astonished at the many different kinds of plants that grow in the marshes and along the mudflats, each one's relative position along the edge determined by the degree of salinity it can tolerate from the rising and falling tides. Lots of nice little "Creatures" live in the mudflats, too.

An attempt to look at "famed wildflowers" inland with a neighbor in April was a bust - the weather had not brought the flowers forth, and what's more, a brief fluke downpour of snow and hail crashed onto us en route as we crossed the mountains between Morro Bay and Atascadero (c.600 ft altitude). Snow almost never occurs here, so that was pretty exciting.

Further afield, the usual things to report--a few trips to San Francisco & environs, for art gallery- and museum-crawling and seeing friends, and one trip to Santa Barbara, for the same (again including an exciting polo match, the Pacific Open Final).

The June San Francisco trip was primarily to attend (and be a volunteer aet) a symposium sponsored by our Wagner Society in conjunction with the SF Opera's production of Wagner's *Der Ring des Nibelungen*, as well as to attend our celebratory banquet party (with a soprano to sing for us). My arduous volunteer "duty" was fun, helping the many visitors from all over the country and from abroad find their name tags from a table at the door. It made my day when a visitor arrived named Isolde. I made a great fuss over her, enthusiastically introducing her to some of our other members nearby--"Steve! Steve! This is **Isolde!**"

(I had not actually attended the operas themselves from this particular San Francisco *Ring* cycle, except for *Rheingold*--which I loathed, finding its interpretation wholly inappropriate, 180° off Wagner's directions. But some of our members apparently didn't mind these productions, and some said the singer portraying Brunnhilde was extremely good.)

Saw the retrospective exhibit of Balenciaga fashions at the DeYoung Museum, excellent. But the art highlight on this trip was the "Stein Show" at the Museum of Modern Art. Curators had gathered together many paintings the American writer Gertrude Stein, her brothers and sister-in-law had collected while living in Paris in the early 20th century--by Picasso, Matisse, *et al.*, before they became famous and sought after. The Stein collections had long since been dispersed among museums and other collectors, so it was quite a treat to see so many all together, and to learn a bit about the Stein family.

I was back in San Francisco in early December and enjoyed several special exhibits at the Museum of the Legion of Honor - "Pissarro's People," (heavy on servants and peasants, and not really as engaging as his landscapes that we're more accustomed to, but actually I liked his lithograph portrait of Cezanne very much). The museum was also exhibiting some exquisite small sculptures ("Mourners") from a 16th century tomb of the Burgundian Court. And, a dramatic marble bust of "Medusa" by Bernini, which was on loan from Italy. She is depicted showing fear and horror as her hair turns into snakes. You could say she was having a bad hair day, or on the other hand, a good snake day.

The timing of the December trip was arranged so I could attend another Wagner Society banquet, the annual

"Cosima Birthday Party," which is our Christmas party, since Wagner's wife was born on Christmas day. This was again at the Marines' Memorial Building, an elegant venue, and we had another young soprano singing some Wagnerian arias and lieder for us. (One of the Society's ongoing projects is raising funds to help young singers with their professional training; they in turn are pleased to sing for us.)

And speaking of Wagner operas, the Metropolitan Opera (New York) HD television simulcasts are shown at the Performing Arts Center in San Luis Obispo, and I've attended several, which are wonderful. I loved their productions of *Das Rheingold, Die Walküre,* and *Siegfried,* and I'm looking forward to *Götterdämmerung* in the Spring!

I've been continuing my weekly one-on-one training sessions (which they call "one-to-one") at the Apple Store in San Luis Obispo, still expanding my grasp of the Mac computer. I've especially enjoyed learning how to make letterhead stationary, notecards and business cards, with illustrations from some of the art work (sketches in pencil and watercolor) by my late father, A. Harold Knott, with text and layout by me. Challenging and fun, and I've had some good results.

There were some difficult times this year with two veterinary hospitalizations for my little orange cat BB (age 10), who somehow acquired a massive infection in his chest cavity. We thought it was cleared up by the end of July, but he gradually deteriorated again--having a great struggle trying to breathe--and had to be re-hospitalized in November. More drainage, more antibiotics, more and more tests, including ultrasound, which revealed that part of his lungs had collapsed. The vet says it will take some time for them to re-inflate. BB came home Dec. 13, but he's still on long-term antibiotics and will need another X-ray in January to check progress. He feels better anyway, is happy to be home, and is eating voraciously to regain the weight he lost while sick. (He's also re-growing the fur shaved off both sides during hospital treatment. Meanwhile his bare rib cage makes him look as if he must be cold without his jacket.)

My other feline, the black & white longhair Jazz (also age 10, is in fine form, and he has fluffed out a thicker, bushier winter coat, thus looking like a lot more cat. He had been in a state of anxiety each time BB was away, and now he is so glad to have his adopted "bro" back home--as am I.

Nature notes--alas, no frogs again this year. I keep looking, and listening, hopefully...

Recent home front events--attended the University Women's Christmas luncheon (which included a concert by a community college corrus to get us into the holiday spirit).

And a Stanford Alumni Club open house Christmas party at the home of one of the members, which is carefully sited part way up a mountain called Bishop's Peak, with fabulous panoramic views on three sides. San Luis Obispo looks rather spectacular from such a height. The members brought a scrumptious array of hors d'oeuvres and desserts, and all kinds of wines and soft drinks were provided. Another good way to get into the holiday mood while increasing one's waistline.

Sorry I'm late getting this letter and the cards done, but I hope that they'll at least be on their way within the Twelve Days of Christmas!

Best wishes for this season and the New Year!

2012

GREETINGS! Running late--my apologies! Only partially a printer problem. The underlying reason--I'm simply late in composing the letter!

To dispense the health news first, I was hit with "hip bursitis" while in San Francisco in March--extreme pain that made standing and walking incredibly difficult. I had to buy a cane. And I had to continue on schedule and get down to Palo Alto the next day on the commuter train for my annual tax prep appointment with the accountant. Then after lunch with a few friends, one ferried me to the Palo Alto Clinic's "Urgent Care" department. I must sing the praises of this place--a model for efficiency. It's like a mini-hospital within their building, and the exam, X-ray (eith extra CD copy for me to bring home to my own orthopedist), diagnosis, cortisone shot, ice bag, and pain prescription filled in their own basement pharmacy--all finished in only two hours! If you're ever in trouble when in Silicon Valley area, that's the place to go.

That evening, I arrived back in SF on the commuter train and then the Muni bus, still in pain, (the cortisone for this joint is slow-acting). It was dark and absolutely pouring rain. I hobbled slowly the one long block from the bus to my motel, hunched over almost double, limping with the cane in one hand and clutching my handbag and tote bag full of tax papers in the other. A grizzled old black man leaning against a wall along the sidewalk greeted me jovially. "That's what you get for living so long!" I had to admire his sense of humor, even in my miserable state.

On return home, despite another cortisone shot from my orthopedist, I was still in pain, and further testing showed me an additional problem had developed--an arthritic lumbar vertebra and disk impinging on a nerve root. I was then sent to a 'rehab" specialist for nerve and muscle testing, and he in turn referred me for extensive physical therapy sessions including spinal traction. By the latter part of August I had regained strength and could again walk without a cane, but I have to continue doing the PT exercises "forever."

A few random brighter points about this experience: During that March trip, when meeting a friend at the Asian Museum in SF for lunch and an exhibit showing the lavish life of Indian Maharajas in their heyday. I spun around the show in style--the museum lends you a wheelchair! And the railroad employees on the commuter trains to Palo Alto are very helpful--when they see one's cane, they pop out of nowhere and arrange for mechanical platforms to hoist you up into the train and then lower you down again when you arrive, so you don't have to struggle to climb and descend the steps. Pretty cool.

Now on to more pleasant news of the year. The major event was a trip to Yosemite National Park. An old family friend was so appalled that I had been literally around the world and had never seen this famous attraction right here in California, that he took me for four days at his guest, June 1st. ("This is your Christmas present!"

Heading there from Berkeley, we went through a bit of the old Gold Rush area (and a reconstructed village of that era) in hot weather--about 103° at one point--but the temp was quite comfortable at Yosemite itself. It is a place heavily frequented by vigorously outdoorsy people--hikers, bikers, rock climbers, campers, etc, and not many, er, "mature" ladies slogging around on canes. Nevertheless, thanks to my friend taking me on a one-person tour, and lodged in the wooden cabins of "Curry Village." I saw all the famous views of massive rock formations, waterfalls, lakes and meadows, and was duly impressed by the sheer magnitude of everything. I was startled each time I looked up and was faced with a huge granite rock wall. Felt very small.

I thought about what this place must have been like zillions of years ago, when it was filled with a gigantic glacier. I kept remembering the eerie sensations I'd felt on a long-ago trip when hiking across the glacier at Mt. Cook in New Zealand. There the hotel fitted us out with boots, alpenstocks and a human guide, and we gingerly trudged among the rough, chunky surface, listening to the moving ice crunching and the slow drip, drip, drip of its water as it melted underneath us.

I loved seeing all the tame deer browsing around the meadows--even the tiniest little patch of meadow near the cafeteria-style restaurant had a few of these gentle creatures munching grass, mindless of the tourists, who were a sight in themselves, gazing in awe and wonder.

The LeConte Memorial Lodge, a small museum built by the Sierra Club in 1903, was a special treat, honoring the early geological work of Prof Joseph LeConte (Univ. of Calif. Berkeley). Dining at the famous Ahwahnee Hotel (1926. pseudo-Indian style decor) was a pleasure, as was lunching not far away at the Wawona Hotel (1879. Anglo-American). I was fascinated by a tour of giant Sequoia redwood trees at the Mariposa Grove with its small museum. One learned how rugged trees can survive partial burning and how two young trees too close together can join their trunks and become one.

Mono Lake has an eerie, lunar-landscape appearance, bristling with an array of "tufa" - tapering stalagmite-like pillars, spiking up out of the water. These are formed by calcium carbonate bubbling up from underwater springs. I wondered if something like that had occured in Biblical times, when someone thought that a certain disobedient wife had been punished by being turned into a pillar of salt. But when I was "swimming" (i.e. floating uncontrollably) in the Dead Sea in Jordan years ago, emerging and drying in the sun to find myself coated with salt, I had mulled over another theory.

We left the area via high-altitude roads, (c.6000-8000 ft.) and found ourselves suddenly engulfed in a <u>snowstorm</u> - - <u>JUNE 4,</u> mind you! It grew heavier and heavier, piling up on the road, and became quite alarming as we passed two cars that had spun out of control in circles and gotten stuck along the roadside. We crept slowly along in the tracks created by two vehicles up ahead, apprehensive at the road conditions, yet awestruck at the beauty of masses of snow-covered trees all along the side of the road--like perfectly-shaped Christmas trees in every size, from baby ones to giants. So one could say this trip was indeed a "Christmas present." When we reached lower altitudes, the snow turned to rain and then stopped, so we got safely back to Berkeley by evening.

After the Yosemite sojourn I spent a few days in San Francisco, which included a Wagner Society lecture meeting and a big party to wind up SF Opera's *Ring* cycle. (I had hated its *Rheingold* production earlier, so I avoided the other three.)

For the Labor Day weekend I went to Santa Barbara for the Pacific Coast Open Final polo match. It was a particularly exciting game--the two teams of top-rated players, running so close, tied at the end. Then the team that had been behind earlier on made the winning goal with a long, spectacular dash by the world-famous Argentine player, Adolfo Cambiaso. The audience was going wild with excitement-- jumping about and screaming their heads off. Me too.

Stanford invited my class year's alumni to attend the four-day October reunion/homecoming of the class three years ahead of ours--to keep them company, presumably because of the dwindling number of ancient beings--and to "celebrate" their entering what the University calls the "Cardinal Society" (class years with so few members still alive or well enough to attend that they're all lumped together). I booked up all the lunches, although you only had to book one in order to attend everything else on the program. The regular lunches are in "class tents" (canopies, actually) with picnic tables and folding chairs on all the lawns, and they consist of cold box lunches and plastic. The Cardinal Society affair on the other hand was indoors in the handsome Alumni Building with real furniture, linen, china, silver and glassware, place cards, and waiters serving an elegant hot meal with wine. Very nice!

Of the "classes without quizzes" I attend, one of my favorites was "Mark Twain and the World" (Prof. Shelley Fisher Fishkin), examining this very American writer who had become a global citizen, what he learned from his travels, and what readers and writers around the world learned from him. (I was pleased to hear that he was an early ardent animal welfare advocate, and I bought a copy of the Prof's compilation book, *Mark Twain's Book of Animals*.)

The class on "The Science of Happiness" (Prof. Fred Luskin) drew a huge auditorium crowd, focusing on what makes people happy and why, with "strategies for finding the good, becoming more peaceful, and improving relationships." This included turning to the person seated next to you and saying "May you be happy!" It did put us all in a good mood.

In "Walt Whitman's Body Language," Prof. Gavin Jones showed lots of photos of the poet (even a few in the nude, and he was no Greek statue) with which Whitman publicized himself. He was an avid self-promoter, yet because his type of poetry was ahead of its time, he never achieved the esteem in his own day that he has now.

The University Roundtable, "Gray Matters: Your Brain, Your Life, and Brain Science in the 21st Century," (held in the basketball pavillion, and taped for television), was another high point. The speakers were Dr. Frank Longo (Chair of Neurology & Neuroscience). Prof Carla Shatz (Biology & Neurobiology), Bob Woodruff (ABC News, Bob Woodruff Foundation, survivor of brain trauma in war), and

Jill Bolte Taylor (Neuroanatomist and author of *My Stroke of Insight; a Brain Scientist's Personal Journey* - re her own recovery from a stroke). <u>One salient point they all stressed: the particular importance of PHYSICAL EXERCISE in keeping one's brain in shape!</u>

Just as at our own class reunion a couple of years ago, I was able to walk to most of the campus venues, and enjoyed the fun of sailing around in golf carts for longer routes. I also enjoyed riding the commuter trains between SF & PA each day, where I'm amused, but not surprised, to find myself almost the only person reading an actual print book or newspaper and not glued to an electronic device.

I went back to San Francisco later in October for a Wagner Society symposium on *Lohengrin,* and I ventured a standing-room ticket for the opening of the opera that night. But I loathed the production (Medieval royalty costumed and behaving like 1956 Iron Curtain-era Hungarian functionaries!) So I walked out early in the second act.

In my local area, I saw an excellent production of Chekhov's *Three Sisters.* PCPA theatre, Santa Maria). I told one of the lead performers I'd seen the Moscow Arts Theatre perform this in London years ago, and I vigorously complimented him on <u>his </u>performance, which I think made his day! Another wonderful production (Pewter Plough community theater, Cambria) of *Six Dance Lessons in Six Weeks* was thoroughly delightful. Odd title, but excellent piece of writing and performing--moving, yet fully laced with humor.

We're fortunate to have most of the Met live in HD opera simulcasts and "encores" (reruns) from the Metropolitan Opera, New York, shown in San Luis Obispo at the theatre on Cal Poly's campus. I <u>did</u> like the Met's production of Wagner's *Ring* cycle--very much!

Can't stay *away* from SF! Went again in early December for the Wagner Society's "Cosima Party" (a Christmas party so-named since Wagner's wife Cosima was born on Christmas). We were entertained by a pianist, and lots of members won gift-wrapped "prizes" (via the drawing of numbered tickets). I won one of these which I didn't open till Christmas. It's a DVD of a production of *Lohengrin* done in

Baden-Baden, Germany, and by serendipity the Music Director was Kent Nagano--world-famous conductor who grew up here in little Morro Bay! I haven't viewed this as yet.

NATURE NOTES: No frogs here again this year! I miss them and their songs! The cats, Jazz and BB, are doing well-- still frisky at their "advanced age" of eleven. BB had been so ill last year (two hospitalizations) but he made an excellent recovery and is still a good gopher-hunter. I let them both out early in the mornings to reconnoiter their territory and hunt any available prey. Jazz likes high places. A woman I don't know but who seemed to know where I live, seeing me at the hairdresser's, told me that one morning before dawn when she was out for an exercise run in my neighborhood, she paused to admire a full moon. She saw my cat Jazz up on the roof-- and he was also gazing at the moon! A pity she didn't have a camera on her--that would have made a terrific picture!

Whew--after all this typing, it seems this was a busier year than I thought. Hope all is well with you and yours. I love hearing your news. And I hope I can get these cards mailed at least within the Twelve Days of Christmas! Herewith my best wishes for the rest of the Christmas Season and a Happy New Year!

2013-2014

I never finished my Christmas cards for 2013, and didn't produce a generic letter at all. My apologies! And once the holidays were past, I couldn't get in the mood. Now I'll try to skim the two years.

2013: The main events were the usual trips to San Francisco and Santa Barbara, but also a bigger trip--to Seattle in **August**, to see its opera's production of Wagner's *Ring* cycle (4 operas). I'd been told they were the only ones doing a "traditional" *Ring* these days, and that I must see it. I'd never been to Seattle.

Went by train-- an all-day, all-night ride, in "coach" -- but a very comfortable part thereof--lower level, meant primarily for people with infirmities, in my case bad knee, arthritis -- thus not having to climb up & down stairs in a moving train. Large seats, with leg supports and lots of leg room, and the seat backs in front of you have tray flaps. And you get food service at your seat! Very good and tasty food! An attendant takes your order from a menu and brings the meal to you. They have electric outlets at each seat so you can use a computer or charge your cell phone, etc. So with all this plus my own large yak-wool shawl to use as a blanket, my own seat cushion and a folded sweater as lumbar cushion, I was very comfortable.

This sounds like a plug for Amtrak. I must say it was indefinitely nicer than the unpleasantries of current-day airplane travel.

I'd never gone that far north by land, so the vast forests we went through were an amazing sight. And Seattle itself was a surprise. What a grand old railway station! Huge, all-white interior, high-ceilinged (moulded ceilings), marble floors, and very efficient organization. A busy travel hub. The city turned out to be lively, with lots of boutiques, shops and all kinds of foreign restaurants. But I didn't try them, as I'd immediately become enamored with the Metropolitan Market right near my hotel, with a delicious variety of hot and cold food cafeteria style (to eat there or take away), plus great pastries, ice creams, groceries and even gift items.

There were a few lectures in conjunction with the operas and one of the singers took part in a lunchtime Q&A while we ate box lunches.

The *Ring* production itself turned out to be too "pretty-pretty" for my taste, and the *Götterdämmerung* absolutely wishy-washy instead of the overpowering end-of-the-world you expect. So that was disappointing.

During a free day I took a sightseeing tour of the city, and was pleased to see the "fish ladder" constructed on the river to enable fish to make their spawning runs upstream and back.

The guide pointed out the gigantic construction to create Amazon's new headquarters. We passed a "sculpture garden" of sorts, which included a large circular object with a slight handle and a brush as the tail. He said Bill Gates sponsored it at the wishes of his mother, since his computers had enhanced its obsolescence. He asked "Can anyone identify that?" The van contained several other "retirement vintage" passengers, but I was the only one who raised my hand and said "A typewriter eraser!" Younger passengers had no idea, and the older ones weren't admitting it if they knew.

We passed an old building which he said had been the headquarters of the L. C. Smith company. "Anyone know what they made?" he asked. My hand shot up again: "Typewriters!"

In **October** I attended a Stanford homecoming (4 days), though this was not the year for my class' 5-year reunion. Once you reach a certain level of antiquity, the University lumps you together with survivors from other long-ago classes, as the "Cardinal Society." If you pay for even one of the events you are entitled to attend all the "classes without quizzes," lectures, roundtable, etc., and can also opt (for another fee) for a first-class luncheon in the Alumni Building, with linen, silver, china, crystal, wine, etc., where you're seated with a handful of people from your class or ones near it.

I particularly enjoy the "classes without quizzes." There are so many intriguing topics offered in each time slot that it's hard to choose, but I picked the following:

"Spytainment: How Fake Spies are Influencing Real Intelligence Policy" (Amy Segart, Senior Fellow, Hoover Inst., Co-Director of Center for International Security & Cooperation)

The government's counter-terrorism building was designed by Disney Engineers, because their old building looked too ordinary and un-spylike!

Fictional characters influence policymakers!

The Pentagon has a liaison in Hollywood for spy stuff!

"Seeing Roman Slavery" (Classics Assoc. Prof. Jennifer Trimble).

(The very visible crucifixion of 5000 survivors of the Spartacus Rebellion on the Via Appia--an excellent warning to others!

Slaves wore collars saying: "Stop me and return me to my master"!

"Landscape as Autobiography: Writers and Painters in America" (Prof. Bryan Wolf, American Art & Culture)

Over the past two centuries they have turned to the landscape to record not just what they see, but what they dream and desire.

"The Monotony of Modernity" (Asst. Prof. Saikat Majumdar, English)

Literary modernity is distinguished by a radical preoccupation with the monotonous, the marginal and the trivial! The modern novel celebrates the banalities of life!

"A Life of Contemplation or Action? Debates in Western Literature and Philosophy" (Assoc. Prof. Blakey Vermeule, English)

What kind of life is best? Can we ever achieve a balance between them?

As at previous reunions, I managed a few long walks but utilized the golf cart transport for most of the longer distances between campus venues, and to get back to the train station. (I stay in San Francisco and run down to Palo Alto on the commuter trains.)

In **December** I was in San Francisco again for the Wagner Society's Christmas party (officially called the "Cosima Birthday Party," since Wagner's wife was born on Christmas day). This was a grand feast with a duo-piano concert (is that the word?) - two pianists playing transcriptions of Wagner numbers on a single piano. They shared a bench, and each -- rather short people-- was seated on a pile of telephone books arranged to elevate him and her to a suitable height.

Back in Morro Bay, the new Rector of St. Peter's Episcopal Church--who had already had a 20-year career as professional actor/director/producer--produced a staged reading of Dickens' *A Christmas Carol*, with a few customers, props and sound effects, and a number of his young relatives taking various roles. (The church got extra value in hiring him!)

2014: In **January** (birthday month) I renewed my driver's license, with splendid eyesight and getting nearly all the written questions right! Though I haven't owned a car for years, I keep the license in case I need to rent one, or if I should be riding with someone who collapses, I can legally seize the wheel and haul them off to the nearest Emergency Room.

In **March**, the usual San Francisco trip to see my tax preparer, and of course to spend a few extra days to see old friends for lunch. A nice bonus to the tax prep--the accountant had an extra ticket to take me to a concert by Schola Cantorum, an auditioned group of amateurs, celebrating its 50th anniversary. They specialize in sacred music, and it was a lovely concert, with one piece specially composed just for the occasion.

In **August** the Stanford Alumni Club of this Central Coast area held a barbecue in a rustic park in San Luis Obispo, to honor young students just accepted for admission to the University, with proud parents basking in their reflected glory,

End of **August-early September**, Santa Barbara again, for the Pacific Coast Open Polo Finals--the top rated players--always an exciting game to watch, with gorgeous horses and handsome riders!

Also in **September**, the City of Morro Bay celebrated the anniversary of its attaining cityhood with a parade, the PRes. of the Historical Society roped me into riding in a trolley with other old-timers. With bells clanging, the exuberant driver exhorted us to shout greetings at various notable spectators. I think there were more people marching and riding in the parade than there were spectators, but everyone seemed to be having a good time at it.

In early **December**, my trip to San Francisco was challenging, since it coincided with storms and long-hoped-for rain. (You have heard of our drought-plagued state.) The day after my arrival I'd planned to ride the ferryboat over to Larkspur to lunch with friends. The storm, wind, rain and rough seas were so bad that per the TV weather announcements, the ferries were not running. Abrupt change in plans.

When I headed out from my motel seeking a hearty, hot breakfast, both places, I use had sustained electric power failure. The first was closed altogether. The second was open but had nothing but fruit and pieces of cake, so all I could get was a banana, to eat in the darkened cafe. It was seriously difficult to walk in this storm-- the wind nearly knocked me over, and my umbrella turned inside out, with all its ribs sticking up and out in all directions like a sculpture of an abstract spider--and no cover for me. I thought I'd have to throw it away and buy a new one. Later I was able to gently get all the spokes back into place and fold it in its normal way.

What else to do? Check out some stores! Bloomingdale's, then Nordstrom's: both places still had full electric power. Stores have a supply of plastic bags just inside the entrance for customers to stuff their dripping umbrellas-- and not drip on the merchandise. Nice Crab Louis lunch at the latter--watching the rain running down the large windows, and pouring down outside. An anomalous "summery" lunch in a winter rain

The Wagner Society's Christmas party was again held in the grand Marines' Memorial Club, with a young bass-baritone singing to us. (Mostly Mahler--?!--but one proper Wagner number, in which Wotan asks his wife to follow him into Valhalla! Now that's more like it!)

My other lunch appointments worked out all right, with just rain and no gales--two in Palo Alto, and one in the East Bay, riding BART [U.S. subway, U.K. underground to Walnut Creek and visiting an old friend in Alamo. On the day of the big storm a neighbor's tree had crashed through her garage roof (luckily not hitting the car), and she'd been without electricity for four days, with neighbors bringing her hot meals. (She'd been "interviewed" on one of the TV channels about this disaster, but I'd apparently been watching a different channel and missed this.)

Back in Morro Bay - the Rector again staged his *Christmas Carol*, this time using parishioners for the cast. My candidate for the Oscar would be the man who played the Ghost of Jacob Marley, draped in heavy chains (fake) with heavy chain (real) sound effects from nearby, and his agonized wailing struck fear into one and all.

ANIMAL NOTES:

It's been years since I had frogs soaking themselves in my "rain barrels" or the cats' water dish. I've missed them.

The cats, Jazz (B&W Tuxedo, Longhair) and Butterball, nicknamed BB (orange stripes, Shorthair) are now both 13 years old, which the vet says corresponds roughly to 60 in humans. Jazz is still in fine fettle, and thinks he's young. BB has developed hyperthyroidism, which we treat with a "transdermal gel" medication specially compounded by a pharmacy in the city of Templeton, northeast of here, for veterinary specifications. (No layman can get a pill into a cat, so this gel is the way to go -- just apply it to the inside of the ear flap and it's absorbed into the cat's system through the skin.)

For our first batch of syringes, a friend happened to be going over that way so he stopped to pick it up for me. He reported that his asking for the prescription for a cat named Butterball Knott (!) in an ostensibly human pharmacy caused some merriment among the other customers!

My cats still catch gophers on occasion, but given the size of the yard, it's too big a job for two cats. To avoid sinking and tripping in gopher tunnels and hoes, I use a cane in my own yard. (Not needed on hard, paved surfaces!)

Squirrels again provided me with Christmas decoration for my front door--they chew off small pine bough tips from a tree across the street (normal dental hygiene procedure of squirrels). (My tree has died.) I attach large red ribbons to the pine--perfect decor for this architecture.

The cats would not hold an interesting pose long enough for me to take some good pictures of them for this letter. What else can I come up with?

This holiday season's gluttony, fueled by a delectable array of gift cheeses, cookies, shortbread, fruit cake, and chocolates, is inimical to waistline maintenance: I feel the pinch around the waist already.

Again my apologies for the tardiness-- I HOPE I can get these mailed at least within the Twelve Days of

Christmas… So, belated Merry Christmas, and best wishes for the New Year!

2015

My apologies for being late! Just picture me still hard at work writing you over the New Year's weekend in a 57° house (heaters skyrocketing that to about 65°). I'm wearing <u>four</u> red sweaters, a charcoal-plaid thick British woolen skirt, regular stockings, and spiffy bright red socks with white polka dots! (Ralph Lauren stops at nothing to get my attention.) (Yes, his logo is on these socks.) And, I'm also wearing fleece-lined house booties.

Looking over the 2015 calendar, I find not much news material. Several "Met Live in HD" operas. Lots of movies. The Palm Theatre in San Luis Obispo, our "art theatre," with three screens, is the venue for most foreign and independent films. It also has once-a-month Sunday matinees of some special "oldies" with discussion by the theatre owner, his pal (a former video store owner) and the audience.

Went to a regional Stanford Alumni Club Christmas party in early December. I was chatting with one of the men about drought-resistant garden plants for our dried-up State of California, when he suddenly changed the subject to ask me if I liked cooking.

"Uh…….sometimes," I murmured.

"Well, you somehow remind me of Julia Child…."

I had to chuckle, and told him that happens quite a bit. The conversation then went on about his admiration for Julia and her TV cookery programs, and those with her subsequent collaborator French chef Jacques Pépin, who still has a show on PBS TV. I told him and another lady who had joined us that I'd heard Pépin interviewed about the time he was introduced to Julia preparatory to their first show together. Pépin said, "And here was this <u>great big woman</u> with a terrible voice!" We had a laugh about that, but agreed that the two had gotten on well together in their cooking shows.

I took only one trip to San Francisco--in March: the usual tax prep appointment, lunch with old pals from my former Stanford Medical Center job, and "doing" museums and art galleries in San Francisco.

At the end of August I was in Santa Barbara seeing friends and attending the Pacific Coast Open Final polo match. There were a few familiar players, and it was exciting, scoring closely till the end, with the Lucchese (boot-makers company) team winning.

A nice piece of news in November: The Carmel (Calif.) Library (Local History Room) wrote asking my permission (*re* my copyright) to put my 1997 speech on DVDs and on the Internet, along with all the other Local History Series lectures over the years.

This April 1997 program was entitled "Enduring Vision: The Camel Art Association Celebrates 70 Years," and honored the anniversary of its founding in 1927. Bill Stone, then President of the CAA and long a mover and shaker in that organization, spoke on the history of the Association, and I spoke on the career of my father, landscape and marine artist A. Harold Knott (1883-1977), as one of its founding members. I displayed several of his paintings "live," and the Librarian had also mounted an exhibit of some of his photos, memorabilia and equipment plus an oil painting in the lobby.

The "Enduring Vision" theme was perfect, and we ran with it: the vision of the founders in creating the Carmel Art Association, still thriving today, and my father's vision as an artist, which the audience could share through looking at his paintings.

Bill and I had so much fun putting on this program that he quipped, "We should take our show on the road!"

So now, 18 years later, the Library is "putting us on the road," as it were! Cool, huh? My 20 minutes of fame will now stretch through eternity!

World news today is horrific. I often think how thankful I am to have visited some of the now-troubled places when everything was peaceful and safe.

In the 1950s, for instance, some British archaeology-and classics-oriented cruises I took included the idyllic little Greek islands of Lesbos and Kos (where Hippocrates taught his medical school students under a tree). Now swamped by desperate refugees and migrants, and dead bodies washed ashore in the attempt to get there.

I visited the vast, magnificent Roman-style site of Palmyra in Syria in 1964--another British archaeologist-led tour, (twelve people in three rickety cars). Much of Palmyra's history and beauty have now been deliberately vandalized and destroyed by ISIS *et al.*

On that same tour, we stayed in one of the most charming hotels I've ever seen, in Homs (Syria)--a city now in ruins from civil war. It was a small house, my bedroom filled with an antique bed, huge pillows, and masses of fresh linens, laces, ruffles and crochet-work. In this Victorian-feeling room, it had seemed such an anomaly to awaken at dawn to the chant outside of a Muezzin calling the faithful to prayer.

That 1964 trip also brought a particularly moving moment to a handful of our group who joined fellow-passenger Bert White in his plea for an impromptu extra excursion. He wanted desperately to go from Homs to Hama (another badly-hammered city today) even though it was late afternoon, to "see the water wheel." This was a huge Roman-era wooden water wheel which creaked slowly round and round, scooping water from the Orontes River into an aqueduct high above. Bert wanted to revisit this site where he'd once been as a Captain in the British Army with Lawrence of Arabia's Arab regiment in the First World War. We arrived as it was growing dusk, and we sat down at the little cafe terrace next to the wheel. Bert fell speechless, eyes moist, thinking of his lost youth and long-lost friends. The rest of us sat in silence sipping our Arak, sharing his moment. The only sound--the creaking of the water wheel.

On a nearby street, a local man in black-and-white *keffiyeh* headdress strolled along nibbling a leaf from a head of Romaine lettuce (the way we might stroll eating an ice cream cone).

[A note about Bert's experience in the Great War--a Turkish soldier had slashed him across the back with a sword, and the only thing that saved his life was the thick leather Sam Browne Belt of his uniform (like a bandolier, worn diagonally over one shoulder across the back and chest).]

In 1976, I was floating up the Nile on a 1920s cruise boat (all wood-panelling, colorfully-uniformed Egyptian waiters and stewards) with another British group, this one led by an English Egyptologist. We trudged around tombs and temples of the Pharaonic era every day, the only inconveniences to speak of being the extreme heat, dust, flies, and sandstorms, and perhaps upset innards ("Gyppy Tummy").

Also in the '70s I went on a totally different type of British "tour" of Tunisia and Algeria, including part of the Sahara Desert, which was designed for people who like Extreme Camping. At that time it was the only tour I could find that included a lot of the wonderful ancient Roman remains--temples, military and domestic buildings, etc., with lovely floor mosaics.* (Camping to me is just a lot of hard work!) But again, no hazards other than extreme heat and dust, scorpions and vipers, and the continual quest for water!

[*Many beautiful mosaics have been lifted up and placed on walls at the treasure--filled Bardo Museum in Tunis, which was not long ago the site of a terrorist attack.]

So--just sharing a few memories of fascinating, long-ago travels in places it would not be convenient or safe to visit today. How lucky I was.

****

NATURE NOTES: As for many years now, no more frogs in the rain barrels. And it has not been a good year for my cats. They are "elderly" (14). Poor Butterball ("BB"), the orange-striped shorthair, was attacked by some creature when he got stuck outdoors and I was away for a few days. When I got back I found him with a gash in his side about 1 1/2 " in diameter with claw marks too wide to be from a domestic cat. I bundled him off to the veterinarian's, where he was hospitalized about a week, being stitched up, hydrated and medicated with antibiotics, etc. The vet could not figure out what had attacked him. A bobcat could have killed and eaten him, so either he escaped with his life from one, or from some other creature coming out of the State Park several blocks away.

My other cat, the Tuxedo longhair Jazz, may have had a bad scare outdoors about the same time; he's refused to go out ever since. Perhaps he escaped some predator unscathed, apart from apparent loss of his normal courage. He used to love to be outdoors all day. Now he just lies around on a table on the porch (after a few weeks on the washing machine).

Although BB was actually injured, once he'd recovered he resumed his daily outings. I've always kept them both indoors at night. However, BB developed another problem. He used to sleep on my bed (as a supplement to the electric blanket) but on several different occasions recently he started using the bed as a toilet! *Quelle horreur!* So I've had to banish him to the kitchen and porch, where Jazz has been sleeping anyway. (The litter boxes are on the porch.) So both cats are shut in there at night, where they can do the least harm. Or so I thought until Jazz knocked out a shaky old windowpane, letting BB out into the cold night and making the porch even colder! Next challenge, get a glazier to make a new window!

Our long California drought has been severe, but lately we've been getting a few light rains--my dead "lawn" came back to life! Weather people keep predicting a winter of heavy rains from the "El Níno" (warm ocean currents) effect, so we are hopeful.

I hope I can get these cards and letters posted at least within the Twelve Days of Christmas! At any rate, here's wishing a belated Merry Christmas and Happy New Year to all!

2016 - 2017

My apologies for the collapse of my Christmas card and letter writing last winter. I was still working on it on Friday, January 6, when my dear cat Jazz (Tuxedo longhair), age 16, became ill. I took him to the Veterinary Hospital on the Monday. He had kidney failure, and the Vet was unable to save him. I made my farewell visit to Jazz there on the Thursday, when he was very far gone, but was able to raise his head a few times. That was his last day of life. I was so upset at losing him, I just could not go on with the Christmas card project, and I piled all the drafts and cards into a box.

My other cat BB (official name Butterball, orange stripes) (same age) was utterly desolated, left forlorn without his adoptive brother, and his own health deteriorated. He already had hyperthyroidism and now developed kidney problems and "tummy trouble.s"

I became his private duty nurse, feeding him prescription diet food about every 2 hours, applying a transdermal gel medication for his thyroid problem twice a day, and cleaning out the litter 3 or 4 times a day, plus numerous "unauthorized deposits outside the box." By June the Vet said he needed subcutaneous hydration twice a week; I was not successful learning how to administer it, so I had to have a Vet Tech make house calls for this. The few times I had to be out of town, I had to board BB at the Vet's for his medical care.

He hung on for a few more months, a determined little fellow despite growing steadily weaker, especially in his legs, and died at home, in an unexpected hiding place, in mid-October.

Both cats were 16 years old, the equivalent of 86 human years. So I keep telling myself they had a very long life--but nevertheless, 16 calendar years seem too short.

Thus it's been a difficult and sad year, losing my "babies," who grew up together from the age of five months, always curling up together for their naps. So cute. I miss their perky, affectionate personalities so much. Rest in soft peace, my dear little furry friends.

****

Not much in the way of more positive news for 2017, just a few movies, Metropolitan Opera HD simulcasts, and the "tax prep trip" to San Francisco/Palo Alto in March, which is at least made more pleasant by seeing carious Bay Area friends. Also made the usual jaunt to Santa Barbara for the polo finals at the end of August.

In September the daughter of an old friend of mine who'd died earlier in the year asked me to be one of the tribute speakers at her mother's memorial service in the Stanford University Church. Daunting to think of "How will I make myself heard in such a huge building?!" But of course they have an excellent microphone system. The attendees were seated mainly in the front, and my friend's two daughters, who were up in the choir loft to sing a Mozart"Ave Verum," said they could hear me there too. I also gave them a printout of my talk, which highlighted some of the fun memories of my long friendship with their parents dating back to the sighteseeing excursions we'd made together when I first went to work in England so many years ago.

****

Thus far (as of December 10) a few pre-Christmas parties, and while I'm drafting this letter, darkness has fallen on the land. Since about 9:30 am it has become so dark with yellowish smoke from the fires in Southern California I had to turn on the lights. [Less smoke here on subsequent days.]

I'll close this 2017 portion with best wishes for Christmas and the New Year. And my many thanks to all who went me cards and letters despite my failure to reciprocate.

****

And I'll append here some of what I'd prepared (as of a 5th draft) for the 2016 letter.

****

2016 (5ᵗʰ Draft)

Attended various Met Live in HD opera performance in San Luis Obispo. I was most keen to see their *Tristan and Isolde,* because the male lead, Stuart Skelton, had some years ago sung for our Wagner Society Christmas party in San

Francisco. A big, happy Australian chap who was then at the "up-and-coming" stage of his career. He had sung *"In Fortnum Land"* for us (from Lohengrin), always a hit with Wagner buffs. The Metropolitan's *Trisan* production didn't grab me, however--the volume was too low. But it was great to see someone I'd met long ago, now a star in the Big Time Metropolitan.

The Pacific Coast Open Final polo match in Santa Barbara (August) provided a bit of a shock when one horse and rider fell. The horse lay motionless on its side, bringing a great cry of anguish from the spectators. Then in a few minutes the horse rallied, scrambled to its feet, and scampered off the field -- "I'm outta here!" -- to hide behind the stalls. Laughter, cheers and applause from the audience! (Note that they were more anxious about the horse than about the rider.)

At midpoint in the game, a female staff member began hurling souvenir polo balls into the audience, as a PR stunt. One ball was coming straight at me, and I ducked to avoid getting hit in the head. It landed--plop!--right in my large open tote bag! (It turned out to be made of soft rubber, a useful hand-squeeze-exercise tool when one is sitting before BBC World News on TV.)

During 2016 my cats, semi-retired, were still quite active indoors and out.

****

TRAVEL MEMORIES:

After reading my 2015 letter, a number of my readers (fans?) wrote me that they'd particularly enjoyed my reminiscences of travel in the Middle East years ago, when all was peaceful and safe. So I thought I'd report on a memorable day in Jordan, part of that British tour I took in 1964 (prior to my leaving my job and residence in London). The tour comprised historic and archaeological sites in Lebanon, Syria, and Jordan, with a few of us afterwards proceeding independently to tour in Israel.

This was a small group, 11 people plus a young English archaeologist as courier/guide/lecturer, traveling in three old cars with local Arab drivers, whose philosophy may have had some effect on their carefree driving style ("nothing happens unless it is written" ?) (e.g. a bit rambunctious in city traffic, or barreling up a highway on the wrong side of the road while approaching the crest of a hill.)

An outstanding site in Jordan is Petra, "the Rose-Red City half as old as time," carved out of the red rock face in ancient times by the Nabatean tribe, who lived on protection rackets, preying on traders' caravans.

The Petra site was approached through a long, narrow, canyon-like defile called the Siq, which then spread out as the center of the bowl-like village, with "buildings" and caves carved out of the high walls of rock all around.

When we were there, it had not yet been much developed for tourism--a bit like roughing it. You had to enter via the Siq on scrawny horses, and the only place to stay inside was a barracks-like building, everyone having to share rooms <u>and beds</u> with 3 or 4 other people. (Imagine the snoring!) Food was tinned stuff like beans, that could be heated up on spirit lamps, which also provided light.

There was another English lady archaeologist having her meals there, who said she had "taken a suite of caves for the season," along with her local guide/assistant.

Our first sightseeing goal was to climb up a rough rock face to a flatter surface on top, where a basin had been carved out by the Nabateans to perform their child-sacrifice rites, slitting teh children open so their blood could run down a carved-out channel. Since I was the youngest member of our group, they said I had to go. So I sat down in the basin while another member took pictures of us, the "grownups" standing behind me in jovial anticipation of my slaughter. (Clambering up and down this rough site was a challenge, I might add, even for "young" me.)

The following day four of us chose to make an optional run down to Aqaba on our own, while the others would stay and climb some more rocky sites. Having learned of Aqaba in the movie *"Lawrence of Arabia,"* I was keen to go there.

As we started our horseback ride out of the Siq, I was photographing the man and horse directly in front of me, Mr. G - a frail little erudite gentleman in his 70's. I had my head down to look in the viewfinder of my old-fashioned Box Brownie camera, and when I looked up, I saw that what I'd photographed was Mr. G falling off his horse, with the Arab groom trying to catch him.

The others in the group froze--a lady in her 70's, and a man in his 50's--neither of whom had any experience of horses. So as the youngest, most agile person, and comfortable with horses, I leapt off my mount and rushed to his rescue. The groom and I managed to hoist Mr. G. back onto the saddle and held him on till we reached the Siq entrance and our car. Mr. G had fainted. My trusty shoulder bag of travel gear contained old-fashioned smelling salts, which I waved under his nose trying to revive him. I sat in the back seat of the car propping him up, while he kept falling over in a faint, and I kept trying to revive him. It seems he had eaten no breakfast after that strenuous climb the day before, and he had low blood pressure.

As we took off, speeding through the Wadi Rum desert, (seen in the *Lawrence* film)--our happy-go-lucky Arab driver pulled out his bottle of Arak (high alcohol content up to 63%), waving it about and swilling it freely as we raced along. ("Don't drink and drive" ?) (Arak is meant to be diluted with water. Based on Anise, it is similar to the Greek Ouzo or Turkish Raki.)

Along the way, coming in the other direction, we passed a grand-looking Arab arrayed in black robes on a handsomely-garbed camel, festooned with fringes and decorations. I was delighted to see an important-looking Sheikh who looked the way Omar Sharif did in the movie!

We came to a government outpost, a Beau-Geste-looking, crenellated mud brick building, with a couple of uniformed police and a couple of Army soldiers on duty, who warmly welcomed us, all smiles, with Bedouin Tea (containing some mint and lots of sugar), served in small glass cups in decorative metal holders. They also served us some lovely chocolate candies, in honor of the Muslim equivalent of Easter, celebrating Mohammed's ascension into heaven. These refreshment perked up Mr. G, and we proceeded on to Aqaba.

At that long-ago time, there was only one very tiny, modest German hotel at Aqaba, with a sprinkling of German sun-seekers. While the "old folks" sat on a shaded veranda taking refreshments that brought Mr. G back to his old self, I rented a floral-patterned German bathing suit and changed in one of the little cabanas, for a swim. Note that the movie sequence of Aqaba was filmed somewhere else, showing ocean waves. There are no waves at Aqaba--it is at the tip of a long, narrow bay off the Red Sea--and the water is absolutely still.

After we'd all had a good lunch at the hotel and everyone felt great again, we drove back to Petra to rejoin our group, where, feigning modesty, I basked a bit in the praises for my "taking care of Mr. G." -heroine of an adventurous day.

I've been shocked to learn over the years how commercialized Petra has become--fancy hotels and restaurants in the area and at Aqaba as well, with "Bedouin-desert-camp excursions," etc. Not only am I happy that I saw this area in time of Middle East peace, I saw things in a far less commercial mode. I can't blame Jordan for capitalizing on a valuable tourist asset--but for me, it was more fun being there in simpler times.

****

In closing I must tell you of the most unusual, colorful Christmas card I received in 2016 from a Japanese lady in Tokyo whom I'd met years ago at the Bayreuth Wagner opera festival. It depicts a large sports arena viewed from high in the stands. Two Sumo wrestlers are grappling it out on a stage in the center. A couple of Christmas trees are positioned among the audience, and the entire audience is wearing Santa Claus costumes!

2018

Another year has flown by--with a few unpleasantries such as repairing gas leaks, replacement of clothes dryer and water heater, and other domestic annoyances, ("What a bore," as some of my English friends would have said.)

But the year had more pleasant highlights too. A few Metropolitan Opera "Live in HD" simulcasts and a few movies (the most fun being "Paddington II"). Several lecture series, two on Biblical topics by a semi-retired professor of Comparative Religion & Philosophy. Another series on topics by speakers in different fields, including one about a favorite American humorist, S.J. Perelman, whose writings I've greatly enjoyed. Now I've learned that he'd also done pieces for the Broadway stage and films.

In March I made my annual trek to San Francisco/Palo Alto for the tax preparer appointment, followed by lunch with a few colleagues from my days in Stanford Medical Center's Cardiology Department.

That trip also included an elegant tea given by the San Francisco Opera for the Bel Canto Society. Beautiful décor (the invitations, place cards and menus all depicting the same floral and leaf arrangement which was "live" on the tables). Oceans of champagne, tea and hors d'oeuvres-type snacks (not the general little English mini-sandwiches), and fancy pastries. An opera official gave a talk on past and future productions, and two young singers rendered some arias for us.

At the end of this party a friend and I stayed at our table a while, waiting for the crowd to thin out so that we could get taxis at the entrance. One of the Opera's lady officials came over to chat with us, and then treated me to a ride with "Lyft" -- showing me how the system works, ordering on the phone, seeing the driver and vehicle identification, and watching it move through the streets on the phone screen. I had never done this before, since I don't have an i-phone. I thought it was a fascinating process, and I enjoyed the ride back to my hotel. This sort of thing is a real asset in a city where it's hard to catch an ordinary taxi.

In June I chanced upon the TV broadcast of the Royal Ascot Races in England, and what a magnificent show that was! The Queen and entourage arriving in horse-drawn carriages (and Her Majesty presenting one of the prize cups). Everyone in fabulous attire--ladies in beautiful dresses and fabulous hats, gentlemen in top hats and tails, etc. (There is a Dress Code!) A happy, enthusiastic crowd, interviews with owners, trainers, jockeys and celebrities etc. Many races, and you also heard heart-warming histories of some of the horses. I happened to catch just the last two days of this five-day event. It's well worth getting up before dawn for such an enjoyable event. I've marked my calendar for next year-- NBCTV is going to continue producing the simulcasts.

I've also seen a few of the major American horse races. (Even just watching on TV one gets caught up in the vigorous enthusiasm of New Yorkers attending the Belmont Stakes!)

I took a short trip to Santa Barbara in July, which included a free concert (a master class in cello -- three young performers) at the Music Academy of the West. (Free because my friend who lives in S.B. is a volunteer usher for some of the Academy's many music festival events that run all summer).

Went to Santa Barbara again over the Labor Day weekend for the Pacific Coast Open Final polo match, always fun. This time we had to book ahead (at greater cost) in order to get our good seats in the shaded grandstand. Previously all seats were the same price and on a "first arrive, first serve" basis.

In November I gave a talk for the local chapter of the AAUW (American Assn. of University Women), along with Marti Lindholm, who is the program chair. Her topic was her Middle East trip earlier this year, with emphasis on the "Palestinian situation." I spoke about my Middle East trip in (gasp!) 1963, which focused on history and archaeology. In my talk I covered mostly experiences in Syria, because obviously she did not go there. I also touched on a few aspects of Palestinian matters and a bit on my adventures in Petra and Aqaba (Jordan).

We displayed some photos and memorabilia on side tables, and Marti also showed some photos from her computer on a large TV screen. We had a full house and a responsive audience, and I garnered some very nice compliments!

My fellow speaker wants us to repeat our program for the parishioners of St. Peter's (Episcopal) Church sometime in the New Year, so you could say we're "taking our show on the road," so to speak -- albeit in the same meeting room, the Church's social hall. OK by me!

NATURE NOTES: As I wrote last year, my beloved cats Jazz and BB died in 2017, and I'm desolated without them. I was so exhausted by almost a year of being BB's private duty nurse round the clock (feeding prescription diet every 2 hours, cleaning up multiple "accidents" every day, etc., that I was not ready to take on a new cat yet. But I hope to get one after the holidays.

Some time after departure of the cats, I acquired a Resident Mouse, who I think may possibly have invited a friend or relative or two as well, to share the great cuisine he finds here. He has gnawed away at avocados and fruit in the fruit bowls, so I had to put heavy covers on the bowls. He has also gnawed into the wrappers of chocolate bars (now secured in a heavily-covered bowl). I never know where he will strike next. I have even seen him scampering in the living room, hoping I'll leave snacks near the TV set. (I've also seen a mouse inside the outdoor garbage can--probably a relative of the Indoor Resident.) I don't want to use traps and poison, so I trust that my next cat will be professional and take care of any rodent invaders--Nature's Way.

I have intermittent plagues of ants, too. They swarm in the thousands -- some for general food scraps before I get them into the garbage -- some preferring greasy things (esp. chicken) and some seeking sweets (even getting into a tightly secured screw-top jaw of sugar -- how on earth do they squeeze through that?)

Ants also seek water -- showing up occasionally in the bathroom (no food there)--and even in the ironing and dryer room (no food there either)-- where they invaded the steam iron! So I have to plug that with a rag when not in use. I may have boiled a few ants when I first turned on the iron, but at any rate it still works.

I'm amazed at how such tiny creatures as mice and ants know exactly where they're going and why, and how to get there -- to obtain food and water.

Even though I have no cat at present, I still put a bowl of drinking water outdoors for such wildlife as turns up (whom I never actually see.) I know I have a skunk who sleeps in the crawl space under the house, because occasionally when some other animal disturbs him, he deploys his terrible scent (his "weapon of mass stinktion," to coin a phrase?). I think I get visits from a raccoon, or a possum as well--or all of these. They drink most of the water and leave a bit of dirt in the bowl, rubbed off their low-lying fur:
I can't begrudge these creatures a drink of water.

****

A few Christmas parties have started off the holiday season, and I've received a lovely arrangement of evergreen foliage for my front door; hand-made by a friend from Washington State. I added my own big red ribbon bow to its top, and it looks splendid--just right for this architecture.

****

That's about all for now. Hope all is well with you and yours, and I look forward to hearing your news. Best wishes for a Happy Christmas and New Year!

Other Writing and Speeches

Travel Writing Workshop - 1985

In addition to her final paper, the following letter to Harleigh's instructor is included to add context. - Editors

Dear Mrs. Z.,

> Re: Travel Writing Workshop
> San Francisco State - Nov. 2 & 3, 1985

Thanks for your postcard. I obtained a catalog from S.F. State and registered. They sent me TWO student body cards! But I'm afraid ONE article is all I can manage at the moment, however!

The enclosed article of about 1000 words may still be too long for newspapers. I seem to have a "pruning problem!" I've hacked away at it and cut out two other episodes which seemed to border on the humorous. Remembering the guidelines about unity of tone I amputated them from the more serious ones that remain. This is in about the seventh draft stage.

I've been studying some 500-word roundups by a regular freelance contributor to the L.A. <u>Times</u> travel section. Fourteen paragraphs of two to four sentences each, first half didactic, second half an ego-trip laundry list of her experiences illustrating her point. She uses the word "I" <u>23 times</u> -- and gets published regularly! She does have a felicitous turn of phrase quite often. But there isn't much feeling or sharing taking place in such a rapid-fire delivery.

Lisl Dennis in her travel photography book points out the growing segment of "fourth tier" in the travelling public which seeks a return to "experiential travel," and this is the audience I most want to address. I want to share more of the experience and the emotions with readers, to "take them with me."

I have a few questions:

(1) Is it really possible to share enough experience and feeling in less than 1000 words??!!

(2) Should this article be chopped down even further than the three examples given, and if so, which should go?

(3) I dislike having to continually refer to myself, "I, I, I" -- yet since this is personal experience and these things happened to me, I don't know how to avoid it.

(4) You have mentioned the use of "authority" as a guideline for nonfiction. Since this piece is personal experience/travel, I haven't really included an authority. I did give occupations of several people in one of the examples as a sort of validation of the point and indication of the type of people I am involved with.

(a) Will that suffice?
(b) Can one do without the "authority" altogether in a purely personal experience piece?

(5) Have I been too didactic and bossy at the start? I would have a tendency to do so, and I don't want to turn readers off.
      I tried to tone it down by saying "I have learned..." etc.

(6) Am I "showing," not "telling"? Find it hard to evaluate after looking at it so long.

(7) I don't know what to call a "horse attendant"--he wasn't a stable boy because there was no stable; he wasn't a groom because the horses obviously got no grooming! There must be a word but nothing in Roget's seems quite accurate at this point. He might even have owned one of the horses, but I think it was more likely he worked for the owner.

(8) The episode in Jordan took place before Arabs and the PLO terrorists had antagonized public opinion. I'm worried that references to Arabs and the Jordanian Army might be a turnoff to editors and readers. Do you think this could still "fly" today?

(9) Have used "CLOUDED TRAVEL, SHINING MEMORIES" as a working title, but am undecided. Other possibilities include:
>Travel Clouds, Shining Silver Memories
>Travel Clouds, Treasured Memories
>Travel Cloud? Polish That Silver Lining
>Clouded Travel or Sparkling Treasure?

Many thanks.   I look forward to the class, your professional critique, and the feedback and reactions of the group.

If I have room in my suitcase (on top of opera clothing!) *I'll try to bring some L.A. <u>Times</u> magazine sections and travel sections for you and the class. Quite a few have stacked up here.

Kindest regards.

Sincerely,

Harleigh
Knott

Encl.

*Maybe there's a story in that--glamorous opera gowns by grotty Greyhound bus!

****

CLOUDED TRAVEL, SHINING MEMORIES

CHRISTMAS GREETINGS FROM A REMARKABLE LIFE

by

Harleigh Thayer Knott
October 21st, 1985

If the cloud of illness or accident starts to cast a pall over a long-anticipated journey, keep an eye out for the sparkle of its silver lining--it could become the sterling highlight of your trip.

During various trips abroad I discovered that some compensating factor arises from mishaps. I learned to enrich my travel experience by focusing on those silver linings instead of grumbling and boring my friends back home with a litany of woes.

One of the woes plaguing the traveller who hurtles from climate to climate, fatigued by jet lag, the common cold can threaten to blight a journey. The weariness and malaise of such sniffles once forced me to forego climbing among all the archaeological excavations of the Hellenistic city Pergamom in Turkey with a Mediterranean cruise group. Discouraged, I sat on the steps of the Temple of Zeus to rest and commune with the ancient gods and ponder ancient history. Instead, contemporary Turkish life headed directly toward me. A colorful group of Turkish women and girls, some in traditional folk costume, some in modern clothes, climbed straight up the hill and arranged themselves and their baskets of food at the other end of the temple.

They removed their tea things from newspaper wrappings and spread them on the steps. One of the girls sang and played a guitar. Wreathed in smiles, they all watched while one of the girls shyly, graciously brought me a glass of sweetened tea and delicate almond cakes.

Moved by this warm hospitality extending across ethnic and language differences, I forgot my respiratory complaints. This wasn't a "tourist thing" — this was real! And so was my cloud's silver lining. I drained tea from a glass in a silver filigree frame; my cup of joy ran over.

I never remember the cold; I never forget the kindness of the Turkish women, the mosaic of colors and patterns of their clothing, the lilt of their folk songs rising up the slopes of the mountain. Their tea had seemed the more refreshing for being served in a glass, their little cakes the daintier for being served in newspaper. Their tea party had become my tea party, and my Turkish delight.

I learned on another trip that an adverse event can lead to ties with strangers from one's own western culture as well. I was eating lunch at an hotel in Potsdam on a hot August day at the start of a British art treasures tour of East Germany. A bee flew in the window and stung me on the arm.

Simultaneously the bee stung my cool, reserved English group into life.

Floods of sympathy, solicitude and tubes of antihistamine ointments poured in on me from all sides.

I became the center of attention for a professor, an architect, a lawyer, an archivist, an author, all sorts of interesting people practically at my feet. My bee sting proved such a great icebreaker that I ceased to notice the pain. It served as a conversation piece as we chronicled my recovery, evaluated the merits of various medications and listened to one another's bee stories.

Conversations progressed from such ephemera to discussions of art history and other deeper aspects of travel. The bee sting was ridiculous, its pain minor and of short duration. It never had a chance to cloud my trip. The whole network of friendships launched in it remain lifelong shining treasures.

At times when I've had no difficulties of my own, I've found that someone else's disaster could cause distress and inconvenience for everyone, yet still add a positive dimension to the trip. Touring the Middle East with a small group before the current rash of wars and terrorism, four of us decided to leave our group at Petra in Jordan for a day in order to cross the "Lawrence of Arabia" country of the Wadi Rhum desert to Aqaba on the coast.

Riding horseback out from the rock-hewn remains of Petra through the long, narrow, steep-walled gorge leading back to our car, I busied myself with my camera. Looking up, aghast, I saw that the elderly man ahead of me had fallen off his horse and lay crumpled and inert on the stony ground.

Our other two companions froze, speechless in fear and horror, inept in the face of emergency, inept even in getting on and off horses.

I leapt off my horse and ran over to administer a whiff of smelling salts from my first aid kit to revive him. It was an old-fashioned effort, but the only thing I knew about at the time, and it seemed to work.

Low blood pressure, we later learned, combined with fatigue and a lack of breakfast had caused his collapse. But because of his age we had all feared the worst possible scenarios. I helped him back on his horse and instructed the Arab horse-attendant to hold him on it until we got safely to our car.

I continued my amateur nursing as our frail friend fainted again in the car. Speeding through the desert, we felt alone and helpless.

Suddenly the Beau-Geste silhouette of crenellated mud brick walls at a Jordanian Army outpost came into view, putting new heart and hope into us. Help at hand! The soldiers brought us glasses of sweet Bedouin tea that perked up our "patient" and lifted our spirits. And they passed around chocolate candies, in celebration of the Muslim equivalent of Easter.

This emergency stop rallied us for the remainder our our excursion. Our friend returned to his normal spry state after a good meal and a rest at Aqaba. We returned to our group thankful and happy at the outcome.

The crisis, a frightening black cloud over our trip, had brought us adventure and the warmth of Arab hospitality. The sparkle from this cloud's sterling silver lining shone in the eyes of our recovered elderly friend. And I have to admit I basked a bit in the praise of the passengers who raved to our courier about how "marvelous" I'd been.

The silver lining's sparkle had even shone on me.

Rachel Knott's "Morro Miscellany"

I was asked to speak about my mother, Rachel Knott, because it was she who took the initiative and did all the groundwork to get this AAUW chapter organized in Morro Bay in the mid-1950's.

Your program chair asked me not only to give my mother's life story but the entire history of Morro Bay. This is not possible.

What I <u>can</u> do is give an overview of my mother' s life, and touch a bit on the creative period here in Morro Bay in the 1930's.

So, like the title of her book, this talk will be a "Morro Miscellany."

I've given two talks to this group in the past about my parents, but we have many new members since then. So anyone who has heard this before may snooze.

****

My mother was born Rachel Louise Thayer in Norwich, Conn., 1892. Her family on both sides was descended from 17th century English settlers. Her father was Mayor of Norwich for many years and her uncle was a Connecticut Supreme Court Justice. Her father even tried for the Governorship, but did not get the nomination. So she grew up with an early awareness of, and interest in, political matters.

She attended a private elementary school and Norwich Free Academy secondary school, as well as a school for young ladies in Virginia.

She then ventured forth to become governess to two little English boys. Their father was running the Cerro de Pasco Copper Mines in Peru.

The long ocean Voyage from New York, down one side of South America and up the other, and then life in a British and American expatriate colony high in the Andes was one of the great adventures of her life.

And then she fell in love with the Canadian doctor on the company's staff, which added romance to the mix.

****

The First World War broke out in 1914 and her Canadian fiancé joined the Army and was sent to the Front in France.

The new Panama Canal had opened up in time for Rachel's return trip home at the end of her South American stay. This made the voyage back to New York much shorter.

While the War was still on, she undertook her second major adventure, sailing from New York to England in the midst of the submarine warfare. Her ship had to zigzag all the way across the Atlantic to avoid being torpedoed by German subs.

(She once told me the way to prevent seasickness was to sip champagne and nibble dainty little chicken tea-sandwiches. I wonder whether these amenities were available on that wartime sailing!)

****

She married Captain Harry Dunlop in London—on leave from his war duties. She stayed in London with the English family she'd been with in Peru, while he returned to duty in France.

Tragedy struck when Captain Dunlop was killed by shrapnel only a week before the war ended in November 1918.

****

Thus Rachel entered a new chapter in her life: As a young widow at loose ends, she returned to the United States to stay briefly with her married sister's family in Connecticut. She did a bit of traveling, including a look at the Wild West on a Wyoming Dude Ranch.

She decided to go to college, and settled on Stanford University, where she had a double major in English and

Classics (i.e. Greek and Latin). Since she was older than the flapper girls in her class, most of her college pals were grad students. She was elected to Phi Beta Kappa and she graduated in 1926.

After college she spent some time in Santa Fé, New Mexico, perhaps drawn by its exoticism, from the east coast point of view, and by the literary and artistic ambiance in that region at the time.

She found the various Indian tribes and their handicrafts of great interest, to the extent that when she moved to Carmel, California, she opened a little shop featuring some of the Indian work in Monterey in 1927.

****

In Carmel she met her second husband, the artist A. Harold Knott, a landscape and marine painter who was also working as a designer of houses for a builder there.

Harold, like her first husband, was also from Canada, born in Toronto in 1883. But when he was about five his family moved to Burlington, Vermont, where he grew up. (He said the Vermont Yankees called them "Redcoats.")

He had studied Applied Design at Pratt Institute in Brooklyn and did his fine art training at the Art Students League in New York and the Byrdcliffe Art Colony in Woodstock, under leading teachers of the day.

He had worked as a designer in New York and Washington, Colorado and Arizona, where he also taught painting, before moving to the art colony at Laguna Beach and then to Carmel by 1922.

****

So romance blossomed once again for Rachel, in Carmel. She and Harold thought Carmel was already "being ruined" by development in 1928. Mind you, it was still all dirt roads! So when they got married that year, they moved to what looked like an "unspoiled" little seaside village at Morro Bay.

Their plan was to spend two years here and then go to England and France. But the stock market Crash of 1929 and the Great Depression put an end to those dreams, and they remained in Morro Bay.

They bought a Cape Cod style house, which they christened "Little House of River Winds," although there' s no river here. It seems to be a romantic name they copied from a place they had seen in Carmel.

****

The Central Coast area was rich in scenery for the artist Harold to paint. There were two other professional artists here, Aaron Kilpatrick, who traveled a lot and had another home in Eagle Rock, and Charles "Robby" Robinson, who had retired here from teaching art in the Midwest. Many other visiting artists painted here from time to time.

Morro Bay had a lively little British colony, which made for a congenial milieu, and enriched the cultural dimensions of the town.

In the early 1930's, Olive Cotter, an Anglo-Irish lady Belfast, opened "The Picture Shop" (nov Pizza Port) , where she sold photos and curios and processed film. She expanded the operation to include an art gallery—the first one in the whole county. Local artists showed their work there, and the gallery received notice in various media.

Local and visiting artists as well as amateurs met at the shop weekly as an informal "Sketch Club." They practiced their drawing skills by doing portraits of anyone they could drag in to pose.

****

Theatrical productions were another highlight Of 1930's Morro Bay. Local citizens, including children, produced and performed in these shows.

(My own show business career aborted after I appeared as Humpty Dumpty in a scratchy white buckram shell.)

Morro Bay's theatre was also used for showing motion pictures. The stage and the projection room are still there. You can find the place by its decorative rows of electric light sockets which remain in place, on the outside of the antique shop opposite the Bank Of America.

****

Rachel Knott's forte was writing, and she wrote and published her own booklet <u>A Morro Miscellany</u>," in 1932. The cover was designed by Harold. This booklet contains verse, notes on the changing seasons in Morro Bay, a short mystery story based on a factual event here on the coast, and a one-act play, based on a local legend.

Rachel was also one of the prime movers and editors in producing the <u>Scribblers' Quarterly</u>. This was Morro Bay's own literary magazine. In addition to Rachel, its editors and contributing writers included, among others, the local doctor Jack Levitt, the Englishman Miles Castle, the artist Robby Robinson, the abalone diver Delmar Reviea, a professional writer Vera Woosley, and the telephone operator Billie Frazier.

(Remember, this is the era when you hand-cranked your telephone to reach the live operator, gave her the number you wanted, and she connected you.)

The covers of one issue of this magazine had a woodblock print design on pieces of wallpaper, soaked in paraffin wax, to simulate a glossy. Other issues also featured woodblock cover designs but on more conventional stock.

The magazine' s subject matter included verse, short-short stories, articles, and essays.

Here is a bit of Rachel's light verse:

The title is "BEAM."

> I am perfect
> That is why
> I pluck the mote
> From my brother's eye.

> Think how much better
> He will be
> When it is delicately
> Removed by me.

And here is her poem about a meeting of the Scribblers' group at Miles Castle's house:

First I'll explain a bit: TUDOR COTTAGE is the adobe house in English Tudor style Miles Castle built for himself. WINDSOR is his dog. ROBBY is the white-bearded artist Charles "Robby" Robinson. The MEDICO is Dr. Jack Levitt. His wife a nurse wearing her white uniform and a blue cape. BILLIE is Billie Frazier, the town's telephone operator. BETTY is a friend of hers whose last name I don't know. POSEIDON'S FOSTER SON is Delmar Reviea, the abalone diver. The ABSENT MEMBER IN gold Country is Vera Woosley, a professional writer. THIS ANCIENT DAME is Rachel Knott who wrote this poem.

The title is "THE SCRIBBLERS AT TUDOR COTTAGE. "

The singing of the kettle on its iron crane
Mingled with moan of wind and beat of rain,
As watery gusts defied the sturdy door,
And crept in stealthy rivulets upon the floor,
The sharp-toothed <u>Findsor</u>, weary of his play,
Curled on the rug and wished we'd go away;
And there was much good talk and laughter ringing
Above the sigh of wind and kettle's singing,
While eight around the hearth and roaring fire,
Pointed the heights to which the <u>Quarterly</u> doth aspire.
Of course beloved <u>Robby</u> graced the Chair,
And strove for order by foul means or fair;
With his benign white head so young, though hoary,
Nodded approval to each new-read story.
Our witty medico roused laughter to high heaven
With his new "Morro Winter Sports of Thirty-Seven";
And his good spouse, a picture was that night

As she stepped from the storm into the light,
In rippling cape of blue and dress of white.
Billie and Betty, that Siamese pair,
Curled on the sofa forsaking his draughty chair,
The deep-sea diver, Poseidon's foster son,
Toasted his shanks, and added to the fun,
Telling how abalones walk and flowers have living light
Beneath the sea, and whether stingraees can really bite!
The host, the Scribbler's poet, the Builder of the House,
Threw on great logs and poked the fire to rouse
New warmth, fresh blaze; bore in the fragrant brew
Of tea and coffee, and this was but the cue
For more good talk and laughter ringing
Above the wail of wind and kettle's singing.
While the Absent Member's spirit hovered there,
Lending an aura to one vacant chair;
She in the cold Gold Country was much missed,
And all to her in thought their fingers kissed!
The clock, had there been clock, would have ticked
To show how swift the wild, wet, windy evening had gone.
Thus to record the Scribbler's hours there came
And went into the mud and storm, this ancient dame.

Rachel also contributed pieces to both the San Luis paper and the Morro Bay <u>SUN</u>.

Incidentally, you would enjoy reading through some of those old SUN newspapers on microfilm at the San Luis library.......

****

      As the Depression wore on, the WPA set up a Recreation Project. Various arts and crafts classes were taught by local people for both children and adults. This was in the Spanish-style building on lover Kings Avenue (now residential).

****

Morro Bay was in the thick of things during WWII. A Japanese sub came here directly Pearl Harbor, torpedoed and sank an oil tanker just off our coast, December 23, 1941. The Navy base where the plant nov stands operated landing-craft rehearsals with the Army from Camp San Luis Obispo. The Army filled the areas where Cuesta College and the prison now stand. Gunfire, flame-throwers burning up the hillsides, tanks, trucks, jeeps and obstacle-course physical training livened up this area considerably.

To help ease the wartime housing shortage the Knotts moved into someone else's tiny vacation home and rented out their house to military families, dividing the place into two apartments.

****

After the war I went away to college and then off to my own life elsewhere. I was working overseas in the 1950's when my mother's letters began to include descriptions of what a time she was having trying to line up enough college-educated women (through an ad in the paper) to form an AAUW chapter. She described the bureaucratic red tape involved in the process.

The population here at the start of the War was about 400 to 500 souls. In such a small town there were not many women as well educated as she was. But the town was growing rapidly in the postwar decade, and was soon to have its own high school. She felt an AAUW chapter would provide a focal point for the handful of educated women already here plus the incoming teachers . She wanted all these women to have a forum where they could meet with people in their own league.

In the early winter of 1956 she wrote that she had finally signed up the requisite number of members and received an official OK from AAUW headquarters. She was asking Clara Froggatt to carry the ball from there, and Clara agreed to do so.

My mother then suddenly died, January 17, 1957.

****

So I have always felt this AAUW Chapter has been a living memorial to her. She would be so pleased to see that her vision came true and that it remains a vital force in the community.

Thank you.

Speech to AAUW on 1964 Trip to Middle East

November 9ᵗʰ, 2018

In 1964 I had been working in London, and in April I went on a British tour through LEBANON, SYRIA and JORDAN. It was led by an English archaeologist with a doctorate and background in working on digs at Jericho. Palmyra Qumran (site of the Dead Sea Scrolls), and others.

I'll focus now mainly on SYRIA, currently in such a troubled state.

A few photos are displayed on the table.....

We'd visited the vast Roman-style site of PALMYRA. Now much of it has been deliberately vandalized or destroyed by ISIS and others.

I've thought of my little hotel room in HOMS, a city now in ruins from the Syrian Civil War. It had an antique bed, huge pillows, masses or fresh white linens, laces, ruffles and crochet work. It felt like a Victorian anomaly, when I awakened at dawn to the chant or a Muezzin calling the faithful to prayer.

Our group comprised 13 people, all British except me, traveling in three rickety old cars with local Arab drivers who had a carefree driving style -- "Nothing happens unless it is written"? In other words, a bit rambunctious in city traffic, or barreling up a highway on the wrong side of the road approaching the crest of a hill.

When we got to HOMS in SYRIA on a late afternoon, Bert White pleaded for an extra impromptu run to HAMA, to see the water wheels. He had been there in the British Army with LAWRENCE of ARABIA'S Arab regiment in FIRST WORLD WAR, and longed to revisit the site. Huge water wheels dating back centuries creak round and round, scooping up water from the Orontes River into an aqueduct above.

So a few of us took off with one of the cars and raced through the desert, passing picturesque mud beehive houses on the way, arriving at RAIVIA as it was growing dusk.

We sat down at a little café terrace next to a water wheel. Bert fell speechless, eyes moist, thinking of his lost youth. The rest of us sat in silence, sipping Arak, sharing his moment. The only sound the creaking of the water wheel.

(Later we learned that HAMA had had a political uprising against the Baathist Regime, a few days after we left. The Syrian Army and Air Force bombed it back into submission.)

Bert's experience in the Great War was our living link with history. A Turkish soldier had slashed him across the back with a sword. What saved his life was the thick leather Sam Browne Belt of his uniform. (That is like a bandolier, worn diagonally over one shoulder across the back and chest.)

Our tour had begun in towns and cities. When we got to a desert area pausing for a brief stop, a Bedouin tribe came heading toward us. We were apprehensive, but Bert strode out toward them alone with a big smile and outstretched hand. They greeted him warmly, effusively. When he returned to us, we exclaimed at his courage. He explained that you must always exude confidence, and must never show fear. If you are part of an Arab military unit and show fear, they will kill you, because you'd be considered a liability in battle.

Bert was a handsome, hearty chap with a shock of white hair, and a civilian career as a prosperous builder. He also pioneered in designing user-friendly houses especially for seniors, a relatively new idea at the time.

Other interesting people in our group were two Jewish women. Lady Choimonderey and her friend Miss Elliot. Since the tour was to Arab countries which were at that time refusing entry to Jews, the travel company had to request passengers to affirm that they were Christian in order to be allowed in. These two ladies said they were so keen to take the tour that they were willing to falsify their religion in order to be allowed entry.

I didn't know Lady Cholmondeley's background at the time, but subsequently learned that she was a member of the Sassoon family, whose forebear was a rich IRAQI Jew with vast trading interests all through the Middle East, India and China. He had been given a title for services rendered to the British Empire and settled in England. She also had a Rothschild in her family tree.

One highlight of SYRIA is the massive Crusader Castle fortress, KRAK DES CHEVALIERS.

The city of DAMASCUS is a high point. It has a large Souk (bazaar) for shopping, and the OMAYYAD MOSQUE with gorgeous Persian rugs that require your changing into floppy slippers to enter.

You'll also see two grand sarcophagi side by side for the Muslims' hero leader SALADIN, who defeated the Crusaders, ejecting them out of the Holy Land. One contains his body, the other being a gift from an admirer, Kaiser Wilhelm of Germany.

There is the STREET CALLED STRAIGHT, where Saul of Tarsus, a dedicated Jewish foe of the new Christian religion, experienced a dramatic transformation. He became the follower and apostle of Christ known as St. Paul.

In DAMASCUS I was invited out to dinner by our local guide, a Palestinian who had been dispossessed of his home by the Israeli takeover of Palestine. Fluent in English, he became a guide in Damascus. Good looking, with European facial features, I wondered about possible Crusader genes. He was about half my size--but I was a bit nervous about going out, and made sure our tour manager knew where we were going, so that if anything went wrong he would get the British Consulate on the case!

But it turned out all very staid. He was gentlemanly, and did not hit on me. We had a good dinner, the guide smoked a water pipe, and we watched a belly dancer floor show.

The next day, the two English married women, who must have seen too many romantic old Sheikh movies, sneaked over so their husbands wouldn't hear, to ask me how the exotic date went! I think they were disappointed, not to hear of a spicy interlude!

Just a few words about some special experiences at PETRA and AQABA in JORDAN.

In 1964 PETRA, you were roughing it, staying in a barracks-like building, everyone having to share rooms--and beds--with several other people--(imagine the snoring!) Food was tinned stuff like beans heated up on a spirit lamp, which also provided lighting.

Our first sightseeing goal was to climb a rock face to a flat surface on top where a basin had been carved out for the ancient NABATEANS' child sacrifice rites, slitting the children open so their blood could run down a carved channel. Since I was the youngest in our group, they said I had to go. So I sat down in the basin while another member took pictures of us, the others standing behind me jovially anticipating my slaughter.

The next day four of us chose to take an optional run down to AQABA on our own.

Elderly Mr. Greeves fainted and fell off his horse on our way out of the PETRA SIQ gorge. Being the most agile person, and comfortable with horses, I leapt off my mount, and with the Arab groom got him on again and out to the waiting car.

We took off, speeding through the WADI RUM desert--seen in the LAWRENCE OF ARABIA MOVIE. Our happy-go-lucky Arab driver pulled out his bottle of Arak (alcohol content about 63%), waving it about and swilling freely as we raced along. (Arak, based on Anise, like the Greek Ouzo, is meant to be diluted with water.)

Mr. Greeves kept passing out in the car, and I kept shoring him up with old-fashioned smelling salts.

Along the way, we passed a grand Arab in black robes on a camel festooned with fringes and decorations, just like Omar Sharif in the movie!

We stopped at a government outpost, a Beau-Geste-looking, crenellated, mud brick building with a few uniformed police and Jordanian Army soldiers on duty. They welcomed us warmly--all smiles--with Bedouin Tea, containing mint and lots of sugar, served in small glasses in decorative metal holders. They also served us some delicious chocolate candies, part of their celebration in honor or of Mohammed's ascension into heaven--the Muslim equivalent of Easter.

These refreshments perked up Mr. Greeves, and we proceeded on to AQABA. There was only one small German hotel there, and a sprinkling of German sun-seekers. The people I came with sat on the verandah taking more refreshments, and I rented a German bathing suit for a swim.

Note that there are no ocean waves at AQABA--it is at the tip of a long, narrow pay off the Red Sea--and the water is absolutely still. (That movie segment was filmed at a different location.)

We had lunch, Mr. Greeves recovered, and we drove back to Petra and rejoined our group.

I loved my long-ago Middle East tour. I'm sad that the region is so filled with strife, but I'm thankful for memories or better days.

Thank you.

Addendum to Speech

At the time in 1964, The Mandelbaum Gate was a powerful symbol of the Israeli takeover of Palestine, including half of Jerusalem.

It was the only way for "non-official traffic," that is, ordinary travelers, to pass from the Jordanian side, through a "No Man's Land" -- a concrete and barbed wire barrier -- into the Israeli side. One way only -- no return.

My group tour, focused on history and archaeology, was through LEBANON, SYRIA and JORDAN. At the end of it, a handful of us from my group went independently, separately, through this Gate into ISRAEL, to visit the historic sites.

It was a bit scary, as I went alone -- the first to go through the Gate. The others came a few days later.

(I took this photo from the Israeli side after I'd crossed though.)

The Israeli passport control staff were shrewd enough not to stamp your passport, so that you wouldn't have trouble if you later wanted to visit other Arab countries.

Regarding the subject of displaced PALESTINIANS, when my group tour started in BEIRUT, LEBANON, I was entertained by a young woman doctor friend whom I'd known in my London *pension*, and her parents. They had been dispossessed of their home, a villa in the part of JERUSALEM taken over by Israel, <u>without compensation</u>. Obviously they were not happy about this.

My friend being a doctor, and her father a lawyer, they were affluent enough to have the flat in BEIRUT as well as another in PARIS.

Our tour guide in DAMASCUS, SYRIA, was also a displaced Palestinian, his home and other properties having been taken over by Israel <u>without compensation</u>. He was unhappy about that, but in business suit and tie, and fluent in English, he was able to earn a living as a guide in DAMASCUS.

The subject of having your home seized by Israel without compensation was clearly a painful subject.

A touching example of the sad situation of Israel's relations with its Arab neighbors was a driver-guide I had on a solo excursion I took in Israel. He said wistfully, "I wish I could see DAMASCUS!" He wanted me to tell him all about it.

The Jordanian side of JERUSALEM was completely taken over by Israel in what is called the "Six Day War" of 1967, and the Mandelbaum Gate demolished.

The United States' recent recognition of Jerusalem as the capital of Israel has created more Arab resentment of the United States.

Timeline

1929	Morro Bay - Harleigh is born – January 21st
1931	Morro Bay - Sister Nona is born – November 27th
1942	Morro Bay - Knott family moves out of their house and into a neighbor's house to make room for officers training in Morro Bay during WWII.
1945	Morro Bay – Chair of Girls League at San Luis Obispo High School
1946	Morro Bay – Receives full scholarship to University of California but decides to go to Stanford, where her mom Rachel went.
1947	Stanford – Member of International Survey Committee and Council for UNESCO at Stanford. Worked the summer at Circle Bar-B Ranch in Goleta.
1948	Stanford – Worked at the Stanford Business Library for two years while a student.
1950	Stanford and Washington DC - Graduates from Stanford with a BA in History. Visited Great Britain (68 days) and France (8 days) and took a summer Economics course at Oxford University in England. Starts work at the US Air Force in Washington DC.
1951	Washington DC – Visits Canada for two weeks.
1955	London – Transfers to Office of the Air Attaché at the US Embassy in London. Visits Ireland for two weeks.
1956	London – Visits Ireland (two weeks) and Holland (1 week).
1957	London – Mother, Rachel Thayer Knott, dies on January 18th at age 64.
1958	London – Three week cruise to Italy, Greece, and Turkey. Two week "convalescent stay" in Mallorca, Spain. Completes two tours of duty with the US Air Force then resigns.

1959	London and Palo Alto – Three week cruise to Italy, Greece, Turkey, and Yugoslavia. Two weeks in Austria. Moves back to Palo Alto to be a Women's Residence Hall director at Stanford.
1960	Palo Alto and Australia. Sails from San Francisco to New Zealand stopping in Canada, Hawaii, and Fiji.
1961	Australia and England – Secretarial jobs in Sydney, Australia. Then sails from Australia to England stopping in Sri Lanka, Yemen, Egypt, Italy, Spain, and Gibraltar. Later visits Italy (three weeks) and Scotland (two weeks).
1962	New York – Secretary at Hazeltine Corporation. Sister, Nona Reynolds Knott, dies on April 16th at age 30.
1963	New York – Three months visiting Belgium, Spain, England, and Denmark.
1964	New York – Three week British-led tour of Lebanon, Syria, and Jordan.
1965	New York and Palo Alto – Attends New York School of Interior Design, earning a Certificate of Interior Design. Moves back to Palo Alto and begins working at the Stanford University Department of History.
1968	Palo Alto – Seriously injured in a car accident in her Volkswagen beetle while driving from Palo Alto to Morro Bay. Recovers over several months in Morro Bay.
1969	Palo Alto – Visits Barbados in November.
1971	Palo Alto – Begins working at the Stanford University Department of Cardiology, where they were preparing to do the first human heart transplant. Ends up not being the first. Visits England for two months, then a cruise to Greece, Turkey, Tunisia, Sicily, and Spain.
1973	Palo Alto – Visits England, Tunisia, and Algeria for two months during the summer.
1975	Palo Alto – Visits England, Portugal, and East Germany for two months during the summer.

1976	Palo Alto – Visits England and Egypt for two months during the spring.
1977	Palo Alto – Father, Arthur Harold Knott, dies on April 16th (same day as her sister) at age 93.
1979	Palo Alto – Visits England, Croatia, Greece, and Turkey for two months during the summer.
1982	Palo Alto – Visits the USSR (Russia, Ukraine, Georgia), West Germany, and England.
1985	Morro Bay – Begins work at the Morro Bay High School as a librarian while living in her childhood home. Takes distance learning French and German classes at Foothill College, and a travel writing class at San Francisco State University.
1988	Morro Bay – Visits England in July.
1996	Morro Bay – Visits France in November after retiring from Morro Bay High School.
2009	Morro Bay - Decides to switch from a PC to a Mac and takes the bus to the Apple Store in San Luis Obispo every week for two months for classes.
2019	Morro Bay – Harleigh Thayer Knott dies on March 2nd at age 90.

Photographs

Passport
1950

Passport
1955

Passport
1960

Passport
1968

Passport
1973

Passport
1979

Passport
1988

Morro Bay
Home,
Garage,
Art Studio
1938

Harleigh
Age 6

Knott
family
picnic at
Morro
Bay Park
1930s

Arthur
Harold
Knott in
Carmel
1923

Obituary, Eulogies, and Memorial Service

Obituary

Harleigh Knott died Saturday, March 2, at 90 years, coincidentally at the very time she was to give a talk on her Middle East travels in the mid-twentieth century. Harleigh (b. 1/21/29) was the elder of two daughters born to Rachel and Harold Knott, in Morro Bay. Her father was a noted landscape painter on the central and north coast; this formed the background for one of Harleigh's three loves—art, ancient history, and opera, especially Wagner's. She held a B.A. in history from Stanford University (1950) and a Diploma from the New York School of Interior Design (1965).

Her work career, her interests, and her travels were wide: She was a civilian employee of the US Air Force at the Pentagon from 1950-55 and at the American Embassy in London from 1955-59. She was Director of a student residence at Stanford 1959-60, travelled and worked in Melbourne and Sydney, Australia 1960-1, and was a secretarial-administrator at the cardiology department of Stanford Medical School during the '60s and '70s. When she came back to live in Morro Bay, she was a librarian at Morro Bay High School.

Her travels took her through Europe and into Egypt, Syria, Turkey, Israel, Jordan and Lebanon, always being alive to the history of the places she visited. Her interests, too, were varied: She loved movies, opera, reading, news, Indy races, polo, horse races, dog shows, baking, sewing, thrift shops, interesting people, good food and wine, cats, and hats, hats, hats. She was a member of St. Peter's Episcopal Church, Morro Bay, AAUW, Stanford Alumni Association, the Wagner Society, Morro Bay Historical Society, (and a contributor to the book, Morro Bay Yesterdays,) Laguna Art Museum, and Monterey Museum of Art.

Services will be held 4 pm Wednesday, March 13, at St. Peter's by the Sea Episcopal Church, 545 Shasta, Morro Bay. Donations in remembrance may be made to St. Peter's or to other charities she supported; the names can be obtained from the church office.

Eulogy by Harleigh's Cousin Janet

Because I am not able to be with you today, I have asked that one of the others in attendance read these thoughts of mine about my cousin Harleigh, one of the most interesting people I have ever had the privilege of knowing. I estimate that we have been "pen pals" for about 30 years or longer, but our first face to face meeting was maybe 16 years ago when I was visiting a friend in Los Angles, and we drove up to Morro Bay and had lunch with Harleigh.

I was prepared for our meeting because of our correspondences. Receiving the Christmas letters always gave me many laughs, but they also showed how many organizations she belonged to, the hobbies she enjoyed, and the constant expanding her knowledge of so many varied subject areas. She never quit learning.

I understand that most of you had the good fortune to be on the Christmas letter list. Did she also send you newspaper clippings concerning subjects she knew interested you?

I regularly received articles from the New York Times and the Los Angeles Times in large envelopes, with extra postage paid, and Scotch Tape sealing them as if they were straight from the Pentagon. There was no way one could use a letter opener, as you could not even get the tip of opener beyond the tape. I always had to cut the ends of the envelopes completely off. The topics sent to me were Jane Austen, Harper Lee, and anything about the Civil War. (Or, as we called it The War Between the States.)

Although I love dogs, birds, some cats, I can't imagine tolerating having a resident skunk. To take a phrase from Robert Browning and twist it a bit, I think perhaps Harleigh with her sympathy for wild animals "…. Had a heart too soon made glad."

May she rest in peace.

Thanks to all who are in attendance and those who have helped with the planning.

Eulogy by Reverend Sid Symington

"When Death comes, like the hungry bear in Autumn; when Death comes and takes all the bright coins from his purse to buy me, and snaps the purse shut, I want to step through the door full of curiosity, wondering what is it going to be like, that cottage of darkness?"

This is part of a poem by Mary Oliver, who died in January. The poem speaks to me of Harleigh, whose hunger for the beauty of life knew no bounds, and whose society saw no limits of inquiry into the wonder of connections among people and places and times.

Dearly Beloved, we are here to express our appreciation and respect for one of God's truly good people, Harleigh Knott, who lived among us as person of principle, integrity and curiosity about the world. She loved the world, the people in it, the books and plays and films that make it speak, the art that makes it rich and the music that makes it sing.

She was truly compassionate, perceptive and wise, as those who were fortunate enough to receive her correspondence and famous newspaper clipping service can attest. And there were many of us, especially among her distant-in-miles, but close-in-spirit extended family. Thank you for sharing her with us.

Harleigh was always looking for connections and meaning, operative principles and telling examples to illustrate what took place in the world. The terrible crash that ended her motoring days did nothing to dampen her hunger for friends, for learning and conversing about things: for life.

She was essentially a private person, but this in no way diminished her interest in other people, nor her concern for their welfare. She managed to get to the heart of any subject – whether policy, event or person -- while never saying an ungracious word. She maintained the highest standards in all her efforts, and her concern for genuineness left no room for doubt.

Harleigh can perhaps best be described by an accolade not much used these days: She was a lady and a scholar. What does a good, long life like hers have to say to us? When anyone dies, some part of us also faces the inevitability of our own death. But a life like hers helps us know that, in its spiritual dimension, life is indivisible and infinite. When a good person dies they continue to speak to us, as they have spoken to us in life. "What would Harleigh have to say about this?" is a question we will ask ourselves as long as we have the capacity.

Perhaps she would say to us that life must be lived in the search for truth but always in the context of love. We have heard the Gospel words of Jesus as reported by John: "I am the way, the truth and the life; no one comes to the Father except by me." Knowing Harleigh helps us understand that these words have no meaning at all unless it is understood that the "Me" they refer to has little to do with one religion (much less one religion over another), and everything to do with love. She would point out that this same evangelist, John, was the one who made the truth most plain: "God is love." Noone comes to God except by love.

"And therefore," says the poet, "I look upon everything as a sisterhood and a brotherhood, and I look upon time as no more than an idea, and I consider eternity as another possibility. When it's over, I want to say all my life I was a bride married to amazement. I was the bridegroom, taking the world into my arms... I don't want to end up simply having visited this world."

God knows Harleigh, beautifully tall and elegant, picture-hatted and wise and graciously-spoken Harleigh was no mere visitor to this world; she was an eager sojourner. And we who knew her will always consider ourselves fortunate to have been along for the ride.

Memorial Service

St. Peter's by the Sea Episcopal Church – Morro Bay
March 13, 2019
4 o'clock in the evening

Preludes: Bist du bei mir, Sheep may safely graze, Sonatina from "Cantata 106," and Jesu, Joy of Man's Desiring, all by J. S. Bach. Laudate Dominum from VESPERAE SOLENNES DE CONFESSORE, by W. A. Mozart. Soloist: Mary Sue Gee, Organist: Martha J. Lindholm

Hymn 287

> For all the saints, who from their labors rest,
> who thee by faith befor_e the world confessed,
> thy Name, 0 Jesus, be forever blessed.
> Alleluia, Alleluia!
> Thou wast their rock, their fortress and their might;
> thou, Lord, their Captain in the well-fought fight;
> thou, in the darkness drear, the one true Light.
> Alleluia, Alleluia!
> The golden evening brightens in the west;
> soon, soon to faithful warriors cometh rest;
> sweet is the calm of paradise the blest.
> Alleluia, Alleluia!
> But lo! there breaks a yet more glorious day;
> the saints triumphant rise in bright array;
> the King of glory passes on his way.
> Alleluia, Alleluia!

The Collect

A reading from the Prophecy of Isaiah - William Morley The 41st Chapter, beginning with the Eighth Verse.

Nunc Dimittis (said by all)

Lord, now lettest thou thy servant depart in peace,
according to thy word;
For mine eyes have seen thy salvation,
which thou hast prepared before the face of all people,
To be a light to lighten the Gentiles,
and to be the glory of thy people Israel.

A reading from Paul's 1st Letter to the Corinthians - Lenny Erickson The Fifteenth Chapter, beginning with the 32nd Verse.

Psalm 46 (said by all)

God is our refuge and strength,
a very present help in trouble.
Therefore we will not fear, though the earth should change,
though the mountains shake in the heart of the sea;
though its waters roar and foam,
and the mountains tremble with its tumult.
The Lord of hosts is with us;
the God of Jacob is our stronghold.
There is a river whose streams make glad the city of God,
the holy habitation of the Most High.
God is in the midst of the city; she shall not be moved;
God will help her when the morning dawns.
The Lord of hosts is with us;
the God of Jacob is our stronghold.

The Holy Gospel according to John, Chapter 14, Verses 1 through 6.

Homily and Remarks --The Rev. Sidney-Symington - Rector, et al.

Hymn 488

Be thou my vision, 0 Lord of my heart;
all else be nought to me, save that thou art--
thou my best thought, by day or by night,
waking or sleeping, thy presence my light.

Be thou my wisdom, and thou my true word;
I ever with thee and thou with me, Lord;
thou my great Father; thine own may I be;
thou in me dwelling, and I one with thee.
High King of heaven, when victory is won,
may I reach heaven's joys, bright heaven's Sun!
Heart of my heart, whatever befall,
still be my Vision, 0 Ruler of all.

Prayers - Please respond: Hear us, Lord

The Peace

Holy Communion -- Book of Common Prayer, Page 361
All present are welcome to come forward for the Bread and
Wine.

Offertory Anthem: Pie Jesu from REQUIEM, by G. Faure

Prayer after Communion (said by all)

Almighty God, we thank you that in your great love you have
fed us with the spiritual food and drink of the Body and
Blood of your Son Jesus Christ, and have given us a foretaste
of your heavenly banquet. Grant that this Sacrament may be
to us a comfort in affliction, and a pledge of our inheritance
in that kingdom where there is no death, neither sorrow nor
crying, but the fullness of joy with all your saints; through
Jesus Christ our Savior. Amen.

Commendation

Celebrant: Give rest, 0 Christ,
to your servant with your saints,

People: where sorrow and pain are no more, neither sighing,
but life everlasting.

Hymn 526

Let saints on earth in concert sing
with those who work is done;
for all the servants of our King in heaven and earth are one.
One family, we dwell in him, one Church, above, beneath,
though now divided by the stream,
the narrow stream of death.
E'en now by faith we join our hands
with those who went before,
and greet our ever-living band on that eternal shore.
Jesus, be thou our constant Guide;
then, when the word is given,
bid Jordan's narrow stream divide,
and bring us safe to heaven.

Dismissal

Postlude in 'F'

Please join us next door in Erickson Hall for a reception following the service. Donations made in Harleigh's memory to St. Peter's by the Sea will support our charitable outreach in the community.

Made in the USA
Middletown, DE
08 May 2019